Storm on Horseback

STORM
ON
HORSEBACK

The Seljuk Warriors of Turkey

JOHN FREELY

LONDON · NEW YORK

To Selçuk Altun

Published in 2008 by I.B.Tauris & Co. Ltd
6 Salem Road, London W2 4BU
175 Fifth Avenue, New York NY 10010
www.ibtauris.com

In the United States and Canada distributed by Palgrave Macmillan,
a division of St. Martin's Press, 175 Fifth Avenue, New York NY 10010

ISBN: 978 1 84511 703 0

A full CIP record for this book is available from the British Library
A full CIP record for this book is available from the Library of Congress
Library of Congress catalog card: available

Typeset in Janson by Dexter Haven Associates Ltd, London
Printed and bound in India by Thomson Press India Ltd.

CONTENTS

ACKNOWLEDGEMENTS

I would like to acknowledge the generous assistance that I have received from the librarians at the American Research Institute in Turkey and Boğaziçi University in Istanbul. I would particularly like to thank Dr. Anthony Greenwood, director of the American Research Institute in Turkey, and Professor Taha Parla, director of the Boğaziçi University Library, as well Hatice Ön, the assistant director. I am very grateful to Professor Hakan Erdem of Sabanci University and Victoria Rowe Holbrook for reading my manuscript and making many helpful suggestions. I would also like to thank my editor, Tatiana Wilde, who as always has been of great help to me in giving my manuscript its final form.

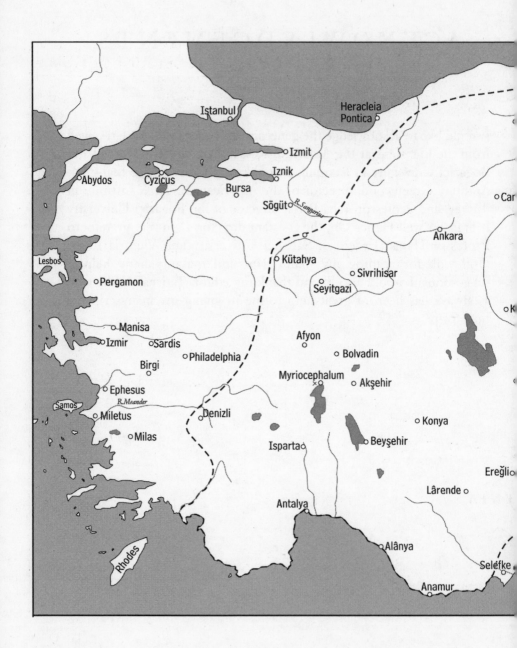

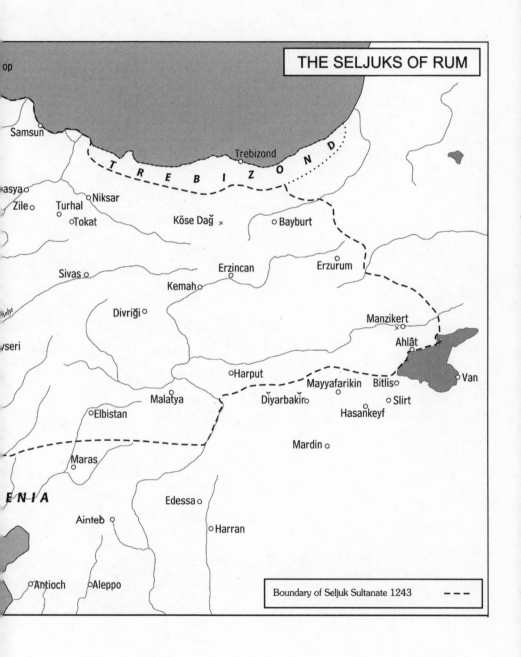

THE SELJUKS OF RUM

op

Samsun

Trebizond

T R E B I Z O N D

asya

Zile

Turhal

Niksar

Tokat

Köse Dağ ×

Bayburt

Sivas

Erzincan

Erzurum

Kemah

Divriği

Manzikert ×

Ahlât

seri

Harput

Mayyafarikin

Bitlis

Van

Malatya

Diyarbakir

Slirt

Elbistan

Hasankeyf

Mardin

Maras

ENIA

Edessa

Ainteb

Harran

Antioch

Aleppo

Boundary of Seljuk Sultanate 1243   – – –

INTRODUCTION

Who are the Turks and where did they come from? This is a perennial question, given the obscure origin of the Turks and the number of nomadic peoples they originally comprised, all of whom adapted to and absorbed the various cultures with which they came in contact during their wanderings. The successive empires that they created stretched from China and Central Asia through the Middle East into the Balkans and around the southern shore of the Mediterranean into North Africa, a whirlwind series of conquests that led one chronicler to call the waves of mounted Turkish warriors a 'storm on horseback'.

This is the story of the Seljuk Turks of Anatolia, or Asia Minor, as the Asian part of modern Turkey is more generally known in the West. The Seljuk Sultanate of Rum was the first Turkish state in Anatolia, lasting from the second half of the eleventh century until the early fourteenth century. The Seljuks were the first Turks to force themselves on the attention of the West, and it was their conquest of a large part of the Byzantine Empire that lead to the First Crusade, whose knights first referred to Asia Minor as Turchia. During the Seljuk period Anatolia, which had been for the most part Greek and Christian, became predominantly Turkish and Muslim, one of the great cultural transformations in human history.

This story also includes the immediate successors of the Seljuks, the Türkmen emirates known as *beyliks*. The *beyliks* emerged after the collapse of the Sultanate of Rum and at the same time continued Seljuk cultural traditions until they were eventually absorbed by the rise of the Ottomans, the westernmost of the emirates, who in 1453 established themselves as a world power by their capture of Constantinople, Turkish Istanbul. This was a great watershed in human history, for the Muslim Ottoman Empire thenceforth replaced the Christian Byzantine Empire astride the straits between Europe and Asia, threatening western Europe

1

for the next four centuries, its influence still evident today throughout the Balkans and the Middle East.

The book is divided into two parts, the first of which is a narrative history of the Seljuks and their immediate successors, the Türkmen *beyliks*. This chronicle involves the internal affairs of the Seljuks and the various *beyliks*, as well as their wars with one another and with the Greeks of the Byzantine Empire, the crusaders of western Europe, the Venetians, the Mongols of Central Asia, and the Mamluks of Egypt, as well as with the Armenians, Kurds, Türkmen tribes and Arabs of eastern Anatolia and the surrounding regions. Those who commanded armies in this epic struggle included the Seljuk sultan Alp Arslan, the Byzantine emperor Alexius I Comnenus, the Norman count Bohemud of Taranto, King Louis VII of France, the Ayyoubid sultan Saladin, the German emperor Frederick I Barbarossa, the English king Richard I the Lion-Heart, the Hungarian regent John Hunyadi and the Ottoman sultan Mehmet II, called 'the Conqueror' after his capture of Constantinople in 1453, and known in the West as 'the Grand Turk, the present terror of Europe'.

The second part of the book is a traveller's guide to the Seljuk heritage in Turkey, described in a continuous series of itineraries that take the traveller all the way from Istanbul through eastern Anatolia. The Seljuk sultans adorned their cities with surpassingly beautiful palaces, mosques, mausoleums and *medreses* (theological schools), including medical schools and hospitals, building roads, bridges and caravanserais along the trade routes throughout the Sultanate of Rum. The viziers of the Türkmen *beyliks* continued this tradition, and their splendid buildings often stand side by side with those of the Seljuks, whose architecture took Bernard Berenson's breath away when he visited Konya, the former capital of the Sultanate of Rum.

> What a miracle is this Seljuk architecture! It has an elegance, a distinction of design and a subtle delicacy of ornamentation surpassing any known to me since French Gothic at its best... Konya was the residence of the Seljuk sultans and is still an unrivalled monument to their taste and love of beauty and magnificence.

The itineraries also bring the traveller into contact with other cultural survivals of this first Turkish period in the history of Anatolia, including the mystical music and dance of the Mevlevi dervishes, the lyrical poetry of Mevlana and Yunus Emre, the love songs of the wandering minstrels known as *aşıklar*, or lovers, and the witty stories of Nasrettin Hoca. These are all elements of the renaissance that took place in Anatolia during the days of the Seljuks, and although they themselves were absorbed and vanished, it would seem, their cultural heritage survives in the deepest roots of Turkish life, just as their monuments still adorn the landscape of Anatolia.

– Part I –

The Seljuks and
Their Successors

– 1 –

Out of Asia

Anatolia, known to the Greeks and Romans as Asia Minor, comprises ninety-three per cent of the land mass of modern Turkey, the other seven per cent lying in Europe, separated from the Asian part of the country by the Dardanelles, the Sea of Marmara and the Bosphorus, the waterway that the sixteenth-century French scholar Pierre Gilles called 'the strait that ends all straits'. The first Greek navigators making their way through this waterway at the dawn of history saw the sun rising over the eastern shore of the strait and so they called that region 'Anatolia', 'the Land of Sunrise', while the country to the west became known as 'Europa', the 'Land of Sunset'.

The topography of Anatolia has made it a bridge between Europe and Asia, and from the beginning of history it has been a battleground between East and West. Much of Anatolia consists of a plateau some 900–1,500 metres above sea level, around which there is a fringe of low-lying coast along the shores of the Black Sea, the Aegean and the Mediterranean. On the south-east the highlands give way to the great Mesopotamian plain, from where the first knowledge of agriculture spread into the central plateau in the Neolithic period, beginning the history of Anatolia.

The first Greek colonies were established along the Aegean coast of Anatolia at the beginning of the first millennium BC, and some five centuries later they were conquered in turn by the Lydians and the Persians. This was the background to the *Histories* of Herodotus, who begins by writing that his 'researches are here set down to preserve the memory of the past by putting on record the astonishing achievements of our own and other peoples; and more particularly, to show how they came into conflict'.

At the beginning of the second millennium AD most of Anatolia was still under the dominion of the Byzantine Empire, the medieval Christian survival of the eastern dominions of the ancient Roman Empire, with its capital in Constantinople on the Bosphorus. The Byzantine Empire in its prime also included all of the Balkans south of the Danube as well as part of the Italian peninsula. The borders of the empire in south-eastern Anatolia marched with those of several Muslim emirates, extending from the Mesopotamian desert to the Zagros Mountains of eastern Iran, while in the north-east they bounded the Christian kingdoms of Armenia and Georgia, the latter extending around the eastern end of the Black Sea into the Caucasus.

The Muslim neighbours of Byzantium referred to it as 'the Land of Rum', since for them it represented the Roman Empire. The Greek-speaking Christians of Anatolia were known to Muslims as 'Rumi', while Byzantine Greeks referred to themselves as 'Rhomoiai'. Greek was the dominant language of western and central Anatolia, and the prevalent religion was Greek Orthodox, headed by the Patriarch of Constantinople under the aegis of the Byzantine emperor. The Christians in south-eastern Anatolia included those under the Orthodox Patriarch of Antioch as well as those belonging to the Jacobite and Nestorian Churches, whose congregations spoke Syriac, a form of Aramaic, the language of Christ. The Armenians, who lived throughout central and eastern Anatolia, belonged to the Gregorian Church. Kurds predominated in south-easternmost Anatolia, with Arabs along the Mesopotamian borderland to their west, where the first Islamic armies had invaded the Byzantine Empire in the eighth century.

During the long struggle between the Greeks and the Arabs, Muslims sometimes ended up within the shifting boundaries of the Byzantine Empire, while Christians often found themselves under Islamic rule. Speros Vryonis writes of the consequences of this ethnic ebb and flow: 'Muslims who survived in areas reconquered by the Byzantines were eventually Hellenised and Christianised, just as many Christians converted to Islam in regions long occupied by the Arabs and other Muslim conquerors, a process that would continue for centuries.'

Such was the situation in Asia Minor at the beginning of the second Christian millennium, when the Turks made their first appearance in the eastern marchlands of the Byzantine Empire, sweeping across the great Anatolian plateau like a 'storm on horseback'.

Both Chinese and Byzantine sources first mention the Turks as a people in the sixth century AD, placing them in the region that is now Mongolia, from which they quickly expanded towards the south and west. Chinese sources write of the T'u-chueh, a Turkic tribe better known as the Gök Turks, who in the mid-sixth century created two khanates (i.e. states headed by a chieftain known as a khan). This first Turkish empire lasted until the second quarter of the seventh century, when it was destroyed by the Chinese emperor T'ai-tsung.

The eastern khanate of the Gök Turks was supplanted in Mongolia by the Khanate of the Uighurs, a nomadic Turkic tribe who first rose to prominence in the seventh century at the crossroads of the Silk Route in Central Asia. The Uighurs were the dominant tribe in central Asia during the years 744–840, after which they were overthrown by the Kirghiz, another Turkic tribe from the north. The dispossessed Uighurs subsequently founded other khanates in Central Asia, one of which lasted until the thirteenth century, and they transmitted their written language and literature to the Turko-Mongol tribes of Central Asia, which earned them the reputation of being 'teachers of civilisation'. Most of the Uighurs eventually adopted Buddhism as their religion, as evidenced by their extant paintings, the earliest in Turkish art.

The Seljuks were Oğuz Turks of the Kınık tribe who entered Transoxiana late in the tenth century, and early in the following century they gained control of the region around Samarkand and Bukhara. According to tradition, the tribe was named for its eponymous founder, Seljuk, who towards the close of his very long life became a Muslim, probably at the end of the tenth century, when all his tribe presumably converted to Islam with him. This and other Seljuk traditions derive from the *Malik-nama*, a work composed in the mid-eleventh century and since lost.

According to this and other sources, Seljuk's sons Israil and Mikail consolidated their tribe's control of Samarkand and Bukhara and in 1034 extended their domains into Khurasan. Then in 1040 Mikail's son Tuğrul, together with his brothers Çağrı and Ibrahim Inal, made war on the Ghaznavids, a dynasty established by Turkic military slaves in what is now northern Pakistan, Afghanistan, Tajikistan and Kirgyzstan, as well as parts of Uzbekistan and Turkmenistan. The Seljuks decisively defeated the Ghaznavids in a battle at Dandarqan, near Merv, opening up the entire Iranian plateau to the victors.

The brothers then separated to establish their own regimes. Çağrı set out to conquer the lands east of the Tigris. Ibrahim established himself in north-western Iran and in 1045 he began raiding into Armenian and Georgian territory, attacking Manzikert, Kars, Erzurum and Trebizond. Meanwhile, Tuğrul conquered all of north-eastern Iran and much of Azerbaijan, forcing his brother Ibrahim to cede Hamadan to him.

In 1055 Tuğrul captured Baghdad and proclaimed himself protector of the Abbasid Caliph, who named him 'Sultan and Sovereign of the East and West'. Tuğrul died in 1063 and was succeeded by his nephew Alp Arslan, a son of Çağrı. Tuğrul (r. 1037–63) and Alp Arslan (r. 1063–72) are considered to be the first two sultans of the Great Seljuks of Iran, a dynasty whose history is usually considered separately from that of the Seljuk Sultanate of Rum in Anatolia.

Turkish raiders made their first appearance in Anatolia in 1016–17, when they attacked the Armenian kingdom of Vaspuracan in what is now the north-eastern corner of Turkey. The Christian chronicler Matthew of Edessa describes the sack of Vaspuracan in apocalyptic terms:

> In the beginning of the year 465 [AD 1016–17] a calamity proclaiming the fulfillment of divine portents befell the Christian adorers of the Holy Cross. The death-breathing dragon appeared, accompanied by a destroying fire, and struck the believers in the Holy Trinity... At this period there gathered the savage nation of infidels called Turks. Setting out, they entered the province of Vaspuracan and put the Christians to the sword... Facing the enemy, the Armenians saw these strange men, who were armed with bows and had flowing hair like women. They were not used to protecting themselves against the arrows of those infidels.

Byzantine sources barely mention this first incursion of the Turks into Anatolia. The Greek chronicler Cedrenus merely notes that the Armenian prince Senecherim, under pressure from his neighbours, abandoned Vaspuracan, which in 1021 was occupied by the emperor Basil II (r. 963–1025) and became part of the Byzantine Empire.

The date given by Matthew of Edessa has been questioned by Claude Cahen, who puts the Turkish attack on Vaspuracan a decade later. The identity of the attackers is also questionable, some authorities holding that they were Seljuk Turks and others that they were Türkmen, the name by which the sedentary population referred to the nomadic Turkish tribes. The Seljuks themselves had been a nomadic tribe before they established their first sultanate in the mid-eleventh century, and their armies were to a large extent made up of Türkmen tribesmen. By that time the Seljuks had added to their Türkmen warriors an army of the traditional Muslim type, with weapons and siege machinery that enabled them to capture walled cities. But the core of the Seljuk army was always its force of mounted archers, which the Greek chronicler Michael Attaliates describes in his account of a battle fought by the Byzantines on the banks of the Euphrates in south-eastern Anatolia: 'The barbarians were good at fighting from a distance and still far off, easily wounding many Romans, while remaining untouched themselves... Those who stood on the banks kept shooting at the Romans, causing a great many casualties, and forced them to turn and run.'

The tactics of the mounted Turkish archers are described by Marco Polo, who refers to them as Tartars, though they were probably Türkmen, but in either case they would have employed the same practices as the Seljuk cavalry.

When these Tartars come to engage in battle, they never mix with the enemy, but keep hovering about him, discharging their arrows first from one side and then from the other, occasionally pretending to flee, and during their flight shooting arrows backward at their pursuers, killing men and horses, as if they were combatting face to face. In this sort of warfare the adversary imagines he has gained a victory, when in fact he has lost the battle; for the Tartars, observing the mischief they have done him, wheel about, and renewing the fight, overpower his remaining troops... Their horses are so well broken in to quick changes in movement, that upon the signal given, they instantly turn in every direction; and by these rapid manoeuvres many victories have been obtained.

When Alp Arslan succeeded to the throne he had to fight a war of succession with Kutalmış, a son of Israil, who even during Tuğrul's lifetime had maintained his own claim to the sultanate. After Tuğrul's death Kutalmış reaffirmed his claim and marched on Baghdad at the head of a powerful army, but Alp Arslan defeated him and he was killed fleeing from the battlefield.

Within a year of his accession Alp Arslan captured Herat, and the following year he recaptured the Holy Cities of Mecca and Medina from the Fatimids and also took Aleppo. His son and eventual successor Malik Şah married the Karakhanid princess Terken Hatun, thus pacifying the eastern boundary of the sultanate. Alp Arslan then turned his attention westward to Anatolia, which since the latter years of Tuğrul's reign had been raided almost annually by Türkmen tribes, beginning with their sack of Melitene (Malatya) in 1057. During the following decade Türkmen raiders penetrated into Byzantine territory all the way to Amorium, far out to the west on the Anatolian plateau.

In 1064 Alp Arslan crossed the river Araxes to invade Anatolia, attacking Ani, the ancient capital of Armenia, which fell after a siege of twenty-five days. The Arab chronicler Sibt ibn al Gawzi quotes a supposed eyewitness in describing the Turkish sack of Ani:

> The army entered the city, massacred its inhabitants, pillaged and burned it, leaving it in ruins and taking prisoner all those who remained alive... The dead bodies were so many that they blocked all the streets; one could not go anywhere without stepping over them. And the number of prisoners was not less than 50,000 souls. I was determined to enter the city and see the destruction with my own eyes. I tried to find a street in which I would not have to walk over the corpses; but that was impossible.

The conquest of Ani occasioned great rejoicing throughout the Islamic world. The caliph in Baghdad issued a declaration praising Alp Arslan and his men for their victory, calling them *gazi*, 'warriors for the faith', giving the sultan the title of 'Abu-'l-Fath', or 'the Conqueror'.

Alp Arslan sent an army into Anatolia the following year under one of his generals, who attacked Caesareia (Kayseri) and defeated a Byzantine army at Sebaste (Sivas), and the year afterwards another Seljuk force penetrated as far as Iconium (Konya).

Byzantium had made several attempts to halt these invasions by negotiations with the Seljuk sultans, first with Tuğrul and then with Alp Arslan, whose reigns overlapped those of eleven Byzantine emperors, three of whom were women. Alp Arslan's first incursions took place during the reign of the emperor Constantine X Ducas (r. 1059–67), who at the same time had to deal with a Norman invasion that cost the Byzantines almost all their remaining possessions in southern Italy. The Byzantines also had to contend with raids by two Turkish tribes – the Patzinaks and the Uze – who migrated south across the Danube and penetrated almost to the walls of Constantinople.

Constantine died in 1067 and was succeeded by his son Michael VII (r. 1067–78), who was so young and backward that his mother Eudocia Macrembolitissa was appointed as regent, vowing that she would not remarry or otherwise support another claimant to the throne. The

Cappadocian noble Romanus Diogenes attempted to usurp the throne, but Eudocia mustered enough support to stop his revolt and have him exiled. But then when the Turkish attacks continued the patriarch of Constantinople, John Xiphilinus, realised that a strong man was needed to rule the empire, and so he persuaded Eudocia to have Romanus returned to Constantinople from exile. The patriarch then released Eudocia from her oath, and at the beginning of 1068 she married the returned exile, who took the throne as Romanus IV (r. 1068–71), ruling as co-emperor with Michael VII Ducas.

Romanus immediately set out to strengthen the Byzantine army, which had been neglected since the time of Basil II. He then mustered his forces in preparation for his first campaign against the Turks. The Greek chronicler Cedrenus describes the motley collection of poorly armed troops under the emperor's command:

> The emperor, leading an army that did not befit the emperor of the Rhomaioi, but one which the times furnished, of Macedonians and Bulgars and Cappadocians and Uzes and other foreigners who happened to be about, in addition also of Franks [Europeans] and Varangarians [the foreign imperial guards], set out hastily... These were bent over by poverty and distress and were deprived of armour. Instead of swords and other military weapons... they were bearing hunting spears and scythes... and they were without war horses and other equipment... These things being observed by those present, they were filled with despondency, as they reckoned how low the armies of the Rhomaioi had fallen... For the older and experienced were without horse and without armour, and the fresh detachments were without military experience and unaccustomed to the military struggles, whereas the enemy was very bold in warfare, persevering, experienced, and suitable.

The emperor's first campaign, in the autumn of 1068, took him down into Byzantine Syria, where he recaptured the fortress city of Hierapolis near Aleppo. Romanus had left a garrison at Melitene to guard his rear, but this failed to stop the Turks, who penetrated all the way to western Anatolia and sacked Amorium.

Romanus returned to Constantinople early in 1069, leaving his Norman mercenaries to guard the Armenian passes under their leader Robert Crispin. Crispin neglected his duties to rob the local tax collectors, and though he was dismissed his men continued to plunder the region.

The emperor again set off from Constantinople in the spring of 1069, to campaign in north-eastern Anatolia. Leaving the Armenian general

Philaretus Brachamius with a large force to guard his rear on the upper Euphrates, Romanus marched farther east, planning to attack the Turkish fort at Chliat (Ahlat), on the northern shore of Lake Van. The Turks attacked and defeated the Byzantine rearguard under Philaretus, forcing Romanus to turn back and pursue the enemy, who evaded him and went on to sack Iconium. Meanwhile, Alp Arslan captured Manzikert (Malazgirt), just to the north of Chliat, thus consolidating the Seljuk position in the Lake Van region. Since it was too late in the season to continue the campaign, Romanus marched his army back to Constantinople, having achieved nothing.

Romanus failed to mount a campaign in 1070, instead concentrating his efforts in an attempt to arrange a truce with Alp Arslan. But nothing came of the negotiations, and in the meanwhile Türkmen raiders penetrated all the way into south-western Anatolia, sacking Chonae (Honaz).

In the spring of 1071 the Normans under Robert Guiscard besieged Bari, the last Byzantine possession in Italy. Romanus, under heavy criticism for his failure to take effective action against the enemies who were invading the empire on all sides, decided that his only hope of survival was to win a major victory over the Turks. He mustered an enormous army, estimated by Muslim sources at between 200,000 and 400,000, though modern Western authorities put the number at about 100,000. It was a very heterogeneous force, the foreign mercenaries including Franks, Arabs, Rus, Uze, Patzinaks, Georgians, Abkazians, Khazars, Kipchak, Scyths, Alans and Armenians.

Before setting off on his campaign Romanus arrested and exiled the Caesar John Ducas, uncle of the late Constantine IX and uncle of Michael VII. The Ducas family had been plotting against Romanus, and so he wanted to have their leader, the Caesar John, removed from the capital while he himself was off on campaign. As an additional precaution, Romanus took John's eldest son, Andronicus Ducas, with him on the campaign, ostensibly as a general but actually as a hostage to guarantee that the caesar's family would not attempt a coup during the emperor's absence from Constantinople.

Romanus set out from Constantinople at the head of his army on 13 March 1071. He planned to recapture both Manzikert and Chliat, which he approached by way of Erzurum. According to Michael Attaliates, an adviser of the emperor who accompanied him on the campaign, when they arrived in Erzurum rations for two months were distributed to the troops as 'they were about to march through uninhabited land which had been trampled underfoot by the foreigners'.

Meanwhile, Alp Arslan, who was about to besiege Aleppo after attacking Edessa, broke off the siege and headed back eastward towards Lake Van as soon as he learned that the Byzantine army was advancing into eastern Anatolia.

As Romanus approached Lake Van he split his forces, sending the larger part on towards Chliat under the Georgian general Joseph Tarchaniotes and the Norman mercenary Roussel of Bailleul, while he himself took the smaller contingent to attack Manzikert. The reasoning behind this was that Romanus expected Manzikert to fall quickly, so that he could rejoin the main army before they reached Chliat.

Manzikert did in fact fall almost without resistance, and after taking it Romanus camped outside the city walls, planning to set out the next day to rejoin the rest of his army before Chliat. At that point the advance guard of the Seljuk cavalry came upon Byzantine soldiers who were foraging in the vicinity of Manzikert. Romanus thought that the horsemen were just a Türkmen raiding party, and he sent Nicephorus Bryennius with a small detachment to deal with them. But Bryennius found the raiders were too strong for him and he sent the emperor an urgent message for reinforcements. At first Romanus accused Bryennius of cowardice, being unaware of the true situation, but eventually he sent another contingent under Basilacius to aid him. Together the two contingents drove back the raiders at first, but then the Turks counter-attacked, capturing Basilacius and wounding Bryennius, who barely managed to make his way back into the Byzantine camp. Romanus then ordered his entire force out to do battle with the raiders, but in the interim the Turks disappeared.

As soon as night fell the Turks returned, attacking a group of Uze mercenaries who were outside the camp buying supplies from the local traders. The Uze fled back inside the fortified camp, while the Turks rode around the periphery shouting war cries and firing arrows into the enclosure, killing and wounding a number of the terrified defenders.

Early the following day a detachment of the Uze mercenaries deserted under their commander Tamais and joined their fellow Turks. This further lowered morale in the camp, Romanus and his generals now fearing that the rest of the Uze might desert. The emperor ordered his archers to march out of the camp and engage the raiders, whom they succeeded in driving away with heavy losses to the Turks.

Romanus wanted to attack the main Turkish force at once, but he hesitated because the majority of his troops were supposedly waiting for him outside Chliat. He sent messengers to summon them to Manzikert, after which he decided to march out against the Turks the next day, even though he knew that his force in Chliat would not be able to join him in time. Unknown to Romanus, both Tarchaniotes and Roussel had fled with their troops as soon as they learned that Alp Arslan had arrived at Lake Van with his army. Thus Romanus and his force at Manzikert were left by themselves to face the Seljuks.

Before Romanus made his move an embassy from the sultan arrived at Manzikert, bringing proposals for an amicable settlement between the Seljuks and the Byzantines. The emperor's generals advised him to reject the offer, arguing that the sultan was just stalling for time, waiting for reinforcements, for the Turks were outnumbered by at least four to one, according to a modern estimate. Also, Romanus knew that he had to take action against the Turks, for his enemies in Constantinople would be able to depose him if he was seen to come to terms with the sultan. So Romanus turned away the sultan's emissaries and prepared to do battle with Alp Arslan, for he felt that this was the only way he could redeem himself, and another such opportunity might never present itself.

The only extant eyewitness account of the battle is that of Michael Attaliates. From his account it would seem that the date of the battle was Friday, 26 August 1071, and the place somewhere on the road between Manzikert and Chliat. Alp Arslan is generally credited by Muslim sources as having 15,000 warriors under his command, while a modern Western authority says that Romanus commanded some 60,000.

On the morning of the day of battle Romanus marshalled all his troops, leaving none in reserve to guard their camp and supplies, since the desertion of his army before Chliat left him no forces to spare. Romanus himself commanded the centre, Bryennius the left wing, and the Cappadocian general Alyattes the right, while Andronicus Ducas was in charge of the rearguard.

Romanus led his army in a frontal attack against the Turks, who retreated in good order, with the emperor in hot pursuit. As sunset approached Romanus ordered a halt, having decided to bring his troops back to their unguarded camp for fear that the Turks might circle around during the night and capture it. When the imperial standard was reversed the troops in the centre of the line began heading back towards the camp. But those who were farther away thought that the reversed standard meant that the emperor had been defeated and was retreating. Attaliates and the other Byzantine sources agree that Andronicus Ducas deliberately started the false rumour that the emperor had been defeated, part of a plan conceived by his uncle, Caesar John Ducas, intended to discredit and overthrow Romanus.

The rumour led to the headlong flight of most of the Byzantine army, which the emperor was unable to stem. The Turks on the heights overlooking the battlefield saw this and informed Alp Arslan, who ordered his troops to regroup and counter-attack. Romanus continued to fight on valiantly along with those around him, while the Turkish cavalry overtook the retreating Byzantine forces and cut them to pieces. Word spread that the emperor himself had been killed or captured, which led the surviving Byzantine troops to desert and flee for their lives. Michael Attaliates describes the scene:

> Outside the camp all were in flight, shouting incoherently and riding about in disorder; no one could say what was happening. Some maintained that the Emperor was still fighting with what was left of his army, and that the barbarians had been put to flight. Others claimed that he had been killed or captured. Everyone had something different to report... It was like an earthquake, the shouting, the sweat, the swift rushes of fear, the clouds of dust, and not least the hordes of Turks riding all around us. Depending on his speed, resolution and strength, each man sought safety in flight. The enemy followed in pursuit, killing some, capturing others and trampling yet others under their horses' hooves. It was a tragic sight, beyond any mourning or lamenting. What indeed could be more pitiable than to see the entire imperial army in flight, defeated and pursued by cruel and inhuman barbarians; the emperor defenceless and surrounded by more of the same; the imperial tents, symbols of military might and sovereignty, taken over by men of such a kind; the whole Roman state overturned – and knowing that the Empire itself was on the verge of collapse?

Eventually Romanus was forced to surrender, after he had been wounded in the hand so that he could no longer hold his sword, his horse killed beneath him. He lay among the dead and wounded Byzantine troops through the night, receiving no special attention from his captors, who the following morning brought him in chains before the sultan.

Alp Aslan at first did not believe that the captive brought before him was the Byzantine emperor. Romanus was eventually identified by the Turkish emissaries who had met with him before the battle, and also by his fellow prisoner Basilacius. Only then did Alp Arslan rise from his throne, ordering Romanus to kiss the ground before him, whereupon the sultan put his foot on the emperor's neck in token of his victory. He then helped Romanus to his feet, bidding the emperor to sit beside him on the throne, assuring his captive that he would be treated with all the respect due his imperial rank.

During the week that followed Romanus was treated as an honoured guest at Alp Arslan's court, eating at the sultan's table and conversing familiarly with him. The sultan, who admired the emperor's dignity in defeat, offered him tolerable peace terms. Romanus, in return for his release, reportedly promised to pay a huge ransom and a large annual tribute. He is also said to have agreed to cede the cities of Manzikert, Edessa (Urfa), Hierapolis and Aleppo, but modern scholars have cast doubt on this.

In any event, Alp Arslan urged Romanus to make his way back to Constantinople without delay, for there was a strong possibility that he might be deposed in his absence, particularly in light of the defeat of the Byzantine army at Manzikert. As it turned out, Manzikert was the second of two disasters suffered by Byzantium in the space of less than five months, for the previous April the Normans had captured Bari, the last Byzantine possession in Italy.

Alp Arslan rode with Romanus on the first stage of his homeward journey, providing an armed escort to accompany him on the remainder of the way. Romanus soon met up with remnants of his defeated army, after which he gratefully dismissed his Turkish escort and sent them back to the sultan. He then rode on with his men to Dokeia (Tokat) in Paphlagonia, where he learned that he had been deposed in Constantinople.

As Romanus had feared, his enemies in Constantinople had taken advantage of his absence to move against him, led by the caesar John Ducas, who had returned from exile. As soon as news of the Byzantine defeat at Manzikert reached Constantinople, Ducas seized power and declared that Romanus was deposed, proclaiming that his nephew Michael VII was now sole emperor. Michael's mother, Eudocia Macrembolitissa, who had been acting as regent, was arrested and exiled to a convent, leaving the caesar John Ducas and his party in power through their influence on the young and ineffective Emperor Michael.

The caesar sent his youngest son, Constantine, with a force to Dokeia, where he defeated the battered veterans of Manzikert and forced

Romanus to flee to Cilicia, on the eastern Mediterranean coast of Asia Minor. There Romanus was defeated by a force led by the caesar's eldest son, Andronicus, who had betrayed the emperor at Manzikert. Romanus surrendered to Andronicus, agreeing to renounce all claim to the throne on condition that he would be allowed to retire unharmed to a monastery.

Romanus was brought back to Constantinople, where his eyes were burned out with a red-hot iron, after which he was confined to a monastery he had founded on Proti (Kınalı), one of the Princes Isles in the Sea of Marmara near Constantinople. He died from his wounds the following summer, after which he was buried in the monastery on Proti. He was only thirty-nine, having ruled for less than four years, most of which he had spent in an unsuccessful attempt to hold back the Seljuk Turks from invading Anatolia.

When news reached Alp Arslan that Romanus had been deposed he renounced the peace agreement he had made with him, which in any event had been rejected by Michael VII.

Alp Arslan himself met his end in Turkestan a few months later, on 25 November 1072, when he was stabbed by the commander of a fortress he had captured. He was forty-five at the time of his death, having reigned for almost a decade, during which time the Great Seljuks of Iran had reached the peak of their power, setting the stage for the eventual Turkish conquest of Anatolia.

– 2 –

The Seljuk Sultanate of Rum

Alp Arslan was succeeded by his son Malik-Şah (r. 1072–92), who when he came to the throne was still a minor and under the guardianship of the powerful vizier Nizam al-Mulk. During the reign of Malik-Şah the Great Seljuks expanded mainly by annexing Muslim states that became vassals, such as the Marwanid emirate in south-eastern Anatolia and the Karakhanid empire in Central Asia. By the end of his reign the Great Seljuks reached the peak of their power, their sultanate stretching from Arabia to the borders of India, including nearly all the Muslim territories in Asia.

At the beginning of Malik-Şah's reign four sons of Kutalmış, who had been under surveillance after the revolt and death of their father, escaped and took refuge with the Türkmen tribes in north-western Anatolia. One of the brothers, Süleyman ibn Kutalmış, established himself as a power in Anatolia, in collaboration with the Türkmen beys Artuk and Tutak, also taking advantage of the disunity among the Byzantines, with whom he occasionally allied himself.

Michael VII Ducas had become sole emperor after his uncle, Caesar John Ducas, deposed Romanus IV Diogenes in 1071. But neither Michael nor John had any talent for administration, and so they gave control of the government to the eunuch Nicephoritzes. Nicephoritzes was soon faced with a revolt in Bulgaria, which he finally suppressed in 1073, after which he turned his attention to the Turkish incursions in Anatolia.

In the spring of 1073 the young general Isaac Comnenus, whose uncle of the same name had been emperor in the years 1057–59, led a small force to drive the Turks out of Cappadocia. He was accompanied

21

by a detachment of Norman mercenaries under Roussel of Bailleul, who had deserted Romanus before the Battle of Manzikert. Roussel was guilty of betrayal again in the Cappadocian campaign, deserting in the face of the Turks, who routed the Byzantine force near Caesareia and took Isaac Comnenus captive. Roussel took advantage of the situation to establish himself as an independent ruler in north-western Anatolia.

Isaac's younger brother, Alexius, escaped capture and made his way back to Constantinople, where he obtained money to ransom his brother. He returned with the money to Cappadocia, where he paid the ransom to Isaac's captors and returned with him to the Byzantine capital, though they were almost captured again by Turks they encountered along the way.

The following spring Nicephoritzes sent a force commanded by the caesar John Ducas to deal with Roussel. The two forces met on the bend of the Sangarius (Sakarya) west of Ancyra (Ankara), where the Norman mercenaries in the Byzantine army deserted to join Roussel, who defeated and captured Ducas. The caesar's son, Constantine, set out with a relief force to rescue his father, only to die in the attempt.

Roussel then moved westward towards Nicomedia (Izmit), where he proclaimed John Ducas emperor, apparently with the caesar's approval. Nicephoritzes then sought the help of the Türkmen emir Artuk, whose tribesmen captured both Roussel and John. Roussel's wife paid a ransom to Artuk to secure the release of her husband, who then returned to his independent principality in north-western Anatolia. Soon afterwards a Byzantine envoy arrived to pay Artuk a ransom for John Ducas, who was allowed to retire to a monastery.

The following year Nicephoritzes sent Alexius Comnenus to deal with Roussel, though they were unable to provide him with any troops. Alexius bribed the Türkmen emir Tutuç to capture Roussel, whom he brought back from Amaseia (Amasya) to Constantinople in chains, ending the Norman's infamous career.

On the final stage of their journey Alexius was forced to take ship at Heracleia Pontica (Karadeniz Ereğlisi) to reach the capital, for the roads were swarming with Turks. The Türkmen tribes were now penetrating as far as the Bosphorus, as Greek refugees fled before them and crowded into Constantinople, causing a severe famine. The princess Anna Comnena, daughter of Alexius Comnenus, describes the situation in her *Alexiad*, a history of her father's times:

The truth was that in this area the Empire was reduced to its last men. Turkish infiltration had scattered the eastern armies in all directions and the Turks were in almost complete control of all the districts between the Black Sea and the Hellespont [Dardanelles], the Syrian and Aegean waters, the Saros [Seyhan] and the other rivers, in particular those which flow along the borders of Pamphylia and Cilicia and empty themselves into the Egyptian Sea.

By the autumn of 1077 the regime of Michael VII was on the verge of collapse, with revolts breaking out in the army in both the Balkans and Anatolia. The army in Europe supported the imperial claim of Nicephorus Bryennius, the duke of Dyrrachium (Durres, in Albania). Bryennius led his supporters towards Constantinople, but their looting in Thrace so angered the people that the rebel army had to retire to Adrianople (Edirne) for the winter. Meanwhile, the army in Anatolia had declared for their general, Nicephorus Botaniates, who occupied a number of towns in Bithynia, the north-westernmost region of Asia Minor, where he proclaimed himself emperor. Botaniates then prepared to march on Constantinople when the time was ripe, having secured his rear by an alliance with the Seljuk prince Süleyman ibn Kutalmış.

While the rebels waited, discontent against the government increased in Constantinople, and in March 1078 the populace rioted and burned down a number of public buildings. Nicephoritzes was seized and killed by the mob, while the emperor Michael took refuge in the monastery of the Studion, where he abdicated and became a monk. Michael's wife, the Georgian princess Maria of Alania, remained behind in the palace with their son Constantine.

Alexius Comnenus, who commanded the imperial forces in Constantinople, sensed that the populace preferred Botaniates rather than Bryennius. Alexius sent word of this to Botaniates, who then marched to Chrysopolis (Üsküdar) and crossed the Bosphorus to Constantinople. There, on 24 March 1078, he was acclaimed as the emperor Nicephorus III, and while he was being crowned by the patriarch, Cosmas, the Turks under Süleyman were sacking Chrysopolis.

Süleyman by that time was in control of large areas of Anatolia from the straits to Cilicia, and had extended his territory into Syria by his capture of Aleppo in 1074. According to the modern Turkish historian Ibrahim Kafesoğlu, Süleyman received from the caliph in Baghdad a robe of honour and a *manshur*, or patent, confirming his sovereignty in

Anatolia. Around that time Byzantine texts begin to use the term 'Sultan' in referring to Süleyman, whose men also started calling him by this title. In 1078 Süleyman took Nicaea (Iznik), the ancient Greek city in Bithynia, and made it the first capital of the Seljuk Sultanate of Rum. Anna Comnena writes of Süleyman's incursions in her *Alexiad*:

> As I have said … the godless Turks were in sight, living in the Propontis [Marmara] area, and Sulayman, who commanded all the east, was actually encamped in the vicinity of Nicaea. His sultanate was in that city (we would call it his palace). The whole countryside of Bithynia and Thynia were unceasingly exposed to Sulayman's foragers; marauding parties on horseback and on foot were raiding as far as the town now called Damalis on the Bosphorus itself; they carried off much booty and all but tried to leap across the very sea. The Byzantines saw them living absolutely unafraid and unmolested in the little villages on the coast and in sacred buildings. The sight filled them with horror. They had no idea what to do.

Nicephorus was seventy-six when he came to the throne, hardly of an age to deal with the grave dangers now threatening the empire. But he did his utmost to restore order, offering the post of caesar to Nicephorus Bryennius, who refused and persisted in his claim to the throne. The emperor sent a force to Adrianople under Alexius Comnenus. Alexius, with the aid of his Turkish auxiliaries, defeated and captured Bryennius, who was blinded to prevent him from ever again claiming the throne. Alexius then went on to put down another rebellion in the European provinces led by Nicephorus Basilacius, whom he also captured and blinded.

Nicephorus sought to legitimise his reign by proposing marriage to the beautiful empress Maria of Alania, although her husband Michael was still alive, confined to the monastery of the Studion. Maria accepted, hoping that her son Constantine would succeed to the throne. The marriage scandalised the patriarch Cosmas and most others in the capital, and even Maria herself realised that she had made a mistake when Nicephorus failed to recognise her son Constantine as his heir.

Late in 1080 another revolt broke out in Asia Minor, where Nicephorus Melissenus, brother-in-law of Alexius Comnenus, declared himself emperor, supported by an alliance with Süleyman ibn Kutalmış. Alexius Comnenus was called on to put down the rebellion, but he refused to take action against his brother-in-law, who continued his rebellion with the aid of his Turkish allies.

Early the following year the emperor named his nephew Nicephorus Synadenus as his successor. This disappointed the empress Maria, who still had hopes that her son Constantine would succeed to the throne, and it alienated both the Ducas family and Alexius Comnenus, whose wife was a Ducas.

Alexius then began plotting to usurp the throne, conspiring together with his brother Isaac, the caesar John Ducas and the empress Maria. He also came to terms with his brother-in-law Nicephorus Melissinus, who agreed to give up his own own imperial claim in deference to that of Alexius, who offered him the title of duke in recompense.

Alexius and Isaac left Constantinople under the cover of night and made their way to Tzurullum (Çorlu) in Thrace, where they secretly gathered an army, which to a large extent was made up of foreign mercenaries, particularly Germans, as was the imperial army in the capital. When all was ready they marched on Constantinople, where the commander of the German mercenaries opened one of the city gates for them. They swiftly seized the capital, but after Alexius lost control of his troops they sacked the city. In the meanwhile, Botaniates saw that there was no point in fighting on, and he was persuaded by the patriarch Cosmas to abdicate. Then, on Easter Sunday, 4 April 1081, Alexius Comnenus was crowned emperor in the church of Haghia Sophia, beginning one of the longest and most illustrious reigns in the history of the Byzantine Empire.

Alexius came to power at a time when the empire was without resources and under threat in both Europe and Asia, attacked on the west by the Normans and Patzinaks and on the east by the Seljuk Turks. The Byzantine emperors had in the past bought off the Patzinaks by settling them in the Balkan territories they had occupied, and now Alexius tried the same strategy with the Seljuks.

Alexius had been skirmishing with Süleyman in an effort to drive the Turks from Nicomedia, the provincial capital of Bithynia. Alexius was forced to send most of his best troops to Europe, because of the threats posed by the Normans and the Patzinaks, and so eventually he was forced to negotiate a treaty with Süleyman, setting the river Dracon (Dragos) as the boundary between Byzantium and the Selçuk sultanate. But, since Alexius was in no position to enforce the agreement, Süleyman violated it, sending his Türkmen tribesmen on raids as far as the Sea of Marmara and the Bosphorus. The princess Anna Comnena describes these raids in her *Alexiad*, where she writes, with some exaggeration, that the effective boundaries of the Byzantine Empire in the east and west were now the Bosphorus and Adrianople.

In 1084 Süleyman went off on campaign in south-eastern Anatolia, leaving his kinsman Abu'l-Kasım in charge at Nicaea. As Süleyman advanced through south-eastern Anatolia the scattered Byzantine commanders gave way before him. The strongest of them, Philaretus Brachamius, surrendered Antioch to him in 1085 and Edessa the following year. Süleyman was advancing into Syria in June 1086 when he was defeated and killed near Aleppo in a battle with Tutuş, a brother of Malik-Şah who had been appointed as sultan of Syria.

When Malik-Şah heard the news of Süleyman's invasion of Syria he marched from Isfahan to besiege Edessa and Aleppo. Süleyman's vizier in Aleppo surrendered to Malik-Şah, to whom he handed over the late sultan's young son and heir Kılıç Arslan. Malik-Şah took Kılıç Arslan back with him to the Great Seljuk capital in Isfahan, where the young prince remained an honoured prisoner for the next six years.

Meanwhile there had been an interregnum in the Seljuk Sultanate of Rum. Abu'l-Kasım, who had been left in charge at Nicaea by Süleyman, took advantage of a Norman invasion of Byzantine territory in Epirus to attack Greek towns throughout Bithynia. He then began building ships in the port of Cius (Gemlik), hoping to establish himself as a naval power, but Alexius Comnenus succeeded in holding him in check.

Malik-Şah decided to put down Abu'l Kasım, and in 1087 he sent an army to Bithynia under the emir Bursuk. Alexius succeeded in reconciling Abu'l Kasım and Malik-Şah, who offered the Byzantines an alliance in which he would remove the Turks from western Asia Minor and the coastal areas. The alliance was never realised, but Alexius took advantage of the offer to recover the Black Sea port of Sinope (Sinop), which had fallen to a Türkmen emir named Karategin.

Five years later Malik-Şah sent another army to deal with Abu'l-Kasım, this one under the emir Buzan. Buzan occupied most of the territory controlled by Abu'l-Kasım, but he was unable to reduce his capital, Nicaea. Abu'l Kasım then thought it advisable to go to Isfahan to seek Malik-Şah's pardon. When he did so the sultan sent him to seek a reconciliation with Buzan, who immediately had Abu'l-Kasım strangled. When news of this reached Anatolia Abu'l Kasım's brother Abu'l-Gazi, also known as Buldacı, hastened from Cappadocia to Nicaea, where he took control without difficulty.

Buzan had presented Alexius with a proposal for an alliance with Malik-Şah, who offered to restore all of Anatolia to Byzantine rule, on condition that a daughter of the emperor be given in marriage to one of his sons. Alexius was unwilling to agree to the marriage, but he played for time by sending an envoy to Malik-Şah with further demands. But en route the envoy learned that Malik-Şah had been assassinated on 20 November 1092, whereupon he returned to Constantinople to inform the emperor.

Malik-Şah was succeeded by his son Bargıyaruk, and in the confusion during the change of regime Kılıç Arslan escaped from the Great Seljuk court and made his way back to western Anatolia. Early in 1093 Kılıç Arslan finally returned to Nicaea, where he took control without opposition, ending the interregnum in the Sultanate of Rum.

During the interregnum the Türkmen emir Çaka had taken control of Smyrna (Izmir) and its hinterland. By 1090 Çaka had built himself a fleet and seized control of the islands of Samos, Chios and Lesbos. He also took the fort of Abydos on the Asian shore of the Hellespont, closing the strait and defeating a fleet that Alexius Comnenus sent against him. Two years later Alexius sent another fleet commanded by his brother-in-law John Ducas, who opened up the Hellespont and drove Çaka's forces from the islands.

Alexius then proposed an alliance with Kılıç Arslan, telling the sultan that Çaka posed a serious threat to him. Kılıç Arslan agreed to the alliance, despite the fact that he was married to a daughter of Çaka. In 1094, when Çaka again besieged Abydos, Kılıç Arslan joined forces with Alexius to defend the fortress. When Çaka saw this he attempted to come to an agreement with Kılıç Arslan, who invited his father-in-law to a dinner, at which he did away with him. Anna Comnena writes of this incident in her *Alexiad*:

> The sultan received him graciously with a pleasant smile, and when his table was laid ready in the usual way, he shared it with Tzachas at dinner and compelled him to drink more heavily than he should have done. Then, seeing him in a fuddled state, he drew his sword and thrust it into his side. Tzachas fell dead on the spot. The sultan then made overtures to the emperor for peace in the future and his proposals met with success, for Alexius consented and a treaty was concluded in the normal way. Thus peace was restored in the maritime provinces.

The Seljuk Sultanate of Rum was only one of several Türkmen *beyliks*, or emirates, contending for power in Anatolia at the end of the eleventh century. The most powerful of these was the Danışmendid tribe of central and eastern Anatolia, the main branches being in Sivas and

Malatya; others included the Artukids in Diyararbakır and Mardin, the Mengücekids in Erzincan, the Saltukids in Erzurum and the Şah Armenids of Ahlat.

Early in 1095 Alexius sent envoys to Pope Urban II, appealing for help against the Muslims who had overrun the Byzantine domains in Anatolia. That fall, during a church council at Clermont in France, Urban called for a great expedition to free the eastern Christians from the Muslims and recapture Jerusalem.

This expedition, which came to be called the First Crusade, got under way the following year, the first contingent being a rabble of peasants who arrived at Constantinople under the leadership of Peter the Hermit. Seeing that there were no soldiers among them, Alexius advised Peter to have his people wait in the vicinity of Nicomedia until the main crusading army arrived. But the Christian rabble went on a rampage when they arrived in Anatolia, and they were soon slaughtered by the Turks. Those who survived were brought back across the Bosphorus by Alexius, who gave them refuge outside Constantinople.

The first of the regular armies of the crusaders arrived at Constantinople in the autumn of 1096, a contingent led by Hugh of Vermandois, brother of King Philip I of France. The next contingent to arrive, on 23 December 1096, was that of Godfrey of Bouillon, duke of Lower Lorraine, with his brothers Eustace and Baldwin of Boulogne. The third was that of the Norman count Bohemund of Taranto and his nephew Tancred, who arrived on 9 April 1097, followed the next day by one led by Raymond of St Gilles. The fourth and last crusader army arrived in May, commanded by Duke Robert of Normandy, who was accompanied by Robert of Flanders and Stephen of Blois. Alexius, after heated arguments and some violence, eventually persuaded all the crusader leaders to sign an oath of loyalty to him, in which they vowed to restore all the Byzantine territory they recaptured from the Turks.

The first objective of the crusaders was Nicaea, capital of the Seljuk Sultanate of Rum. The various crusader contingents reached Nicaea between 6 May and 3 June, while Alexius set up his camp at Pelecanum, on the northern shore of the Gulf of Nicomedia.

Meanwhile, Kılıç Arslan had been in eastern Anatolia besieging Malatya, which he was trying to take from the Danışmendid. As soon as he heard that the crusaders were threatening his capital he made a truce with the Danışmendid and rushed back to Nicaea, where he had left his wife and children and much of his treasure.

The advance guard of the Seljuk army arrived at Nicaea around 18 May, by which time the crusaders had surrounded the city, which was protected on all sides by powerful Roman walls, the eastern side bordered by Lake Ascania.

Kılıç Arslan arrived with the main Seljuk army on 21 May and immediately attacked the southern section of the city walls, defended by Raymond of St Gilles. The crusaders defending the other sides of the city walls were afraid to leave their sections unprotected to come to the aid of Raymond, but he fought off the Seljuks in a day-long battle that resulted in heavy casualties on both sides.

After the battle Kılıç Arslan abandoned Nicaea to its fate and departed with his army. Alexius then marched his own army to Nicaea, bringing a flotilla of warships to Lake Ascania under the command of the admiral Butumites. The Turkish defenders in Nicaea secretly made contact with Butumites, opening negotiations to surrender to Alexius rather than to the crusaders, playing for time in the hope that Kılıç Arslan might return to save them. The allies agreed to make a general assault on 19 June, but when the day dawned the crusaders saw the imperial Byzantine banner flying from the defence towers of the city. It turned out that during the night the defenders had surrendered to Butumites, who had rushed his troops through the gate that opened on to the lake.

The crusaders were then allowed into Nicaea in small groups, so that the Byzantine garrison could prevent them from looting the city and harming the populace, both Greeks and Turks. The sultan's family and the Seljuk nobility were escorted to Constantinople, where the nobles arranged for ransom to be paid for their release. Alexius, after a delay of some months, sent Kılıç Arslan's wife and children back to him without a ransom. The emperor then mollified the crusader leaders by giving them gold and jewels from the sultan's treasury.

Meanwhile Kılıç Arslan had made an alliance with the Danışmendid of Sivas and Hasan Bey, the Türkmen emir of Kayseri, agreeing to take joint action against the crusaders. Then, together with his allies, he headed westward to confront the enemy.

The crusaders had decided to march across Anatolia in two sections of about equal numbers. The first section of the crusaders, commanded by Bohemund of Taranto, set out from Nicaea on 26 June, accompanied by a detachment of Byzantine troops, while the second left the following day, led by Raymond of St Gilles. The first stage of their march took them to Dorylaeum (Eskişehir), where on 1 July the force under Bohemund was ambushed by Kılıç Arslan and his allies. The Turks surrounded Bohemund's troops and rained arrows upon them, putting the crusaders in a perilous position. But then at midday the second section of the crusader army under Raymond of St Gilles arrived and broke through to join up with Bohemund's beleaguered troops, forcing Kılıç Arslan and his army to flee.

Kılıç Arslan by now realised that the Turks were no match for the more numerous and better-armed crusaders, and he gave up active resistance, other than ordering that the Christians be harried and that their route across Anatolia be stripped of supplies.

Later that summer, near Cybistra Heracleia (Ereğli) in southern Cappadocia, the crusaders were attacked by Türkmen tribesmen under Hasan Bey, whom they drove off easily. A detachment of crusaders led by Bohemund and Tancred defeated Hasan Bey again near Augustopolis in Cilicia. The Christian army then passed through the Cilician Gates and captured Tarsus, where the Turkish defenders managed to kill 300 Normans.

The crusaders went on to capture Antioch on 3 July 1097; on 6 February 1098 they took Edessa; and on 11 July 1099 they conquered Jerusalem, the ultimate goal of the First Crusade. Each of the three cities became the capital of a crusader principality. Godfrey of Bouillon was elected king of Jerusalem, and when he died on 18 July 1100 he was succeeded by his brother Baldwin. Raymond of Toulouse established himself as count of Edessa, and Bohemund of Taranto became count of Antioch.

In mid-August 1100 Bohemund was ambushed while en route from Antioch to Malatya, and after a brief struggle he was taken captive by the Danışmendid emir Malik-Gazi Gümüştigin of Sivas. Malik-Gazi took his captive to Neocaesareia (Niksar), where Bohemund was held for ransom, while his nephew Tancred ruled Antioch in his absence. Tancred was not anxious to ransom his uncle, who remained captive in Niksar for nearly three years.

Meanwhile, Kılıç Arslan established his capital at Konya, where he was in a better position to contend for power in central and eastern Anatolia. There his principal rival was Malik-Gazi, whose possession of Bohemund gave the Danışmendid emir a great potential advantage in negotiating with the various powers in the region.

Pope Urban II died on 29 July 1099 and was succeeded by Paschal II, who continued the crusading policy of his predecessor. As a result of his appeals a new wave of crusaders began arriving at Constantinople early in 1101. The first group to reach the capital comprised 20,000 Lombards; followed by two successive contingents of French knights, the second commanded by Count William of Nevers; and finally an enormous Franco-German force headed by William, duke of Aquitaine, and Welf, duke of Bavaria.

The first to leave Constantinople were the Lombards, under the command of Raymond of Toulouse, who had returned to the capital to visit Alexius. Rather than starting out directly for the Holy Land, the Lombards insisted on first heading for Niksar to liberate Bohemund from Malik-Gazi. En route they captured Ankara, but soon afterwards they were ambushed at Mersivan (Merzifon) by the Seljuks and their Danışmendid allies. Four-fifths of the Lombard soldiers were killed and many others were captured, along with the women and children who accompanied them, while Raymond of Toulouse was among the few who escaped and made their way back to Constantinople.

The French knights left Constantinople in June under the command of William of Nevers, who led his army via Ankara to Konya, which he tried to capture from its Seljuk garrison, but without success. Kılıç Arslan and Malik-Gazi then ambushed the French in southern Cappadocia near Ereğli and virtually wiped them out, William of Nevers being among the few to escape.

The Franco-German army suffered the same fate not long afterwards, again ambushed by the Turks near Ereğli. Once again the leaders, William of Aquitaine and Welf of Bavaria, were among the few to survive, though they had to throw away their weapons and flee to Cilicia incognito. Thus the crusade of 1101 ended in disaster for the Christian cause.

Kılıç Arslan had grown jealous of the influence that Malik-Gazi had gained through his possession of Bohemund. The wily Bohemund took advantage of this by offering Malik-Gazi favourable terms, including an alliance against both Kılıç Arslan and Alexius Comnenus in return for his freedom. Bohemund's friends finally raised the ransom demanded by Malik-Gazi, who freed his captive in May 1003. Bohemund then returned to Antioch, where he resumed his rule of the principality, relegating Tancred to the governorship of two small towns.

Although Kılıç Arslan and Malik-Gazi had been allies in resisting the crusaders, the Seljuk sultan and the Danışmendid emir were rivals in the struggle for dominance in central and eastern Anatolia. Kılıç Arslan captured Malatya from the Danışmendid in 1104, which brought him into conflict with Muizz-ud Din Malik Şah, whose death the following year averted open warfare.

Kılıç Arslan then turned his attention to south-eastern Anatolia and upper Mesopotamia, where the emirs of Harran and Mosul called on him for aid against their master Sultan Muhammad, son of Malik-Şah and ruler of the branch of the Seljuks in Iraq. Kılıç Arslan succeeded in capturing Mayafarrekin, the capital of the Diyarbakır region, after which he went on to take Mosul.

But then in 1107 he came up against the emir Chavli Saqaveh, who had been appointed governor of Mosul by Sultan Muhammad. The two armies met on the Khabur, a tributary of the middle Euphrates, where Chavli defeated Kılıç Arslan, who was drowned in the river during the fighting. Thus for the second successive generation a Seljuk sultan of Rum had died in an attempt to expand his domains, leaving his sultanate in a precarious position.

– 3 –

Konya, the Capital of Rum

The death of Kılıç Arslan in 1107 left the Sultanate of Rum in a state of crisis. Kılıç Arslan's son Melik was captured during the battle on the Khabur by Chavli Saqaveh, who sent him as a prisoner to the court of Sultan Muhammad. Melik was regarded as Kılıç Arslan's heir, but since he was a prisoner his cousin Hasan Bey of Cappadocia served as regent of the Sultanate of Rum. Two years later Hasan secured the release of Melik, who made his way back to Konya. There he succeeded to his father's throne under the name of Melikşah, though he is sometimes called Şahanşah.

Kılıç Arslan had left three other sons – Ruknuddin Mesut, Arap and Tuğrul – complicating the succession to the throne and, for a time, causing divisions in the sultanate. Ruknuddin Mesut, the eldest, was held hostage at the Danışmendid court in Anatolia; Arap was a prisoner at the Great Seljuk court in Iran; while Tuğrul, the youngest son, was with his mother in Malatya.

Tuğrul's mother, originally named Isabella (her Muslim name is unknown), was a sister of the crusader Raymond of St Egidier. When she heard of Kılıç Arslan's death she quickly moved to establish Tuğrul as ruler of Malatya and the eastern provinces, acting as regent for her son. She retained power during the next decade by marrying in turn three Türkmen chieftains, to each of whom she gave the title of *atabeg*. The office of *atabeg* in the Seljuk dynasty was normally held by a military chief to whom the sultan entrusted the education and welfare of his son and heir, and who in some cases ultimately married his pupil's mother. The third of the three *atabeg* was Balak, whom Tuğrul's mother married in 1118. Balak was a descendant of the Türkmen emir Artuk, founder of the Artukid dynasty, which from the beginning of the twelfth century until 1408 was the dominant power on the upper Tigris, one branch of the clan ruling in Diyarbakır and the other in Mardin and Mayyafarikin.

Ruknuddin Mesut had in the meanwhile married a daughter of Amir Gazi Gümüştigin, the Danışmendid emir in whose court he was being held hostage. Amir Gazi ruled from the Halys to the Euphrates, and he used his power to support the claim of his son-in-law to the Seljuk throne occupied by Mesut's brother Melikşah. Thus three of Kılıç Arslan's sons were contending for power in Anatolia, while the deceased sultan's fourth son, Arap, was still a captive in the court of the Great Seljuks in Iran.

Melikşah mounted an offensive in western Anatolia in 1111, attacking the Byzantine cities of Philadelphia (Alaşehir) and Pergamon (Bergama) as well as other places in the Aegean provinces of the empire. Sultan Muhammad, Malikşah's former captor, sent a contingent to aid him in this campaign. At the same time, a fleet of Pisan, Genoese and Lombard ships threatened to ravage the Byzantine ports along the Aegean coast of Anatolia, forcing the emperor Alexius to fight on two fronts at once.

The following year Alexius entered into negotiations with Sultan Muhammad, leaving Melikşah aside, and the two monarchs came to terms. The details of the agreement are unknown, but Muhammad withdrew his troops, and the Great Seljuks never again intervened in Anatolia.

Three years later Melikşah launched another expedition into western Anatolia, this time without the aid of Sultan Muhammad. Alexius was suffering from an acute attack of gout, and so he was unable to mount an offensive until the following year, by which time Melikşah's army had penetrated as far as Nicomedia. As Alexius advanced Melikşah retreated, his men burning the countryside behind them and harrying the Byzantine troops with frequent raids. Anna Comnena describes the Turkish style of attack:

> ...Their right and left wings and their centre formed separate groups with their ranks cut off, as it were, with one another; whenever an attack was made on right or left, the centre leaped into action in a whirlwind onslaught that threw into confusion the accepted tradition of battle. As for the weapons they use in war, unlike the Kelts they do not fight with lance but completely surround the enemy and shoot at him with arrows; they also defend themselves with arrows at a distance. In hot pursuit the Turk makes prisoners by using his bow; in flight he overwhelms his

pursuer with the same weapon and when he shoots, the weapon in its course strikes either rider or horse, fired with such force that it passes clean through the body. So skilled are the Turkish archers.

Alexius led his army as far as Philomelion (Akşehir), which he captured from the Seljuks. The emperor than sent out several detachments into the countryside around Konya, in the hope of rescuing the Byzantine soldiers and Greek civilians who had been captured by the Turks. But he rescued so many refugees that he decided to start back with them to Constantinople rather than going on to attack Konya.

The Byzantine force was followed by the Turks, who laid ambushes on either flank. Then as the Byzantines approached Acroenos (Afyon) the Seljuks attacked them in force, though they were beaten off with heavy casualties, while Melikşah was almost captured in the Turkish retreat.

Melikşah attacked again the next day, but once more he was beaten back with heavy casualties. Then, after consulting with his generals, the sultan decided to sue for peace, after which he and the emperor came to terms. Before they went their separate ways Alexius gave Melikşah generous presents, including a silver candelabrum.

Meanwhile, news arrived that Mesut had taken Konya with the aid of his father-in-law, Amir Gazi, and was plotting to supplant his brother Melikşah as sultan of Rum. Alexius advised Melikşah to wait with him until he had more information about the plot. But Melikşah was intent on leaving, and so Alexius offered to have a company of heavily armed Byzantine soldiers accompany him, but the sultan was too proud to accept the escort.

Mesut was now approaching with a large army, forcing Melikşah to take refuge in the fortified town of Tyragion near Philomelion. The garrison surrendered to Mesut, who captured Melikşah and usurped the throne. Anna Comnena describes Melikşah's fate in ending her account of this singular campaign:

> They [Mesut's soldiers] arrested the sultan and blinded him. As the instrument normally used for this purpose, the candelabrum given to Melik-Shah by the emperor took its place – the diffuser of light had become the instrument of darkness and blinding. However, he could still see a small ray of light and when he arrived at Iconium, led by the hand of some guide, he confided this fact to his nurse and she told his wife. In this way the story reached the ears of Mesut himself. He was greatly disturbed and extremely angry. Elegmon, one of the most prominent satraps, was sent to strangle the sultan with a bowstring. Thus ended the

career of Melik-Shah – the result of his own folly in not heeding Alexius' advice. As for the latter, he continued his march to Constantinople, maintaining the same discipline and good order to the very end.

Thus began the reign of Ruknuddin Mesut I (r. 1116–55), the longest in the history of the Seljuk Sultanate of Rum. Although his predecessors had set up their court in Konya, Mesut was the first to establish the city as the capital of Rum. The earliest western description of the Seljuk capital is by an anonymous knight of the Third Crusade who passed through Konya in 1190; he describes it as being the size of Cologne, surrounded by defence walls enclosing a citadel.

The victory that Alexius Comnenus won over Melikşah was the emperor's last campaign. After his return to Constantinople his health steadily declined, and he finally passed away on 15 August 1118, after thirty-seven years of rule. He was succeeded by his eldest son, John II Comnenus, who was nearly thirty-one at the time of his accession.

The year after his accession John set out on his first campaign, his goal being the reconquest of some of the Byzantine cities in Anatolia that had fallen to the Seljuks. His commanding general was John Axouchos, a Turk who in infancy had been captured by the crusaders at Nicaea. Axouchos had been adopted by Alexius Comnenus and brought up in the imperial household together with Prince John, the two of them becoming close friends.

On this first campaign the imperial forces recaptured Laodicea (Denizli) and Sozopolis (Uluborlu), along with a series of fortresses leading up from the Maeander (Menderes) valley to the central Anatolian plateau. By late autumn the Byzantines had also reopened the road from the plateau to Attaleia (Antalya), their main port on the Mediterranean. There is no record of any reaction from Mesut during this campaign, his policy apparently being to avoid direct battle with the Byzantine army, leaving armed resistance to the Türkmen tribes.

The following year John may have resumed his campaign in Anatolia, but it is difficult to be sure since the chronology of the Byzantine sources is vague on this point. In any event, in 1121 a Patzinak uprising in Thrace turned John's attention towards Europe, and he was not able to resume his campaign against the Turks in Anatolia until the end of the decade.

Meanwhile, in the years 1118–20, Mesut's brother Tuğrul, who was ruling in Malatya under the aegis of his *atabeg* Balak, had been at war with the Türkmen emir Mengücek Gazi, who had founded a dynasty in Erzincan and Divriği. Mengücek received reinforcements from the

Greek duke of Trebizond (Trabzon), Constantine Gabras, who was in rebellion against Emperor John Comnenus. This led Balak to seek help from Amir Ghazi, whose Danışmendid tribesmen defeated and captured Mengücek and Gavras, both of whom were ransomed.

After Balak's death in 1124 two of his cousins, Süleyman and Timurtaş, in turn tried to overthrow Tuğrul as ruler of Malatya, but both failed to seize power. Amir Gazi, with the support of Mesut, took the opportunity to attack Tuğrul and capture Malatya, which from 1124 onward again became part of the Danışmendid emirate. Amir Gazi then went on to take the districts of Kayseri, Ankara, Çankırı and Kastamonu, so that the Danışmendid emirate became the largest Türkmen principality in Anatolia, surpassing the Seljuk Sultanate of Rum in its extent.

Tuğrul was eventually killed, removing him as a rival to his brother Mesut. But then in 1125 Mesut's brother Arap, who had been held captive in the Great Seljuk court in Iran, obtained his release and rushed back to Anatolia. There he gathered support from the Türkmen tribes and captured Konya, overthrowing Mesut and establishing himself as sultan.

Mesut fled to Constantinople, where he was given refuge by the emperor John. John allowed his guest to obtain help from Amir Gazi, who assisted Mesut in recapturing Konya and regaining his throne. Arap fled and took refuge with Prince Thoros, the Armenian ruler of upper Cilicia. Arap enlisted both Armenian and Türkmen troops in an attempt to regain his throne, but after some initial success he failed. He was then given refuge by the emperor John Comnenus in Constantinople, where he remained as an honoured guest for the rest of his days.

The emperor turned his attention to Anatolia once more in 1130, beginning with the fortification of Lopadium (Ulubat) in Bithynia, where Türkmen tribes had again been raiding. John then mounted a campaign against Amir Gazi and the rebel Constantine Gabras. But at the beginning of his march into Anatolia the emperor learned that his younger brother Isaac was plotting to usurp the throne, whereupon he quickly returned with his army to Constantinople.

Isaac fled to Anatolia, where he sought help in turn from Sultan Mesut, Amir Gazi, Constantine Gabras and the Armenian king Leo of Cilicia, but to no avail. Finally, after nearly a decade of exile, Isaac was pardoned by his brother John, who allowed him to live in retirement in Heracleia Pontica.

Meanwhile, the emperor, having secured his position in Constantinople, set out in 1132 with an even stronger army than before to campaign in

Paphlagonia, in north-central Anatolia. He captured Kastamonu from the Danışmendid, received the submission of several of Amir Gazi's governors and slaughtered Turkish settlers, after which he returned to Constantinople in triumph the following year.

Amir Gazi responded by attacking Sozopolis, trying to cut off the Byzantines from their port at Attaleia. When that attempt failed, he marched his army north to Paphlagonia and captured Kastamonu. But then in 1134 Amir Gazi died, to be succeeded by his son Malik Muhammad. The succession left the Danışmendid emirate in a state of disarray, which the emperor took advantage of by recapturing Kastamonu and Çankırı in 1135.

Malik Muhammad attempted to recoup some of the territory that the Danışmendid had lost to John Comnenus, and in 1135 he reconquered most of Paphlagonia. He also continued the Danışmendid policy of supporting Constantine Gabras, duke of Trebizond, in his revolt against the emperor.

John Comnenus responded by mounting a campaign against Malik Muhammad, enlisting the aid of Sultan Mesut. John and Mesut set off together on campaign in the autumn of 1135, when they besieged the town of Gangra (Çankırı) in Paphlagonia. But Malik Muhammad conspired with Mesut to abandon the campaign, forcing the emperor to lift the siege and encamp for the winter.

John resumed the campaign early the following year, when he took Gangra and Kastamonu, after which he put the Danışmendid stronghold of Niksar (Neocaesarea) under siege. During the siege his nephew John, son of the sebastocrator Isaac Comnenus, defected to the enemy, after which he converted to Islam and married a daughter of Sultan Mesut. The emperor was forced to raise the siege that summer, but then he sent a contingent against Gabras that finally regained Trebizond for the empire. By the time that John returned to Constantinople early in 1141 he had reconquered the entire Black Sea coast of Anatolia.

When Malik Muhammad died in December 1141 disputes arose among his sons and brothers, breaking up the Danışmendid emirate into three separate branches. Yağıbasan ruled as emir in Sivas, Ayn-ad-Din controlled Elbistan and Dhu'l-Nun held power in Kayseri. Sultan Mesut took advantage of the situation and invaded Danışmendid territory, capturing Ankara, Çankırı, Kastamonu and their surrounding areas. Yağıbasan and Ayn-ad-Din became frightened by this, and in 1143 they agreed to a treaty with John Comnenus, becoming in effect his vassals.

The break-up of the Danışmendid emirate negated their threat to the Byzantines, allowing John Comnenus to concentrate his attention on a campaign into south-eastern Anatolia and Syria. He set off in the spring of 1142 along with his four sons, Alexius, Andronicus, Isaac and Manuel. Alexius died of disease in Attaleia, and when Andronicus fell ill as well John sent him back him back to Constantinople with his brother Isaac, who was also unwell. Andronicus died on the way, and Isaac brought his body back to Constantinople for burial.

The emperor continued on the campaign with his son Manuel, spending the winter in Cilicia, where he reduced a number of Danışmendid fortresses. He was preparing to set out again in March 1143 when he was accidentally wounded by an arrow while hunting. The wound became badly infected, and by the beginning of April it was clear that he was approaching death. He finally died on 8 April 1143, having designated his youngest son Manuel as his successor. Manuel led the army back to Constantinople, where he secured his position as emperor, briefly imprisoning his brother Isaac to prevent a war of succession.

On Christmas Eve in 1144 Edessa fell to Imad al-Din Zengi, the Great Seljuk *atabeg* of Mosul and founder of the Zengid dynasty. After Zengi was assassinated in 1146 Edessa was recovered by its former Christian ruler, Count Joscelin II. A few days later the city was recaptured by Zengi's son and successor, Nur al-Din Mahmud, who put all the Christian men to the sword and sold the women and children into slavery. The fall of Edessa made a profound impression on Europe, leading Pope Eugenius III to proclaim the Second Crusade.

The year after his accession Manuel went on a brief campaign against Sultan Mesut, who had been raiding in Bithynia as well as in the Aegean area. But Mesut invaded the empire again in 1145, capturing the fortress of Pracana just north of Seleuceia (Silifke), threatening Byzantine communication with Syria.

Manuel responded in the summer of 1146 by proclaiming a formal declaration of war against Mesut, marching his army into Anatolia with the intention of capturing Konya, the Selkuk capital. The contemporary chronicler Nicetas Choniates describes the first phase of the campaign, in which Manuel was wounded:

> At Philomilion he [Manuel] engaged the Turks in battle. There he was struck by an arrow shot by a certain Turk overthrown by the emperor's lance; as he fell backward, the discharged arrow pierced the sole of

Manuel's foot. Manuel, who appeared awesome and daring and more venturesome than his father John, did not choose to turn back, nor would he be persuaded by those who counseled him to consider returning home lest the Turks, in desperation, regroup and batter his forces.

Choniates then goes on to describe the anticlimactic conclusion of this campaign, in which Mesut's daughter dissuaded Manuel from attacking Konya, a remarkable story told by no other chronicler of this period.

Indeed, he [Manuel] rode on to Iconium with heightened enthusiasm. Mesud, who had departed, had set up camp at Taxara, the ancient Koloneia [Şebenkarahisar]; one of his daughters, reportedly married to the emperor's cousin, John Comnenus, the son of the sebastocrator Isaac who, because of some trifling vexation against his uncle, Emperor John Comnenus, had fled and defected to Mesut, peered out from above the walls and delivered a persuasive defence on behalf of her father, the sultan. The emperor reached the outskirts of Iconium with his troops, but after he had allowed the archers to aim their arrows at the battlements…he turned back without further ado.

The emperor then retreated to Lake Caralis (Beyşehir Gölü), beating off Türkmen raiders, after which he led his army back to Constantinople.

In the spring of 1147 Mesut opened negotiations with Manuel, suggesting a truce and offering to give back Pracana and other recent Seljuk conquests. Manuel agreed to a twelve-year truce with Mesut, for which the crusaders would call the emperor a traitor to Christianity.

The German crusaders crossed the Danube in the summer of 1147, led by their emperor, Conrad III, Manuel's father-in-law. They were followed soon afterwards by the French crusaders under their king, Louis VII.

When the Germans arrived at Constantinople Manuel had them ferried across the Bosphorus to Chalcedon (Kadıköy). Conrad was eager to be on his way, and was unwilling to wait for the French to arrive. Manuel was equally anxious to see him off, for the Germans had committed acts of violence against the local population.

Conrad asked for a guide to lead him across Anatolia, and Manuel entrusted the task to Stephen, head of the Varangarian guard. Manuel advised Conrad to avoid the direct road across Anatolia that had been taken by the First Crusade, for this would expose them to attacks by the Turks. Instead, he strongly urged that they take a more indirect route, which would keep them within Byzantine-controlled territory. Manuel also advised Conrad to send home all the non-combatants, mostly pilgrims, because their presence would only hamper the army.

When Conrad reached Nicaea he decided to divide his forces. One group, which included most of the non-combatants, was to be led by Otto of Freisingen, and would take the more indirect route via Laodiceia, while Conrad himself would lead the main army along the route that had been taken by the First Crusade.

Conrad's army left Nicaea on 15 October 1147, and for the next eight days they marched eastward without incident. On 23 October they were approaching Dorylaeum, where half a century earlier the knights of the First Crusade had defeated the Seljuks under Kılıç Arslan. At the end of their march that day the German knights dismounted from their exhausted horses, after which they began to set up their encampment for the evening. At that moment a Seljuk force suddenly attacked the crusaders, who were totally unprepared for them. Conrad tried to rally his men, but by evening he was forced to flee back towards Nicaea with the few others who had survived, having lost nine-tenths of his army and all his supplies.

Meanwhile, King Louis and the French army had passed through Constantinople, and at the beginning of November they reached Nicaea, where they learned of the German defeat. Conrad had already arrived at Nicaea, and Louis hastened to confer with him. The two kings decided to join forces and follow a route that in its initial stage would take them along the Aegean coast of Anatolia as far as Ephesus, from where they would head inland along the Maeander valley, hoping thus to avoid the Seljuks. Conrad became ill at Ephesus and returned to Constantinople, while Louis led the army on, reaching Pisidian Antioch (Yalvaç) on 1 January 1148. There the crusaders were attacked by a Türkmen force, but they fought them off and continued on their way, reaching Pisidian Laodiceia three days later.

From Laodiceia the crusaders started south across the Taurus Mountains, continually harried along the way by Türkmen raiders. At the beginning of February they arrived at Attaleia, where the Byzantine governor, Landolph, arranged for ships to take them to Saint Symeon, the port of Antioch. When the flotilla arrived there were not enough ships to take the entire company, and so King Louis filled them with his own company and as many cavalrymen as he could fit aboard, leaving the rest of the army to make its way along the coast under the command of Counts Thierry of Flanders and Archimbald of Bourbon.

The day after the king's departure the Turks attacked the crusader camp, forcing them to take refuge within the walls of Attaleia. Landolph arranged for more ships to take them to Saint Symeon, but once again there was not enough room for everyone, and so the two counts embarked with their friends and the remaining cavalrymen, leaving the foot soldiers and pilgrims to fend for themselves. The latter made their way along the coast, under constant attack by Türkmen raiders, and in late spring they finally arrived at Antioch, having lost half of their number along the way. Kings Louis and Conrad were already there, the latter having come by ship from Constantinople.

The crusaders decided to attack Damascus before going on to liberate Edessa. They reached Damascus on 24 July 1148, but after four days of heavy fighting they were forced to retreat, harried along the way by Türkmen cavalry. The failure of the expedition against Damascus was a great humiliation for the Western knights, demoralising them to the extent that they abandoned the expedition. And so the Second Crusade ended in a total fiasco, leaving Nur al-Din Mahmud in possession of Edessa, while the Latin ruler of the county, Count Joscelin II, controlled only the town of Turbessel.

Meanwhile Mesut, his western frontier secure through his peace treaty with Manuel Comnenus, took advantage of the situation and invaded the Latin County of Edessa. Mesut had prepared for this invasion by making an alliance with Nur al-Din Mahmud, to whom he married off one of his daughters.

Mesut captured Germaniceia (Maraş) in 1150, and then in the spring of the following year he took four other towns in the former County of Edessa, most notably Ainteb (Gaziantep), giving two of them as an appanage to his son Kılıç Arslan. Nur al-Din took Turbessel and captured Joscelin, who was blinded and imprisoned in Aleppo, where he died in 1159. This effectively ended the history of the Latin County of Edessa, one of the two crusader principalities in south-eastern Anatolia. The other one, the County of Antioch, was only a shadow of its former self, most of its territory being occupied by Nur al-Din Mahmud.

Meanwhile, Mesut had received the submission of the Danışmendid emir Yağıbasan, which gave him control of Sivas and the surrounding area. He died soon afterwards, around April 1155, having divided the sultanate between his heirs, as Nicetas Choniates reports in his chronicle.

Many were the sons and daughters born to Mesut, the ruler of the Turks. As he was about to depart this life and go on to the tortures of the next because of his impiety, he distributed among some of his sons the cities and provinces which had once been included within the boundaries of the Roman empire and were now under his rule, and to some he bequeathed other provinces as their paternal inheritance; the metropolis of Iconium and all that was subject to it he assigned to his son Kilij Arslan. To his son-in-law Yaghi-basan he allotted Amaseia, Ankara, the fertile province of Cappadocia, and all the adjacent lands and cities; and to his son-in-law Dhu'l Nun, he portioned out the great and prosperous cities of Kaisareia and Sebasteia.

Mesut had ruled for nearly forty years, during which time he fought off two Byzantine emperors and the kings of both Germany and France in the Second Crusade. He had also broken the power of the Danışmendid, extending the bounds of his territory from the Sakarya to the Euphrates. At the same time, Mesut had established the city of Konya as capital of the Sultanate of Rum, where he had begun construction of the great mosque that would later be called Alaeddin Camii, one of the landmarks of Seljuk architecture.

– 4 –

Kılıç Arslan II

Mesut, in dividing the Sultanate of Rum between his heirs, had given Konya, the capital, to his eldest son, who succeeded as Kılıç Arslan II. Şahanşah, the younger son, established himself as an independent ruler in Ankara and Çankırı.

Şahanşah immediately set out to supplant his brother as sultan, and towards this end he entered into an alliance with Yağıbasan, the Danışmendid emir of Sivas, who was in turn supported by Nur al-Din Mahmud, the powerful *atabeg* of Mosul and Aleppo. Aided by his allies, Şahanşah took possession of Ainteb and the other towns of the former County of Edessa that had been conquered by his father Mesut, winning the first round in his war of succession with Kılıç Arslan.

Kılıç Arslan, for his part, had secured support from the other two rulers of the now divided Danışmendid principality, the emirs Dhu'l-Nun of Kayseri and Dhu'l-Qarnayn of Malatya.

On his western frontier Kılıç Arslan was in conflict with the emperor Manuel Comnenus, who on returning from a campaign in Cilicia in 1159 had passed through the sultan's lands and had been attacked by Türkmen raiders. The following year Manuel supported the Danışmendid emir Yağıbasan in making war on Kılıç Arslan, who was forced to sue for peace with the emperor. Manuel had been playing the various Turkish factions against one another, particularly Kılıç Arslan versus Yağıbasan, a double-dealing policy that was crowned with success when the sultan was forced to go to Constantinople to seek the emperor's help.

Nicetas Choniates describes Kılıç Arslan's reception in Constantinople, where he was Manuel's guest in the Great Palace during the spring of

1162, remaining for eighty days. Manuel entertained Kılıç Arslan regally and showered him with rich gifts, according to Choniates, as the emperor strove to impress the sultan with the magnificence of the Byzantine capital, though the festivities were interrupted by an earthquake that the clergy interpreted as divine wrath at the Turk's presence in the 'God-guarded city of Constantinople'.

John Kinnamos records the details of the treaty signed by the sultan in 1162 while he was in Constantinople. Kılıç Arslan swore to have the same friends and enemies as the emperor; to hand over to the emperor any important cities that he captured; to make no treaty without the emperor's consent; to serve the emperor with all his forces, in east or west, when required; and to punish the Türkmen who raided imperial territory.

When the other Turkish emirs learned of this treaty they sent envoys to Constantinople, seeking an agreement with the emperor and reconciliation with the sultan. Kinnamos writes of how Manuel referred the envoys to Kılıç Arslan, who was still enjoying the emperor's hospitality in the Great Palace:

> This [the treaty] was achieved in Byzantion, but a rumour [thereof] had previously crossed from Europe to Asia. The tribal leaders there, deeming it would not be to their advantage if the emperor dealt with the sultan, sent envoys and begged to be reconciled with the sultan. He [Manuel] listened to them [the envoys] with undoubted satisfaction, but supposedly put everything at the sultan's discretion and referred them to the latter at his quarters in the Palace. As soon as they had spoken with the sultan, they persuaded him to dissolve his enmity towards them and to supplicate with the emperor on their behalf. The latter on receiving his intercession then ranked them too among his friends, and the Roman power enjoyed stable peace.

When the time came for Kılıç Arslan to leave Constantinople he was dismayed to learn that his youngest son, Giyaseddin Keyhüsrev, his favourite, was to be kept as a hostage by Manuel, who promised to return the boy when he was sure that his father was living up to the terms of the treaty. Keyhüsrev, whose mother was a Christian, and who himself later married a Greek woman, was eventually allowed to rejoin his father in Konya.

Kılıç Arslan's treaty with Manuel now gave him security on his western frontier, allowing him to take action against his Muslim adversaries in the east. Choniates tells of how Kılıç Arslan, despite the gifts and arms given to him by Manuel, and disregarding the agreements he had made with the other Muslim rulers, began attacking them as soon as he returned to Konya, his principal adversary being Yağıbasan, the Danışmendid emir who had been supporting Kılıç Arslan's rebellious brother Şahanşah.

Yağıbasan died in 1164 and was succeeded by his nephew Ismail. Revolts broke out against Ismail, and Kılıç Arslan took advantage of this to reoccupy the towns of the Ceyhan, the area in the northern part of the former County of Edessa that had been conquered by his father Mesut. In 1168 Kılıç Arslan had broken with his Danışmendid ally Dhu'l-Nun, from whom he had taken Malatya as well as Kayseri. Then the following year Kılıç Arslan took Ankara and Çankırı from his brother Şahanşah, who had been forced to take refuge with Manuel Comnenus in Constantinople.

The dispossessed Danışmendid emirs received support from Nur al-Din Mahmud, but when he died in 1174 they were defenceless against Kılıç Arslan. During the next four years Kılıç Arslan captured Sivas, Niksar, Tokat and Amasya. The defeated Danışmendid emirs fled to Constantinople and were given refuge by Manuel Comnenus, who thus saw himself deprived of the places that Kılıç Arslan was supposed to return to him, according to their treaty of 1162. The emperor sent a force to recover the towns of Amasya and Niksar from the sultan, but the campaign was a failure.

Matters were made worse by the fact that the Türkmen tribes were once again raiding into Byzantine territory, penetrating as deep as Bergama and Edremit. This was in further violation of the treaty of 1162, and so Manuel began preparations for an offensive against the Seljuk sultan. He began by rebuilding and fortifying the towns of Dorylaeum and Sublaeum, the first of which dominated the approach to Konya from the north and the second from the west. Dorylaeum had been one of the most important and prosperous towns of Anatolia, but the Türkmen raids in the century after Manzikert had left it an abandoned ruin until Manuel rebuilt it.

On 11 January 1176 Manuel wrote to Pope Alexander III asking for Western support against the Turks. The pope in turn wrote to Cardinal Peter of St Crisogono, asking him to transmit Manuel's appeal to the king and nobles of France, mentioning the efforts the emperor had made in rebuilding Dorylaeum so that pilgrims could once again make their way across Asia Minor to the Holy Land. According to the pope:

He [Manuel] has constructed a great and populous city in the middle of the land of the Sultan of Iconium, where he has placed Latins and Greeks to defend it, and by this city he dominates a great region of the Turks, so much so that he has restored the road for all Christians, both Greeks and Latins, to visit the Lord's Sepulchre.

The contemporary Byzantine texts show that Manuel advertised the rebuilding of Dorylaeum and Sublaeum as the first step in a holy war, a crusade against the Seljuks in which the emperor himself was willing to lay down his life. Nicetas Choniates records the skirmishing between the imperial forces and the Seljuks that occurred frequently during the rebuilding of Dorylaeum, including an incident in which Manuel himself was involved:

Once, when the emperor had turned aside to eat and was peeling a peach with a knife, a Turkish attack against those gathering food was announced; casting aside the fruit at once he girded on his sword, donned his coat of mail, and mounted his horse to ride on at full speed. The barbarians in battle array quickly broke rank when they saw him; then, feigning flight, they wheeled around and smote their pursuers, putting their rout to advantage by shooting and overthrowing those who pressed upon them.

In September 1176 Manuel launched a massive expedition against Kılıç Arslan, with contingents from Serbia, Hungary and the crusader states of the Levant, as well as Cumans from the Balkans, the total number of troops being estimated at 150,000.

Manuel sent a force under his nephew Andronicus Vatatzes to take Niksar in Paphlagonia, while he himself led the major part of his army towards Konya. Kılıç Arslan withdrew before Manuel, burning the villages and crops along the route so as to deny supplies to the Byzantine forces, as well as contaminating the wells with dead animals to deny them clean drinking water. Manuel's progress was also slowed by the Türkmen tribes, who in groups of 5,000 to 10,000 continually harassed the imperial army.

Meanwhile, the Byzantine force that had been sent to Paphlagonia under Andronicus Vatatzes was defeated at Niksar by the Turks. Vatatzes was captured and killed by the victors, who sent his severed head to Kılıç Arslan as a trophy of their victory.

Kılıç Arslan sent an embassy to Manuel asking for peace, but the emperor ignored the advice of his senior generals and rejected the offer.

Manuel's route took him past the ruined fortress of Myriocephalum to Tzybritze, the long and narrow pass through Sultan Dağı, above Eğirdir, which the imperial army entered on 17 September 1176. Manuel later wrote to King Henry II of England that in going through the pass his army and its enormous baggage train stretched for more than 10 miles along the road.

Kılıç Arslan had massed his troops on the heights above both sides of the pass, and as soon as the imperial army was completely within the defile the Turks attacked. The Turks concentrated their attack on the baggage train, killing so many horses and mules that the narrow road became blocked, trapping the imperial army inside the pass. Baldwin of Antioch, the emperor's brother-in-law, led his cavalry regiment in a charge up the hill, but he and all his men were killed. A blinding sandstorm had by then swept down upon the pass, so that the Greeks and Turks could hardly distinguish one another in the hand-to-hand fighting, with heavy losses on both sides. When the storm subsided at day's end it became obvious that the Turks had the advantage, and as night fell they withdrew to the heights above the pass, surrounding the demoralised survivors of the imperial army below. Then at dawn the Turks attacked again, an action described by Nicetas Choniates:

> The Turks... moved out at the crack of dawn to encircle the Romans like wild beasts rushing to gulp down a prepared dish or to carry off both abandoned eggs and undefended nest. Riding in a circle around the entrenched camp and raising their barbarian war cry, they struck down those within with their arrows. The emperor therefore commanded John, Constantine Angelos' son, to attack the Turks with his troops; obedient to the imperial command, he attempted to repulse them, but he was unable to perform any noble deed and returned. Next, Constantine Makrodoukas led out his forces mustered from among the eastern divisions, but he too turned back after making a brief showing.

Manuel panicked, and for a time he considered secretly fleeing for his life, leaving his army to be slaughtered by the Turks. But at that point Kılıç Arslan called a halt to the fighting, sending an envoy to offer peace terms to the emperor, the principal demands being that the newly built fortifications at Dorylaeum and Sublaeum be destroyed. Manuel accepted, whereupon he led his surviving troops out of the pass to begin the retreat to Constantinople. En route the imperial forces were continually harassed by Türkmen raiders, who ravaged the countryside, killing the stragglers of the defeated army and carrying off what was left of the baggage train as booty. Manuel protested this violation of the peace treaty to Kılıç Arslan, but the sultan replied that the Türkmen were acting independently of him, and that in any event he had no control over them. The attacks continued until the imperial army reached Chonae, where they were safely within Byzantine territory.

The Battle of Myriocyphalum was the single most important military action in Anatolia since Manzikert, a little more than a century before. Manuel was well aware of the significance of the disaster his empire had suffered, which he himself, in a letter he wrote to Constantinople, compared to the catastrophe at Manzikert, although he pointed out that, unlike Romanus Diogenes, he had escaped capture and was able to lead his army home, having made peace with Kılıç Arslan.

But, whereas Byzantium had recovered after Manzikert through the heroic efforts of three generations of the Comneni dynasty, the situation was different after Myriocephalum, for Manuel Comnenus was now growing old, and neither he nor his empire had the resilience necessary for another recovery, as events were soon to show.

When the army reached Sublaeum Manuel ordered that its fortifications be destroyed, in accordance with the treaty he had signed with Kılıç Arslan. But he failed to do the same at Dorylaeum, incurring the fury of Kılıç Arslan. In 1177 the sultan sent his army deep into imperial territory, sacking Tralles (Aydın) and other towns in the Maeander valley, though his forces were defeated by Manuel on their way home.

That same year Kılıç Arslan took Malatya and the following year he completed his conquest of the Danışmendid emirate, bringing their history to an end. The following year he mounted a campaign against Raban, a fortress on the Euphrates on the road between Samosata and Aleppo. But this brought him into the sphere of influence of Saladin, the Kurdish warrior who in 1171 had overthrown the Fatimids and founded the Ayyubid dynasty. Saladin sent a nephew to maintain the existing border, whereupon Kılıç Arslan withdrew his forces from Raban. Then in 1180 Kılıç Arslan captured Sozopolis, and later that year he sacked Cotyaeum (Kütahya) and subjected Attaleia to a long siege.

Towards the end of 1180 a more serious dispute arose between Kılıç Arslan and Saladin, this time over a family matter. Kılıç Arslan had given his beloved daughter Selçuka Hatun in marriage to Nur ed-din Muhammad, son of the emir of Hasankeyf. Soon after their marriage Nur ed-din abandoned his bride in favour of a beautiful dancing girl, and the outraged Selçuka appealed to her father to avenge her honour. Kılıç Arslan immediately mounted a campaign against Hasankeyf, and the terrified Nur ed-din Muhammad fled and took refuge in the court of Saladin. Kılıç Arslan and Saladin almost went to war over the matter, but Nur ed-din Muhammad settled the dispute by giving up the dancing girl and returning to Selçuka Hatun.

Meanwhile, in the spring of 1178, Manuel had received a visit from Philip, count of Flanders, who was on his way back to France from the Holy Land. The emperor presented to him his son Alexius, who was then eight years old, and suggested to Philip that on his return to France the count might sound out King Louis VII on the possibility of a marriage between the young prince and one of the king's daughters. The king agreed to the proposal and sent his daughter Agnes to Constantinople as a bride for Alexius. Agnes, who took the Greek name Anna, was married to Alexius in the Great Palace on 2 March 1180; she was then barely nine years old, while her husband was only ten.

During the winter of 1179–80 Manuel had mounted a campaign to relieve the fortress of Claudiopolis (Bolu), and when his army appeared the Türkmen raiders who had been besieging it withdrew without a fight. This was to be Manuel's last campaign, for he passed away on 24 September 1180, aged about sixty, having ruled for thirty-seven years.

Manuel was succeeded by his son Alexius II, who was then twelve years old. Because of his youth, the young emperor's mother, Maria of Antioch, governed as regent in his stead. Maria became very unpopular with the people of Constantinople, particularly because she favoured her fellow Latins, who were despised by the Greeks. This led to a coup by Andronicus Comnenus, a son of the sebastocrator Isaac, brother of John II. Andronicus, who had been living in exile in a town on the Black Sea, marched on Constantinople and seized control of the capital in August 1182. Then, after having Maria of Antioch executed for treason, Andronicus had himself declared co-emperor with Alexius II in September of the following year.

At the time of his accession Andronicus was sixty-five years old. But despite his age, according to Nicetas Choniates, Andronicus was still vigorous and in superb health: 'The condition of his body was excellent, of venerable aspect, of heroic stature, and even in his old age he had a youthful face. His body was outstandingly healthy because he was neither voluptuous nor gluttonous, nor a drunkard, but like the Homeric heroes lived simply and moderately.'

Shortly after his accession Andronicus had Alexius strangled, leaving the empress Anna a widow at the age of eleven. Towards the end of the year Andronicus married Anna, though they differed in age by more than half a century, scandalising both Byzantium and western Europe.

When Andronicus came to power there were rebellions against him in Lopadium, Nicaea and Prusa (Bursa). The rebels called in the Turks to aid them, but Andronicus put down the revolts with savage reprisals. Andronicus soon began a reign of terror, executing anyone he thought might be a threat to the throne. At the same time the empire came under attack by the Seljuks, the Hungarians and the Normans, the latter invading Greece. The Normans took Thessalonica in the summer of 1185 and advanced on Constantinople. The populace panicked at the approach of the Normans and castigated Andronicus for not making adequate preparations for defending the city. Andronicus responded by arresting all his opponents and condemning them to death. Among them was a distant relative of the Comneni named Isaac Angelus, who escaped from his captors and took refuge in Haghia Sophia, where he called on the populace for support. The people of the city responded to his call, and on 12 September 1185 he was raised to the throne as Isaac II.

Andronicus tried to flee, but he was captured and tortured before being put to death. His death ended the illustrious dynasty of the Comneni after more than a century of brilliant rule, during which Byzantium had recovered from the disaster of Manzikert, only to suffer another catastrophe at Myriocephalum.

The chaos in the Byzantine regions of Asia Minor increased markedly during the reign of Isaac II Angelus. At the time of his accession many of the Byzantine soldiers in the Aegean provinces were transferred to Europe, and Kılıç Arslan took advantage of this to invade the empire's territory. These raids led the emperor to seek peace with the sultan, which Isaac achieved by agreeing to pay Kılıç Arslan an annual tribute.

Around 1186 Kılıç Arslan began thinking about retirement, for he had reached the age of seventy and had ruled for three decades. Two years later he announced his abdication, noting in his diary that he was dividing the Sultanate of Rum between his eleven sons. Sivas and Aksaray were given to Küthuddin Melik Şah II; Tokat and the lands towards the Black Sea to Ruknuddin Süleyman Şah II; Ankara and Eskişehir to Muhuddin Mesut Şah; Kayseri to Nüreddin Mahmud Sultan Şah; Elbistan to Müizeddin Tuğrul Şah; Malatya to Müizeddin Kayser Şah; Niksar and Koyluhisar to Nasreddin Bargıyaruk Şah; Amasya to

Nizamuddin Argun Şah; Niğde to Arslan Şah; Ereğli to Sencer Şah; and Konya, Kütahya and Uluborlu to Giyaseddin Keyhüsrev I.

At the beginning Kılıç Arslan seems to have intended to keep only Konya for himself, living there in retirement while Giyaseddin Keyhüsrev, his youngest son, ruled that portion of the sultanate. He also noted in his diary that he expected all of his sons to join him in an annual campaign, but during the remaining four years of Kılıç Arslan's life this never came to pass, because of the inevitable disputes between his heirs. The first of these disputes arose in the winter of 1188–89 when Küthuddin Melik Şah, the eldest son, forced Kılıç Arslan to let him share power in Konya with his younger brother Giyaseddin Keyhüsrev.

Earlier in 1188 the emperor Isaac was faced by a revolt that erupted in the city of Philadelphia, led by Theodore Mangaphas. Recruiting Türkmen from the local tribes, Mangaphas set himself up as an independent emperor in Lydia, even minting his own coins, ravaging the towns of Caria and enslaving the local inhabitants, both Greeks and Turks. Isaac was forced to recognise Mangaphas as de facto ruler of Philadelphia, on condition that he gave up his imperial claims and sent his two sons to Constantinople as hostages.

Meanwhile events of profound importance were taking place in the Holy Land. On 4 July 1187 Saladin destroyed the allied army of the Latin Crusader states in a battle at Hattin, on the Sea of Galilee. Then on 2 October of that same year Saladin accepted the surrender of Jerusalem, which he took without bloodshed, in contrast to the Christian massacre of Muslims that had occurred when the city fell to the Crusaders in 1099.

News of the fall of Jerusalem to the Muslims reached Rome on 20 October, so shocking the ailing Pope Urban III that he died of grief that same day. His successor, Gregory VIII, immediately sent out a circular letter to inform Christians in the West to join in another crusade to liberate the Holy Land. But Gregory never saw this come to pass, for he died on 11 December of that same year, to be succeeded by Clement III. The new pope in his turn immediately took up the cause of his predecessors, setting in motion the great expedition that came to be called the Third Crusade, the principal contingents of which were the armies of Emperor Frederick I Barbarossa, Richard I, Lion-Heart, king of England, and Philip II, Augustus, king of France.

Frederick Barbarossa set out from Ratisbon in Germany early in May 1189, accompanied by his second son, Frederick of Swabia. The emperor's army, estimated to number 100,000 foot soldiers and 50,000 cavalry, crossed the Danube at Belgrade on 23 June, entering Byzantine territory. Frederick spent the winter at Adrianople, and then in March 1190, after lengthy disputes and negotiations with the emperor Isaac II Angelus, he led his army across the Hellespont.

Before he set out on the crusade Frederick had written to Kılıç Arslan, asking for permission to cross Seljuk territory in Anatolia on his way to the Holy Land. Kılıç Arslan had answered courteously, giving his permission, but by the time Frederick began his march across Anatolia the old sultan had abdicated and divided the Sultanate of Rum among his sons. Thus he was unable to guarantee safe passage for the crusaders, particularly since neither he nor his sons had full control over the unruly Türkmen tribes. Frederick was unaware of this, and he was infuriated when his army was twice attacked by Türkmen raiders as soon as they crossed into Seljuk territory.

On 3 May, after the second of the Türkmen raids, Frederick's army passed Myriocephalum, where the battlefield was still strewn with the bones of those who had died in battle there fourteen years beforehand. Two weeks later they reached Konya, the Seljuk capital, which Frederick, angered by the Türkmen attacks, was prepared to take by storm. Nicetas Choniates describes the fighting that took place between the Germans and the Turks, who attacked the crusaders outside the walls of Konya:

> The Turks stole into the ditches of the gardens and the trenches which form a continuous line around Iconium and surrounded themselves with stone enclosures as a wall of defence, thinking with these to check the passage of the Germans into Iconium, for they were all mighty archers and, assembled in one place, an easy match for men in heavy armour on horseback riding through rough terrain. But these tactics were also foiled. The Germans, who observed the Turks as they slipped behind the stone walls of the gardens and shot their arrows from there as though from a military emplacement, did the following: each knight lifted an armed foot soldier onto his horse, and setting them on top of the enclosures where the Turks were formed in close order, they left them to engage the enemy while they came to their aid by charging through the enemy's ranks wherever possible.

The German crusaders quickly defeated the Turkish defenders and broke into Konya. They then started to plunder the city, but Kılıç Arslan entered into negotiations with Frederick and persuaded the emperor to remove his troops from Konya the following day. The agreement signed by Kılıç Arslan included a fresh guarantee that the crusaders would have safe passage through Seljuk territory, although the old sultan knew that the Türkmen tribes would undoubtedly continue their raids against the Christian army.

After resting for two days outside Konya, Frederick led his army southward across the Taurus Mountains towards Seleucia, on the Mediterranean coast in Cilicia. On 10 June 1190, when they finally came in sight of the Mediterranean, Frederick fell from his horse while crossing the river Calycadnus (Göksu) and was drowned. The emperor's untimely death was a severe blow to the morale of the German knights, many of whom turned back at this point, with only a part of the powerful army continuing on to Antioch under the duke of Swabia, Frederick's son. The duke carried his father's corpse along, preserved in a cask of vinegar. Some of the emperor's bones were set aside at the burial in Antioch and carried to the Holy Land by the remnants of his army, 'in the vain hope', as Steven Runciman writes, 'that at least a portion of Frederick Barbarossa should await the Judgement Day in Jerusalem'.

Meanwhile, Richard and Philip had met in France on 4 July 1189, ready to embark on the crusade. But it was late in April 1191 before they arrived at Acre in Palestine, having come by ship across the Mediterranean. When they arrived in Acre, which had been captured by Saladin in 1187, the city was being besieged by the Latins of the crusader states in the Levant. Richard and Philip arrived with their armies essentially intact, and so they were able to join in the siege of Acre, whose Muslim garrison finally surrendered to the Christian allies on 4 July 1191.

This was the high point of the Third Crusade, which ended when Saladin and King Richard signed a peace treaty on 2 September 1192. Jerusalem remained in the hands of Saladin, while Acre became the capital of a Latin kingdom in Palestine. As Steven Runciman writes in ending his account of this campaign: 'The Third Crusade had come to a close. Never again would such a galaxy of princes go eastward for the Holy War.'

That same year Sultan Kılıç Arslan II died in Konya. He was buried there in Alaeddin Camii, the great mosque that he had built on the foundations laid by his father, Ruknuddin Mesut I. Kılıç Arslan's grave can still be seen there today in one of the two mausolea attached to the mosque, the decagonal *türbe* to the north. He and his father had established Konya as capital of the Sultanate of Rum, which by the last years of Kılıç Arslan's reign had become the dominant state in Anatolia, although his division of this heritage between his sons would now imperil the Seljuk state.

– 5 –

The Sons of Kılıç Arslan II

When Kılıç Arslan II divided his realm between his eleven
sons he endangered the unity of the Seljuk Sultanate of Rum,
and even before his death his heirs began fighting one
another over the inheritance.

The youngest of the brothers, Giyaseddin Keyhüsrev I, had, by
his father's testimony, inherited the title of sultan and ruled in
Konya, the Seljuk capital. Küthuddin Melik Şah, the eldest son, was
not satisfied with Sivas and Aksaray as his share, and so he tried to
take Konya from his brother Giyaseddin Keyhüsrev, but to no avail,
though he did manage to gain control of the Seljuk treasury. He then
tried to take Malatya from his brother Müizeddin Kayser Şah, who
forestalled him by receiving support from Saladin, whose niece he
had married.

During the winter of 1193–94 Küthuddin took Kayseri from his
brother, Nüreddin Mahmut Sultan Şah, whom he then executed. The
following winter he tried to take Elbistan from his brother Müizeddin
Tuğrul Şah, who fought him off with the help of the Armenian prince
Leo, whose vassal he became.

Küthuddin died soon afterwards, whereupon his share of the sultanate
was taken over by his brother Ruknuddin Süleyman Şah, who already held
Tokat and the lands towards the Black Sea. He also forced his brother
Muhuddin Mesut Şah in Ankara to give up part of his share of the
sultanate. Then in 1196 Ruknuddin seized Konya from Giyaseddin
Keyhüsrev I, supplanting his brother as sultan and forcing him to flee, first
to the court of Leon I, king of Lesser Armenia. But Leon refused to give

Keyhüsrev refuge, for he feared that this would provoke Ruknuddin to attack him.

Keyhüsrev was finally given refuge by Manuel Mavrozomes, a Byzantine noble with a large estate in the Maeander valley. Mavrozomes gave Keyhüsrev one of his daughters in marriage, for which he was richly rewarded when his son-in-law eventually regained power in Konya.

Around the same time Rukneddin took Niksar from his brother Nasreddin Bargıyaruk Şah and Amasya from another brother, Nizamuddin Argun Şah. Then in 1201 he took Malatya from Müizeddin Kayser Şah. Soon afterwards he captured Erzurum from the Saltukids, another Türkmen dynasty. He then installed as governor his brother Müizeddin Tuğrul Şah, who in return ceded Elbistan to him. Finally, in 1204, he occupied Ankara and executed his brother Muhuddin Mesut Şah, who was accused of being in league with the Byzantines.

Five days after taking Ankara, Ruknuddin suddenly and quite unexpectedly died. He was succeeded by his young son Izzeddin Kılıç Arslan III, who ruled for only a short while before being deposed. Izzeddin was succeeded by Giyaseddin Keyhüsrev I, who thus began his second reign as sultan, after having spent much of the interim as a refugee with the Byzantines.

Meanwhile, the Byzantine Empire had been in serious decline since 1185, when the last of the Comneni emperors was replaced by Isaac II Angelus, the first of the short-lived dynasty of the Angeli. The internal conflicts in the Sultanate of Rum after its division by Kılıç Arslan II allowed Isaac to make limited headway against the Seljuks, and he was able to drive them out of parts of north-western Anatolia. But then in 1192, the year in which Kılıç Arslan II died, a number of rebellions against Isaac II broke out in imperial territory.

The most serious rebellion was that of the pretender known to historians as Pseudoalexius, so called because he claimed to be Alexius II Comnenus, son and successor of Manuel I Comnenus, who had been killed in 1180 by his uncle Andronicus. Nicetas Choniates tells the story of how this imposter passed himself off as the late Alexius II to Kılıç Arslan shortly before the old sultan died:

> ...A certain Alexius, who claimed to be the son of Manuel, emperor of the Romans, so excellently played his role in the drama and so brilliantly donned the mask of Emperor Alexius [II] that he dyed his hair the same yellowish brown colour and even affected the young emperor's stammer. The lad set out from Constantinople and was first seen in the cities along

the Maeander [1189]. He took up quarters in a small town called Harmala, and there he was entertained as the guest of a certain Latin to whom he announced his identity... Together they traveled to Iconium, where the old sultan [Kılıç Arslan II] looked upon him as the true son of Emperor Manuel and never addressed him or dealt with him as an outsider and an imposter.

Kılıç Arslan allowed Pseudoalexius to recruit an army to advance his imperial claim, which gained widespread and enthusiastic support. Choniates then concludes his account by telling how the emperor Isaac II sent his older brother, the sebastocrator Alexius, on an ineffective expedition against Pseudoalexius, who in the end was killed by a Greek priest in a drunken brawl.

> As the issue thus hung in doubt, and Pseudoalexius gained ground and waxed strong while the sebastocrator cowered and shunned face-to-face conflict, God, in a novel manner, terminated the civil war in a manner as only He knows how. After a drinking bout in Harmala, to which Pseudoalexius had returned, a certain priest cut his throat with his own sword, which was lying by his side. When his head was carried back, the sebastocrator Alexius gazed at it intently; picking it up frequently by the golden hair with a horse's spur, he commented: 'It was not altogether out of ignorance that the cities followed this man.'

Another imposter, also known as Pseudoalexius, appeared shortly afterwards in Paphlagonia. The emperor Isaac sent a force to Paphlagonia under Theodore Choumnos, who defeated and killed the second Pseudoalexius.

Still another rebellion broke out under the leadership of Theodore Mangaphas, who had been recognised as de facto ruler of Philadelphia by Isaac II. Isaac later sent a force under Basil Vatatzes, who drove Mangaphas from Philadelphia and forced him to take refuge in Konya with Sultan Keyhüsrev.

The reign of Isaac II came to an end on 8 April 1195, when he was deposed and blinded by his older brother, the sebastocrator, who then succeeded to the throne as Alexius III. The new emperor then imprisoned both Isaac and his son Alexius in the dungeon of the palace of Blachernae in Constantinople.

A third Pseudoalexius appeared in 1196 and allied himself with Muhuddin Mesut Şah in Ankara. Alexius III sent an army against Pseudoalexius, and when they were unable to capture him they destroyed those places that had supported the pretender. Muhuddin took advantage of the situation by attacking Dadybra (Dodurga), which surrendered to him after a four-month siege. By the terms of the surrender, the Greek populace were forced to leave the town, after which they were replaced by Turkish colonists. Soon afterwards, in December 1196, Alexius III signed a peace agreement with Muhuddin, in which the emperor agreed to pay him an annual tribute.

Choniates writes of a war that broke out at about this time when Sultan Keyhüsrev violated the terms of a treaty that he had made with Alexius III. According to Choniates, Keyhüsrev treated the Greek captives he took during the conflict very humanely, which in some ways marked a turning point in the struggle between the Byzantines and Seljuks in Anatolia, for it convinced some of the Christians living there that they were better off under the rule of the sultan than that of the emperor.

> The sultan took pains that the captives should not lack the necessities of life, and providing them with bread did not ignore the pernicious cold of the season; taking up a two-edged ax, he himself split into billets an old tree nearby which had fallen long ago... When the Turk came to Philomilion with his horde of captives, he assigned them to unwalled villages and apportioned fertile land for cultivation; he then provided grain and seed for the sowing of crops. Indeed, he filled them with high hopes, assuring them that once he and their emperor were reconciled and had renewed their former treaties, their reward would be their return home... His humane pronouncement had two effects; it did not permit any of the captives to remember their homeland and it also attracted to Philomilion many who had not fallen into the Turks' hands but who had heard what the Turk had done for their kinsmen and countrymen.

During the summer of 1201 the emperor went off on campaign in the southern Balkans against the Vlachs, accompanied by his young nephew Alexius, whom he had released from the prison where he continued to hold the blinded Isaac II, his brother and the father of Alexius. Alexius took the opportunity to escape from his uncle and fled to take refuge with his sister Eirene and her husband, Philip of Swabia.

At Philip's court the young Alexius met another of his relations by marriage, Marquis Boniface of Montferrat, who had just been chosen to lead the Fourth Crusade, which Pope Innocent III had proclaimed in January 1198. Alexius pleaded with Boniface to help him regain the Byzantine throne for his blinded father and himself. They almost certainly discussed the possibility of diverting the crusade to Constantinople, although Boniface lacked the authority to make such a decision on his own.

The knights of the Fourth Crusade had planned to meet in the summer of 1202 at Venice, where the Venetians had contracted to ferry them to Egypt for a payment of 85,000 silver marks. But many fewer crusaders arrived than had been expected, and between them they could raise only 51,000 marks. The Venetian doge, Enrico Dandolo, offered to postpone payment of the balance if the crusaders helped him recapture the Dalmatian city of Zara, which had defected to the Hungarians. The knights agreed, whereupon they embarked at Venice on 8 September 1202, bound for Zara in a Venetian fleet of 480 ships led by the galley of the doge.

The fleet reached Zara on 10 November and attacked the city, which surrendered after a two-week siege. The garrison and populace were unharmed, but the Latins stripped the city of all its movable belongings, dividing the loot between them. It was then too late in the season to sail on into the Aegean, so the expedition wintered in Zara.

Boniface joined the crusaders at Zara in mid-December. Two weeks later envoys arrived bearing a message from young Alexius Angelus, promising that if the expedition restored his father Isaac II to the throne he would agree to a union of the Greek and Roman Churches under the papacy. Moreover, he would give a huge sum of money to the Latins, as well as paying all their expenses for an additional year. The crusaders accepted the offer, and Doge Dandolo agreed to divert the expedition to Constantinople.

The knights of the Fourth Crusade and their Venetian allies attacked Constantinople on 17 July 1203, breaking through the sea walls along the Golden Horn. That night Alexius III escaped from the city, and soon afterwards the Latins released the blind Isaac II from prison, restoring him to the throne with his son, who now ruled as the co-emperor Alexius IV. The crusaders then waited for Alexius to make good on the extravagant promises he had made to them, and in his efforts to satisfy the Latins the new emperor became extremely unpopular with the people of Constantinople.

Late in January 1204 a revolt among the people of Constantinople, led by Alexius Ducas Murtzuphlus, deposed and imprisoned Isaac II and his son Alexius IV. Then on 5 February 1204 Murtzuphlus was crowned as Alexius V. The new emperor executed Alexius IV, whose father Isaac II died of natural causes at about the same time.

As soon as Murtzuphlus was in full control he issued an ultimatum to the Latins to leave Constantinople and its environs within a week. The crusaders, who were camped outside the city, took this as a declaration of war and on 9 April 1204 they attacked and captured the city, forcing Murtzuphlus and his supporters to flee. The Latins then proceeded to sack Constantinople, stripping it of all its treasures and sacred relics, burning down a large part of the city in an orgy of killing, raping and looting in which some 2,000 Greeks lost their lives. Murtzuphlus was captured and executed by the Latins later that year, while Alexius III remained a fugitive.

The Latins met on 9 May 1204 to choose an emperor, forming a committee of twelve, half of them Venetians. On the second ballot Count Baldwin of Flanders was chosen emperor of Romania, as the Latins called their new kingdom. The Latins then divided up the Byzantine Empire in an agreement called the *Partitio Romanum*, the final details of which were set forth in October 1204. The treaty divided the empire into three major shares: a quarter for the Latin emperor, and three-eighths each for the Venetians on one hand and all the other crusader leaders on the other, with the portion of each beneficiary further subdivided into a share near Constantinople and a share more remote. The share of Venice also included the great church of Haghia Sophia, where Thomas Morosini, a Venetian, was appointed as the Roman Catholic patriarch of Constantinople.

Most of the Greek Orthodox bishops in Constantinople either refused to recognise Morosini or else fled to Nicaea, where a fragment of the Byzantine Empire was now developing in exile. This was one of three Byzantine states that emerged after the fall of Constantinople in 1204, the others being the Empire of Trebizond and the Despotate of Epirus. The Empire of Nicaea was founded by Theodore I Lascaris, son-in-law of Alexius III Angelus, who was crowned emperor in 1205. The Empire of Trebizond was established by two grandsons of Alexius I Comnenus, the brothers Alexius and David Comnenus, aided by their aunt, the Georgian queen Tamara. Alexius declared himself emperor and David took the title of duke and commanded his brother's army. The foundations of the Despotate of Epirus were laid by Michael II Angelus, bastard son of Michael I of Epirus, a great-grandson of the emperor Alexius I Comnenus.

Late in 1204 Emperor Baldwin mounted an expedition under the command of his brother Henry into north-western Anatolia, which he expected to annex to the Latin empire. Theodore Lascaris quickly mustered a force to oppose Henry, but his army suffered two successive defeats at the hands of the Latins, first at Poemanenum in December 1204, and then near Adramyttium in March 1205. The Latins were then poised to attack Nicaea, the Byzantine capital, but the Bulgar tsar Kaloyan invaded Thrace and Baldwin had to move his army across to Europe to meet the threat. The Bulgars decisively defeated the Latins near Adrianople on 14 April 1206; the emperor Baldwin was captured and died not long afterwards in prison. As a result, the Latins had to give up all the territory they had taken in north-western Anatolia, which reverted to the Byzantine empire in Nicaea. Baldwin's brother, Henry of Hainault, served as regent until 20 August 1206, when he was crowned emperor in Haghia Sophia by the Latin patriarch Thomas Morosini.

Henry then allied himself with David Comnenus against Theodore Lascaris. When Theodore was marching on Pontica Heracleia, David's headquarters, Henry attacked him from the rear, forcing him to turn back and fight off the Latins. During the winter of 1206–7 Henry invaded Theodore's territory again, capturing Nicomedia and Cyzicus (Erdek). Theodore retaliated by persuading Tsar Kaloyan to attack Adrianople. This forced Henry to sign a truce with Theodore, to whom he returned Nicomedia and Cyzicus.

Theodore signed a non-aggression pact in 1206 with Sultan Keyhüsrev, although neither party was committed to a long-term peace. A series of multiple conflicts then broke out in Anatolia, the first of them involving the two fragmentary Byzantine empires in Asia Minor contending with one another for territory along the Black Sea coast, while Manuel Mavrozomes, the Greek father-in-law of Sultan Keyhüsrev, was trying to establish his own kingdom with Turkish help. Theodore Lascaris won the first phase of this three-sided conflict, prevailing in turn over the forces of Manuel Mavrozomes and David Comnenus, who was aided by Latin troops from Constantinople. Theodore then forced David to come to terms, limiting his westward expansion to the town of Heracleia Pontica, which thereafter marked the boundary on the Black Sea coast between the Byzantine empires of Trebizond and Nicaea.

Meanwhile, Keyhüsrev attacked the Mediterranean port town of Attaleia, known to the Turks as Antalya, which he captured in March 1207. He then established Antalya as the capital of a new Seljuk province, under a government headed by Mübarizeddin Ertöküş ibn 'Abd Allah, a former Greek slave who had converted to Islam. This finally gave the Seljuks a port on the Mediterranean, which they would soon exploit to their great advantage.

Keyhüsrev then launched a campaign against the Armenian king Leon II, whom he defeated and took prisoner, annexing some of his territory in Cilicia. He also forestalled the invasion of northern Syria and south-eastern Anatolia by the Ayyubid ruler al-Malik al -'Adil

Meanwhile, the deposed Alexius III Angelus suddenly reappeared on the political scene. After he had fled from Constantinople in 1203 he made his way to Mosynopolis in Thrace, where at the end of the following year he was captured by Boniface of Montferrat. In 1209 he was ransomed by his cousin Michael II Ducas, despot of Epirus, after which he made his way to Konya in the hope that Sultan Keyhüsrev could help him regain his throne. Keyhüsrev, for his part, welcomed Alexius, whom he thought would be of great use to him in his struggle with Theodore Lascaris, the deposed emperor's son-in-law.

That same year the Latin emperor Henry of Hainault entered into an alliance with Sultan Keyhüsrev, in which they agreed to take action against their common enemy, Theodore Lascaris. As part of the agreement a contingent of Latin troops was sent to Konya, where they joined the sultan's forces in preparation for the coming campaign.

Keyhüsrev invaded Nicaean territory in 1211, ostensibly to overthrow Theodore Lascaris and replace him with Alexius, who accompanied the sultan on the campaign. The two sides were evenly matched, the Turks reinforced with Latin auxiliaries, Theodore's army strengthened by Frankish, Bulgar and Hungarian units.

The two armies met in the upper Maeander valley near Antioch on the Maeander. According to popular legend, Keyhüsrev, seeking to avoid unnecessary casualties, challenged Theodore to settle the issue by meeting in single combat, in which the emperor killed the sultan. But the Muslim historian Ibn Bibi tells the story differently, saying that in the battle between the two armies Theodore was unhorsed and the sultan's servants were about to kill him when Keyhüsrev came to his aid, helping Lascaris remount and allowing him to escape. When the Christian soldiers saw Lascaris fall, according to Ibn Bibi, they thought that the battle was lost and fled, whereupon the Turks set off in pursuit, leaving the sultan unguarded. A Frankish cavalryman spotted Keyhüsrev and killed him with a javelin, after which he began stripping him of his valuables. Word of this came to Lascaris, who had the Frank and Keyhüsrev's corpse brought to him. On recognising the corpse he wept and ordered that the Frank be executed. The emperor then had a local Turk wash and embalm Keyhüsrev's corpse according to Islamic rite, after which the sultan was honourably buried in Philadelphia. Meanwhile, news of the sultan's death spread through the Turkish forces and caused them to abandon the fight, giving the victory to Lascaris.

Alexius Angelus was left behind by the Turks and captured by Lascaris. Alexius was then brought back to Nicaea, where he was tried and convicted of treason, after which he was confined to a monastery where he spent the rest of his days.

The death of Keyhüsrev was the end of an age, for he was the last of the sons of Kılıç Arslan II to rule in Konya, and with his passing a new chapter in Seljuk history began, one in which the Sultanate of Rum would reach the apogee of its power and prestige.

– 6 –

The Seljuk Apogee

K eyhüsrev I left behind three sons, Izzeddin Keykavus, Alaeddin Keykubad and Keyferidun Ibrahim, all of whom contested the throne. Keykavus, the eldest, was governor in Malatya; Keykubad controlled Tokat; and Keyferidun, the youngest, was in Antalya. The majority of the Seljuk emirs supported Keykavus, but Keykubad had the support of his uncle Müizeddin Tuğrul Şah of Erzurum, as well as Leon II, king of Lesser Armenia, and the Danışmendid emir Zahir al-Din.

Keykavus came to Kayseri to be enthroned as sultan, whereupon his brother Keykubad put the city under siege in an attempt to seize the throne himself, but he failed and was forced to withdraw. Keykavus moved to Konya to set up his government there, after which he defeated Keykubad, who was then removed to comfortable confinement in a fortress near Malatya.

Keyferidun, his other brother, had in the meanwhile obtained support from the Latins in Cyprus, who helped him take control of Antalya. Keykavus besieged Antalya by land and sea until he recaptured the city; he then confined Keyferidun in a remote fortress, where he died soon afterwards.

Keykavus rebuilt the ancient defence walls of Konya, a project that he completed by 1213, as evidenced by an inscription. By then he had arranged for the reburial of his father Keyhüsrev, who was finally laid to rest in one of the tombs in Alaeddin Camii, which Keykubad completed in 1219.

According to the Muslim chronicler Ibn Bibi, Keykavus was a good man of admirable character, handsome and of regal appearance, and although he was peaceable by nature, devoted to literature and the arts, he was forced by circumstances to spent most of his reign in warfare, in which he proved himself a brave and able leader.

Keykavus secured his western frontier by signing a favourable agreement with Theodore Lascaris of Nicaea. He then signed a commercial treaty with Hugh I, the Lusignan king of Cyprus, which allowed him to develop Antalya as a port for the Mediterranean trade. The pact, which was signed in 1214, facilitated commercial relations both for the caravan trade in Asia and for maritime commerce between Anatolia, Palestine and Egypt via Cyprus.

Meanwhile the Latin emperor Henry invaded the territory of Nicaea and defeated Theodore Lascaris, occupying the north-western corner of Anatolia. A peace treaty was signed in 1212, leaving the Latins in control of the territory they had conquered, by which they gained the coast from Edremit to Izmit, with a hinterland extending to Achyracus (Balıkesir), with the Empire of Nicaea holding the territory to the south of that.

Theodore Lascaris, after recovering from his defeat by the Latins, attacked David Comnenus, the brother of the emperor Alexius of Trebizond. Theodore captured Heracleia Pontica, David's headquarters, forcing him to flee to Sinop.

Keykavus then attacked Sinop, defeating and killing David Comnenus in a battle outside the city. Alexius Comnenus hastened from Trebizond to relieve the defenders in Sinop, but he was captured by the local Türkmen while on a hunting expedition outside the city walls. Alexius, to regain his liberty, had to surrender Sinop to Keykavus and agree to become the sultan's vassal. The treaty fixed the annual tribute of the emperor to the sultan at 12,000 gold pieces, 500 horses, 2,000 cattle, 10,000 sheep and fifty bales of precious goods.

After the treaty was signed Alexius and Keykavus rode together into Sinop on Sunday, 1 November 1214, a date given by a bilingual inscription in Greek and Arabic on the city walls. Another inscription on one of the towers records that the walls were rebuilt by the Seljuks in 1215. Their possession of Sinop now gave the Seljuks a wedge between the territories along the Black Sea of the Byzantine Empires of Nicaea and Trebizond, the latter emperor now acknowledging that he was a vassal of the sultan. This deflated Alexius's claim to be the true Byzantine emperor, and thenceforth the Empire of Trebizond had little more than local significance.

The capture of Sinop now gave the Seljuks a port on the Black Sea. Keykavus invited merchants from elsewhere in Anatolia to resettle in Sinop, which he sought to develop as a major port, particularly for trade with the Crimea. He rebuilt its harbour installations, establishing Sinop as the base for the Seljuk Black Sea fleet. This, together with the new Seljuk port on Mediterranean at Antalya, opened up the Sultanate of Rum to trade from both the north and the south, greatly increasing its economic potential.

In 1216 Keykavus besieged the Armenian fortress of Gaban, which commanded a mountain pass on the road between Kayseri and Maraş. The Seljuks defeated a force sent to relieve Gaban, capturing a number of Armenian nobles, but the fortress itself continued to hold out. Leon II, king of the Cilician Kingdom of Armenia, then personally led an army that succeeded in relieving Gaban. Nevertheless, the prisoners were released only after the surrender of two other Armenian fortresses, Loulon and Lauzada, both near the Cilician Gates.

The following winter Keykavus went on to besiege Seleucia (Silifke) on the Mediterranean coast, which at the time was occupied by the Knights Hospitallers of St John of Jerusalem, a crusading order, who held it under Armenian suzerainty. But the knights held out against Keykavus and he was forced to lift the siege.

During the next year Keykavus defeated the Armenians in several engagements, and either captured or destroyed a number of their fortresses. Leon II was forced to submit to Keykavus as his vassal, agreeing to pay an annual tribute and to supply troops to the Seljuks when needed on campaign. Keykavus, for his part, was to inform the Türkmen tribes on the frontier that merchants from both sides should be allowed to come and go without interference.

The Fifth Crusade began in 1212 when Pope Innocent III issued a proclamation calling on Christians to come to the aid of the besieged Kingdom of Acre, the crusader state that had been established in the Holy Land after the Third Crusade. The first of the crusaders did not arrive in Acre until 1217 and they did not go into action until the following year, under the leadership of John of Brienne, when they engaged the forces of the Ayyubid Sultan Saif ad-Din al-Adil, brother and successor of Saladin.

Al-Adil's nephew, az-Zahir of Aleppo, died in 1216 and was succeeded by a child named al-Malik al-Aziz, for whom the eunuch Togril was appointed regent. Saladin's oldest son al-Malik al-Afdal, az-Zahir's brother, the Ayyubid emir of Samosata, disputed the succession and called on Sultan Keykavus to help him. Early in 1218 Keykavus and al-Afdal invaded the territory of Aleppo and advanced on the capital. Togril, knowing that al-Adil was dealing with the threat of the Fifth Crusade and could not help him, appealed to al-Aziz's cousin al-Malik al-Ashraf, al-Adil's third son, the Ayyubid emir of Urfa and Harran.

Keykavus captured Manbij, north-east of Aleppo, as well as several other fortresses, but because of the treachery of al-Afdal, who retired to Samosata, he was badly defeated by al-Ashraf near Buza'a, as a result of which he had to retreat to Elbistan. He was pursued by al-Ashraf, who recaptured the fortresses that had fallen to the Seljuks.

Keykavus immediately began preparing for another campaign against al-Ashraf, in preparation for which he received the allegiance of Nasir al-Din Mahmud, the Artukid ruler, and Muzaffar ud-Din Kök-Bori, the emir of Erbil. Together with his allies, Keykavus set out against al-Ashraf in 1220 at the head of his army, but when he reached Malatya he suddenly died. Some suspected that Keykavus had been poisoned, but others felt that his death was caused by the defeat that he had suffered at the hands of al-Ashraf. Keykavus was buried in a tomb in the *darüşşifa*, or hospital, that he had erected in Sivas.

Though the reign of Keykavus had lasted just a decade, he left the Sultanate of Rum more powerful and prosperous than he found it, with Konya renowned as the capital of the dominant state in Anatolia, with a strong army, an efficient administration and a flourishing trade, which now, because of the acquisition of Antalya and Sinop, extended into the Mediterranean and the Black Seas and to their surrounding shores.

Keykavus was succeeded by his brother Alaeddin Keykubad, who was released from his place of confinement near Malatya and returned to Konya. Soon after his return he completed Alaeddin Camii, the great mosque that bears his name.

Keykubad proved to be an excellent and just administrator, and during his reign the Sultanate of Rum reached the peak of its prosperity, as he built roads, bridges and caravanserais throughout central and eastern Anatolia, encouraging agriculture and trade as well as developing industries such as sugar refineries. He was astute in foreign policy and an able commander, holding back the forces that confronted the Seljuk Sultanate of Rum along its now lengthy periphery, defeating enemies both Christian and Muslim. He also prepared to meet the threat posed by the Mongol conquests by fortifying the main cities of the Sultanate of Rum, particularly Konya, Kayseri and Sivas.

Meanwhile, Henry of Hainault, the Latin emperor in Constantinople, had died in 1216, without leaving a son or heir apparent. After an interval the Latin leaders in Constantinople elected the husband of his sister Yolanda, Peter of Courtenay, who was then in France with his wife. Peter was killed the following year before he could arrive in Constantinople, whereupon his widow Yolanda succeeded to the throne as empress. She died in 1219 and was succeeded by her son Robert of Courtenay, who did not arrive in Constantinople until 1221.

Leon II of Armenia also died in 1219, after a reign of thirty-two years, during which time he had been an obstacle to Seljuk expansion towards the south-east in Anatolia. He was succeeded by his daughter Zabel, who in 1222 married Philip of Antioch, fourth son of Baldwin IV of Antioch. Philip was executed in 1225, and the following year Zabel married Hetoum, son of Constantine the Constable, lord of Babaron and Partzapert. Hetoum ruled until 1270 and was the founder of the Hetoumid dynasty, who ruled the Armenian Kingdom of Cilicia for nearly a century and a half.

Theodore Lascaris died in the autumn of 1221, and since he had no son he was succeeded by his son-in-law John III Ducas Vatatzes. The following year Alexius Comnenus of Trebizond died, to be succeeded by Andronicus Gidus Comnenus. Thus in a span of five years there was a complete change in the cast of characters in the endless drama of Anatolian history.

At the beginning of his reign Keykubad signed a political and commercial treaty with Venice. According to the terms of this pact, the peace treaty was to be renewed every two years; merchants of both states would pay reduced customs fees in one another's ports; Venice would have a monopoly in trade to the Orient passing through the Sultanate of Rum, and in return would carry Seljuk goods to Europe in Venetian ships; and the sultan would be obliged to protect Christian pilgrims passing through Anatolia on their way to and from the Holy Land.

During the first year of his reign Keykubad captured Kalonoros, the great rocky promontory on the Mediterranean shore of Pamphylia, which had previously been held by the Armenians and before them by the Byzantines. The town was then renamed Alaiye (Alanya) after Alaeddin Keykubad, who soon afterwards erected the magnificent fortress that still crowns the great rock above the port. Keykubad also built the harbour works that can still be seen in Alanya, most notably the *tershane*, or naval arsenal, and the adjoining *tophane*, or armoury. Thus the Seljuks of Rum became a major naval power, their warships guarding their maritime commerce and extending their influence around the shores of the eastern Mediterranean as well as the Black Sea. As a result, Keykubad now entitled himself 'Sultan of the Two Seas'.

During the next four years Keykubad extended his territory eastward from Alanya, along the inhospitable Mediterranean coast known as Rough Cilicia. His most important conquest in Rough Cilicia was the great fortress of Anamur, at the southernmost point on the Mediterranean coast of Anatolia, which Keykubad took soon after his capture of Alanya. By 1225 he had expanded Seljuk control as far east as Silifke, which was still held by the Knights Hospitallers of St John under Armenian suzerainty.

At the same time, Keykubad extended Seljuk influence into the hinterland above the Mediterranean coast known as Isauria, which now became a marchland between the Seljuk Sultanate of Rum and the Armenian Kingdom of Cilicia. He also launched expeditions from Maraş, and these, together with Seljuk incursions in Isauria, forced King Hetoum to submit to terms. Hetoum literally became a Seljuk vassal, paying double the indemnity that had been imposed on Leon II, and in addition he had to supply the sultan with troops and even to mint coins in the name of Keykubad.

Keykubad was also active on the Black Sea coast of Anatolia, where in 1223 a conflict broke out between Andronicus Gidus, the Byzantine emperor in Trebizond, and the Seljuk governor in Sinop, an Armenian named Hethoum who may have been a convert to Islam. The dispute involved a group of merchants from the Crimean port of Sughdaq, who had settled on the Black Sea coast of Anatolia to escape the Mongol invasion of Russia. Through them trade was established between Sinop and the Crimea, whose principal port of Cherson was part of a colony belonging to the Byzantine Empire of Trebizond.

According to the Muslim historian Ibn al-Athir, one of the ships involved in the Crimean trade was wrecked off Sinop, and the Seljuk authorities, according to local maritime law, took possession of the cargo. The Byzantine government in Trebizond claimed that the ship was bringing tribute from their colony at Cherson, and that it had been deliberately wrecked by Hethoum. As a result, war broke out later that year between the Seljuks and the Byzantines of Trebizond.

The Seljuks attacked Trebizond in 1223 under the leadership of an emir referred to in the Greek sources as Melik Gazi, who may be Müizeddin Tuğrul Şah, Keykubad's uncle. The siege failed and Melik Gazi was captured by the forces of the emperor Andronicus, who forced him to submit to a humiliating peace treaty, in which he had to accept the status of being a Byzantine vassal.

Sultan Keykubad mounted a naval expedition against the Crimea in 1225 under the command of Husam al-Din Chupan, Seljuk governor of the Kastamonu province, who captured Sughdaq. A Seljuk protectorate was then established in Sughdaq, which was protected by a Turkish garrison, and a mosque was erected in the city for them and the local Muslim traders.

Meanwhile, Keykubad had been engaged in intermittent warfare with John III Vatatzes, the Byzantine emperor of Nicaea. One of the historical sources for this conflict is the Syrian chronicler Ibn Natif, who in an entry for 1225 states that Keykubad seized several fortresses in the course of a war with John Vatatzes. Ibn Natif reports that the war resumed in 1227 when the sultan seized one of the Nicaean emperor's 'great fortresses' after a hard-fought siege of eight days, but that Vatatzes counter-attacked and defeated the Seljuks, capturing part of Keykubad's army in the process. Some of the details of Ibn Natif's account of this conflict are corroborated by the Byzantine chronicler Nicodemus Hagiorites, who records that in the fourth year of the reign of John III Vatatzes, i.e. 1225–26, the emperor waged successful war against the Seljuks, who had attacked Phrygian Antiocheia and other cities in the upper Maeander valley.

Ibn Natif reports that Vatatzes and Keykubad were still involved in indecisive combat as late as 1229, after which the sultan had to direct his attention eastward to meet a threat from the revived Khwarizmid kingdom, while the emperor had important matters to deal with in the Marmara region, Thrace and the Aegean. Peace was thus in the best interest of both parties, and Ibn Natif reports that Vatatzes and Keykubad signed a non-aggression pact in 1231. This ended six years of intermittent and indecisive war between the Byzantines and Seljuks, which Greek chroniclers refer to as a great crusade that Vatatzes waged victoriously against the Turks, grossly exaggerating its importance and misjudging it as a Greek victory.

Meanwhile, the Fifth Crusade had ended in 1221, when the Latins had failed to capture Damietta on the Nile delta. Another Christian expedition, sometimes numbered as the Sixth Crusade, began when Emperor Frederick II of Hohenstaufen, king of Germany and Sicily, landed at Acre early in 1228. Later that year Frederick came to terms with the Ayyubid sultan al-Kamil, son and successor of al-Adil, who agreed to return Jerusalem to the Latins, although Muslims would still be allowed to visit the Islamic shrines in the city.

That same year Robert of Courtenay, the Latin emperor of Constantinople, died. The Latin nobles of Constantinople then elected as his successor the aged John of Brienne, who had commanded the army of the Fifth Crusade and had been king of Jerusalem.

Keykubad also sought to extend his influence in upper Mesopotamia and northern Syria. Having been reconciled with al-Ashraf, Keykubad went to his aid against the Artukids of Hasankeyf and Diyarbakır, both of which he conquered, along with their fortresses west of the Euphrates. At the same time he took Erzincan from the Mengücek emir Daudşah, and soon afterwards he captured Şebinkarahisar, another Mengüçek town.

Meanwhile, the Khwarizmid kingdom had revived under Jalal al-Din Manguberti, son of Khwarizmshah Muhammad, who had been driven from Central Asia in 1217 by the Mongols. Mustering an army of Kipchak cavalrymen, Jalal al-Din carved out a kingdom centred in north-western Iran and extending into Azerbaijan and Georgia, threatening eastern Anatolia. Jalal al-Din conquered Ahlat in 1229 after a long siege, forcing the emir Jahanshah of Erzurum to break his ties with Keykubad and enter into an alliance with the Khwarizmids. This led Keykubad to establish an alliance with the Ayyubids of Mesopotamia and Syria against Jalal al-Din, who for his part entered into an alliance with Andronicus Gidus of Trebizond.

Keykubad assembled his army in Sivas, including the regular Seljuk army and Türkmen cavalry, a force of 5,000 Ayyubid troops from Aleppo and Diyarbakır under al-Ashraf, and a contingent of Armenian and Latin troops sent by King Hethoum of Cilicia in accordance with his status as a vassal of the Seljuk sultan.

Jalal al-Din had been besieging Malazgirt, and when he learned that Keykubad had mounted a campaign against him he immediately invaded Anatolia. The two armies met on 29 July 1231 in the valley of Yassıçimen west of Erzincan. The battle lasted for three days, with Keykubad emerging victorious, largely through the efforts of the Ayyubid troops from Syria. Most of the Khwarizmid army was killed or captured, forcing Jalal al-Din to flee, abandoning Malazgirt and Ahlat as well as his treasure. Seventeen days later he was killed by a Kurdish peasant in the mountains near Diyarbakır. His ally, the emir Jahanshah, was captured and his emirate of Erzurum was annexed to the Seljuk Sultanate of Rum.

Shortly afterwards a Cypriot plot to recapture Antalya forced Keykubad to move his army south to the Mediterranean coast, while al-Ashraf marched his Syrian troops eastward to retake Malazgirt and Ahlat. The Mongols, who had by now penetrated into Azerbaijan, took advantage of the dispersal of the Turkish forces to invade Anatolia, raiding as far as Malatya and Sivas.

Keykubad responded by sending a Seljuk force under his general Kamyar to invade Georgia, whose Queen Russudan had aided the Mongols. After the Seljuks captured a number of frontier strongholds Russudan was forced to sue for terms, which included the betrothal of her daughter to Keykubad's son, the future Keyhüsrev II.

Keykubad's victory over Jalal al-Din effectively destroyed the Khwarizmid kingdom, which had been a buffer between Anatolia and the rapidly expanding Mongols of the Golden Horde, with whom the Seljuks now came into direct contact. A Mongol army of 30,000 men under the commander Chormagan was encamped in north-western Iran, whence in the decade 1231–41 they made regular raids into eastern Anatolia, ravaging the region and terrifying the population, both Christian and Muslim.

Meanwhile Keykubad, having put down the attempted coup in Antalya, returned to eastern Anatolia. He then expelled the Ayyubid troops from Malazgirt and Ahlat, after which he had all the fortresses in eastern Anatolia repaired as a precaution against an invasion by the Mongols, who were now his eastern neighbours. At the same time he signed a treaty with Ögedei, the Great Khan of the Mongols, who seems to have treated the Seljuk sultan as an equal. Keykubad now felt that his eastern frontiers were secure, for besides making peace with the Mongols his sovereignty was recognised by the Artukids of Diyarbakır and the Ayyubids of Syria.

In 1232 the sultan of Egypt, al-Kamil, launched a campaign into south-eastern Anatolia, his aim being to recapture Ahlat, which had belonged to the Ayyubids before it had been taken by the Khwarizmids three years beforehand. The invasion was thwarted in 1234 by a Seljuk army commanded by Kamyar, who held all the passes leading from Mesopotamia up onto the Anatolian plateau. The Seljuks then went on to take Harput, which thereafter became part of the Sultanate of Rum, ending the history of that branch of the Artukids. Soon afterwards the districts of Urfa, Harran and Raqqa came under Seljuk rule. Meanwhile, the retreating Ayyubid army took a fearful revenge by ravaging the region as far as Mardin, killing everyone they encountered.

Keykubad responded to this by marshalling all his forces near Kayseri, in preparation for a great campaign. He came to terms with Sultan al-Kamil, inviting him to send an ambassador to a conference of all the states in the region, Christian as well as Muslim, the aim being to establish an alliance against the imminent threat posed by the Mongols, whose raids had now carried them to Mosul. The meeting, which was held at the end of May 1237, commenced with a great banquet given by the sultan for the ambassadors, but shortly afterwards Keykubad died, general suspicion being that he was poisoned by his son and successor, Giyaseddin Keyhüsrev II.

The reign of Alaeddin Keykubad I is considered to mark the apogee of the Seljuk Sultanate of Rum, which under his rule reached its greatest territorial extension as well as the peak of its power and prosperity, his brilliant court at Konya and in his palaces of Kubadabad and Kubadiye giving rise to what would be the first flowering of Turkish culture in Anatolia.

His reign probably also marked the arrival of the Osmanlı Turks in Anatolia. According to some Ottoman sources, the Mongol invasions in the early thirteenth century drove the ancestors of the Osmanlı, a tribe of Oğuz Turks, from their homeland in Central Asia into eastern Anatolia, where they settled first in the region around Erzincan. Around 1230 they moved westward into the Sultanate of Rum. According to tradition, the newcomers came to the aid of the Seljuks in a battle near Ankara against Mongol raiders, and as a reward for this the sultan settled them in the western part of his domain, in the marchlands between the Seljuks and the Byzantine Empire of Nicaea. There the Osmanlı lived in obscurity until the first quarter of the fourteenth century, when they emerged as a major power, soon to become a world empire.

– 7 –

The Mongol Conquest

When Alaeddin Keykubad I died in 1237 there was a crisis of succession between his three sons, Izzeddin, Ruknuddin and Keyhüsrev, the first two of whom were the sons of his Ayyubid wife, while the third had a Greek mother. Since the latter was the eldest the great emirs supported him, and so he succeeded to the throne as Keyhüsrev II. As soon as Keyhüsrev secured his hold on the throne he had his two brothers executed, along with their mother. This was the first example in Turkish history of royal fratricide, which was to be practised as a matter of course by the Osmanlı when they came to power.

When Keyhüsrev first came to the throne he was under the influence of the vizier Sadettin Köpek, who had been his father's minister of buildings and hunting. Köpek (which means 'Dog') was extremely ambitious and eliminated all those who threatened his power, and one of the first to go was Kamyar, commanding general of Keykavus I, who was executed at the same time as Keyhüsrev's brothers.

The Egyptian sultan al-Kamil and his brother al-Ashraf died within a few months of one another, which led Köpek to take advantage of the situation by having Keyhüsrev join a coalition to seize Ayyubid territory in Mesopotamia and northern Syria. But the campaign had just modest success, and Köpek was able to add only Samosata to the Seljuk realm.

Köpek's intrigues eventually led Keyhüsrev to lose trust in his vizier, who was executed by the sultan in 1240. Influence then devolved to three of the sultan's advisers, Celaleddin Karatay, Shams al-Din al-Isfahani and Muhadhdhab al-Din. The three of them arranged for the marriage of Keyhüsrev with a daughter of the Georgian queen Russudan, the two having been betrothed some time before. The Georgian princess was Keyhüsrev's second wife, for he was already married to a daughter of the Ayyubid prince of Aleppo, but he clearly preferred the Christian princess to the Muslim one.

Keyhüsrev's almost total reliance on his advisers was evidence of the weakness of his rule, which marked the beginning of the decline of the Seljuk Sultanate of Rum. Dramatic evidence of this weakness came with a violent and widespread Türkmen revolt that broke out in Anatolia c. 1239–40, led by a self-proclaimed prophet named Baba Ishak. Baba Ishak preached his messianic message to the Türkmen tribes between Amasya and the Taurus Mountains, increasing their disaffection with the Seljuk state, particularly the corrupt administration of Keyhüsrev, which had left them unassimilated and in dire poverty. The rebellious Türkmen in Maraş and Adıyaman organised themselves and defeated the Seljuk forces sent to quell them in Elbistan and Malatya. They then marched on to sack Sivas, after which they headed to Amasya to join their leader Baba Ishak, only to learn that he had been killed by the Seljuks.

But the Türkmen tribespeople refused to believe that Baba Ishak was dead, for in their eyes he was an immortal prophet, a mahdi, or messiah. So with renewed vigour, and joined by increasing numbers of rebels, who brought along their families, the Türkmen defeated the Seljuk army. The defeated army, which included Latin mercenaries, retreated in disarray towards Konya, causing the terrified Keyhüsrev to flee from the capital to take refuge in the palace of Kubadabad. Another Seljuk army arrived from Erzurum as reinforcement, and together the two armies managed to stop the rebel force near Kırşehir in 1240.

The anti-Ayyubid coalition was revived in 1241, and later that year the Seljuk army captured Diyarbakır. The Seljuks then launched an expedition against Mayyafarikin, capital of the Ayyubid Emirate of Diyarbakır, but it was aborted when word came that the Mongols were preparing to invade Anatolia.

Keyhüsrev's military power at the time would appear to have been about the same as that of his late father, at least on paper. According to the contemporary Latin chronicler Brother Simon of Saint Quentin, the king of Armenia had to provide Keyhüsrev with 1,400 lances for four months; the emperor of Nicaea with 400, with no limit of time or place; the emperor of Trebizond with 200; and the Ayyubid emir of Aleppo with 200. Nevertheless, despite these forces the revolt of Baba Ishak had shown that there were serious weaknesses in the Seljuk state, particularly in its army, which only with the greatest difficulty was able to put down the Türkmen insurrection. What is more, these weaknesses were soon to be tested by the gravest threat ever faced by the Seljuk Sultanate of Rum: the imminent Mongol invasion of Anatolia.

Beginning in 1237 the Mongols had swarmed out of Central Asia in an invasion that took them through Russia and into Poland, Bohemia, Moravia, Croatia, Bulgaria and the lands north of the Black Sea. The destruction and slaughter were so widespread that an anonymous chronicler of the time remarked, 'No eye remained open to weep for the dead.'

The Mongols then moved down into the great grazing lands of Azerbaijan, from where they could threaten the Christian kingdoms of the Caucasus and the Muslim states of Iraq, Syria and Anatolia. The Georgian kingdom was ravaged, and Queen Russudan was forced to flee from Tiflis to Kutaisi. In 1239 the Mongol commander Chormaghan captured and sacked Kars and Ani, the ancient Armenian capital, massacring the entire population of both cities. Then in the winter of 1242–43 one Mongol army invaded Upper Mesopotamia, while another, under the commander Bayju, captured Erzurum, opening the way into eastern Anatolia.

When news of the fall of Erzurum reached Keyhüsrev he marshalled his forces at Sivas, summoning all his vassals, Christian and Muslim, to send him reinforcements. The emperor John Vatatzes of Nicaea sent him troops, but King Hethoum of Armenia played for time, for he was trying to stay on good terms with the Mongols. Keyhüsrev managed to muster about 80,000 troops, including about 3,000 Greeks and Latins, giving the overall command to the Georgian prince Shervashidze. Then, without waiting for the Armenians, the sultan marched his army to the mountain pass of Kösedağ, nearly 100 kilometres north of Erzincan.

The Mongol army under Bayju was somewhat smaller than the Seljuk force, though it was reinforced by Georgian and Armenian mercenaries, but it made up for its fewer numbers by its greater discipline and experience and its far better leadership. The pass at Kösedağ was a difficult position for the Mongols to take, for there was no escape from it once the attackers had committed themselves. The two armies clashed on the morning of 26 June 1243, with the Mongols defeating the vanguard of the Seljuk army, Prince Shervashidze dying in battle. Keyhüsrev fled in panic with the rest of the Seljuk army, leaving their camp with the tents of the sultan and other notables to be plundered by the Mongols.

After Bayju's victory he marched the Mongol army to Sivas, which surrendered without a struggle. The Mongols plundered the city, but they did not destroy it or massacre its inhabitants. Tokat and Kayseri, on the other hand, tried to resist, and as a consequence they were brutally sacked and their people were put to the sword.

Meanwhile Keyhüsrev had collected his treasure in Tokat and escaped to Ankara, sending his mother to take refuge with King Hethoum of Cilicia, who promptly handed her over to the Mongols. Keyhüsrev then finally made his way back to Konya, his sultanate a shambles, as the Turkmen tribes ran rampant throughout central and eastern Anatolia.

The sultan's vizier Muhadhdhab al-Din, on his own initiative, had gone in search of Bayju. After they made contact, Bayju took the vizier to Mughan near the south-eastern end of the Caspian Sea to meet with the Mongol chieftain Jurmaghun, his superior. Jurmaghun was probably already aware that a complete conquest of Anatolia was far too large a task at the moment, and one that was not essential for the security of the territory that he already held. Consequently, he concluded a peace agreement with the vizier on condition that the Seljuks become vassals of the Mongols and pay an annual tribute in gold and silver. Muhadhdhab then returned to Konya, where Keyhüsrev undoubtedly received him with great satisfaction, for the vezir had saved the Sultanate of Rum from destruction at the hands of the Mongols.

After Muhadhdhab's return to Konya he sent an embassy to Batu, founder and Khan of the Golden Horde and ruler of the western part of the Mongol Empire. The leader of the Seljuk embassy was Shams al-Din al-Isfahani, whom Keyhüsrev had appointed as deputy to Muhadhdhab. Shams al-Din obtained from Batu a *yarligh*, or diploma, which certified that Keyhüsrev was his representative in Konya, thus legalising the status of the Seljuk sultan as a vassal of the Great Khan of the Mongols.

Muhadhdhab had died while his deputy was away on the embassy, and so when Shams al-Din returned he succeeded him as vizier, and as a token of the sultan's esteem and gratitude he was also appointed governor of Kırşehir. Plans were then made to send Keyhüsrev's young son Ruknuddin on an embassy to pay homage to Batu, for this was part of the agreement that had been signed by Shams al-Din.

At around that time another Türkmen revolt erupted, this one in the mountains between Konya and Alanya, led by an obscure figure whom the chronicler Ibn Bibi refers to only as Ahmad, who rallied 20,000 men to his cause. According to his mother's testimony, Ahmad was a son of the late Sultan Keykubad I, and he claimed that he alone was worthy of the succession, since his 'half-brother' Keyhüsrev had shown himself to be incompetent. Keyhüsrev called on Constable Constantine, the Armenian lord of Lambron, for help in putting down the revolt. Constantine was at the time in revolt against Hethoum, the Armenian king of Cilicia, and it was in his interest to put down the Türkmen, whose revolt continued until the pretender Ahmad was captured and hanged at Alanya. Keyhüsrev for his part wanted to show that the Seljuks of Rum were still a force to be reckoned with in Anatolia, despite their defeat at the hands of the Mongols, who probably gave their tacit approval for this campaign.

Keyhüsrev died shortly after this campaign, passing away early in 1246. He left behind three young sons, who were raised to the throne as a triumvirate. These were: Izzeddin Keykavus II, aged eleven, son of the daughter of a Greek priest; Ruknuddin Kılıç Arslan IV, aged nine, son of a Turkish woman of Konya; and Alaeddin Keykubad II, aged seven, whose mother was a daughter of the Georgian queen Russadan.

The fact that the late sultan's successors were all minors added to the difficulties of the Seljuk state, leading to a power struggle between the great emirs. Shams al-Din succeeded in defeating his rivals in turn and then married the mother of Ruknuddin. He then shared out the principal posts in the sultanate to his friends, after which he sent Ruknuddin on the embassy to Batu, planned three years earlier.

Batu granted Ruknuddin a *yarligh* conferring the sultanate upon him. As Ruknuddin returned from the embassy, escorted by a Mongol detachment, the *yarligh* won him recognition in the eastern parts of the sultanate. The emir Celaleddin Karatay, who was Izzeddin's *naib*, or chief adviser, felt that he had no choice but to acquiesce. But at the same time he plotted against Shams al-Din, whose execution he arranged in March 1249, after which he became the power to be reckoned with in the Sultanate of Rum.

Karatay wanted to preserve the unity of the Seljuk state, and so he sought to support the original triumvirate between the three brothers. Other emirs wanted to divide the sultanate between Ruknuddin and Izzeddin, the former to rule the eastern half and the latter the western, the river Halys (Kızılırmak) to be the boundary. It appears that this solution was adopted at first, but then the two brothers, urged on by their respective advisers, went to war with one another, though neither had many troops. They met in battle at Aksaray, where Izzeddin's force emerged victorious. The emirs on both sides then came to terms with one another, with Karatay and his supporters persuading their rivals that an undivided sultanate was preferable. The government of the restored triumvirate was reorganised in June 1249, with all three brothers ruling together over a united sultanate, though the real power was in the hands of Celaleddin Karatay, who held the title of *atabeg* to Izzeddin.

Meanwhile, another crusade had begun under the leadership of King Louis IX of France, who on 5 June 1249 captured Damietta from Sultan Ayub. But the expedition ended in disaster early the following year, when the crusader army was utterly defeated by the Egyptian forces, who captured King Louis and all the other nobility who survived the battle, freeing them only after the payment of an enormous ransom. Meanwhile, Ayub had died on 23 November 1249 and was succeeded by his son Turanshah, who at the time was governing as emir in Diyarbakır. Turanshah reached Cairo at the end of February 1250, but on 2 May he was assassinated by a group of Mamluk officers led by Rukn ad-Din Baibars. The officers then appointed the senior Mamluk commander Izz ad-Din Aibek as regent, and after he had married the dowager Sultana, Shajar-ad-Durr, he gained enough legitimacy to be accepted as sultan of Egypt.

Thus began the first Mamluk dynasty, which replaced the Ayyubid dynasty in Egypt but not in Syria. The word *mamluk* in Arabic means 'owned' or 'belonging to', and in particular it applied to white male slaves, often Turks, who were taken as prisoners of war or purchased in the slave market. The Mamluk dynasty begun by Aibek were known as the Bahri, from the isle in the Nile at Cairo where they lived when they were slaves of the Ayyubids.

Five years later the Mongols asked that Izzeddin be sent to them on an embassy, as had his brother Ruknuddin when he paid homage to Batu. But the Seljuk emirs were reluctant to let Izzeddin leave, for his sybaritic lifestyle had made him very unpopular with his subjects, and it was feared that they might rebel against him in his absence. The three sultans met in Kayseri in 1254, and it was decided that Alaeddin, the youngest, should be sent to the court of the Great Khan of the Mongols in Karakorum.

After Alaeddin departed Izzeddin and Ruknuddin returned to Konya, where they soon fell into disagreement. Izzeddin, who, as may be recalled, had a Greek mother, had established ties with John Vatatzes, the emperor of Nicaea, whose daughter he may have married. Advised by

Karatay, he represented the party that wanted to revive some semblance of Seljuk independence, while Ruknuddin and his advisers stood for unconditional acquiescence to the Mongols.

Accompanied by his supporters, Ruknuddin fled to Kayseri. There he was proclaimed sultan, in his name alone, a claim that was recognised in most of the principal towns in the eastern part of the sultanate. Izzeddin and his advisers then mustered an army to deal with the secession, and after a futile attempt at reconciliation Ruknuddin's forces were defeated. Ruknuddin was then confined at Burghlu (Uluborlu), in the western part of the sultanate, where he would be safe from intervention by the Mongols.

That same year, 1254, John III Vatatzes died and was succeeded by his son Theodore II Lascaris. Soon afterwards Theodore signed a peace treaty with Izzeddin, the emperor and the sultan meeting at Tripolis in the Maeander valley to sign the pact. One of the terms of the agreement was that the Seljuks would return Laodiceia to the Byzantines, but before the transfer could be made a Türkmen tribe seized the town for themselves.

Around that time Theodore came into conflict with Michael Palaeologus, a general and high government official whom he suspected of having designs on the throne. Michael was put on trial for treason, which led him to flee to Konya, where in the summer of 1256 he was given refuge by Izzeddin. The sultan appointed Michael to a military command, his troops being exclusively Anatolian Greeks and other Christians. The contemporary chronicler Nicephorus Gregoras says that Michael's troops wore Byzantine uniforms and were armed in the Greek manner.

Soon afterwards, news came that Bayju had begun another Mongol incursion into Anatolia. The Great Khan of the Mongols, Möngke, had appointed his brother Hülagü, founder of the Ilkhanid dynasty, to govern Iran and to supervise the Seljuk protectorate, which until that time had been the responsibility of Bayju. At the beginning of 1256 Hülagü took up his post in Iran, bringing a large force of cavalry that required extensive grazing lands. This displaced Bayju, who was ordered to find pasturage for his cavalry on the Anatolian plateau. Thus Bayju's move into Anatolia was not an invasion, but it was still a serious matter for the Seljuks, for his large army would be a great drain on their finances, and at the same time it would inevitably lead to Mongol interference in Seljuk affairs. The first such intervention came almost immediately, when Bayju, in response to an embassy from Izzeddin, asked that his friend Muineddin Süleyman be appointed to a high post in the Seljuk government.

Alaeddin, who was still en route to Karkorum, sent a message to his brothers saying that it was absolutely essential that they comply with the Mongol demands. But Izzeddin's advisers persuaded him to resist, particularly the strict Muslims, who called for a *jihad*, or holy war, against the infidel Mongols. Thus an army was mustered and placed under the overall command of a vizier, while Michael Palaeologus led his contingent of Greek troops.

Bayju penetrated quickly into eastern Anatolia, where all the towns submitted to him without a struggle. He came up against the Seljuk army south of Aksaray and defeated them decisively, for many of them were so terrified of the Mongols that they fled from the field. The Seljuk vizier was killed and Michael Palaeologus fled for his life, finding refuge with a Türkmen ally in Kastamonu before eventually making his way back to Nicaea.

Konya was spared only through the intervention of Muineddin Süleyman, who had been appointed as Izzeddin's *amir-hajib* and *pervane*, titles that made him the sultan's exclusive authorised spokesman. Muineddin was the most famous and powerful official ever to hold the title of *pervane*, which literally means 'butterfly', and so he came to be better known by that name than his own.

Izzeddin then took his treasury and fled from Konya to find refuge in Byzantine territory. Meanwhile, Ruknuddin was released from captivity in Burghlu and returned to Konya, where he was proclaimed sultan in his own right. Although Bayju spared Konya, he ordered that the city's defence walls be demolished, and Ruknuddin promptly complied.

Ruknuddin felt insecure in Konya, and so he moved to Tokat, the residence of Muineddin, who persuaded the sultan to pay obeisance to Hülagü. This left an opening for Izzeddin, who had obtained Greek troops from Emperor Theodore by agreeing to give back the town of Laodiceia to the Empire of Nicaea. Izzeddin was thus able to return to Konya, where in May 1257 he re-established himself as sultan.

A general uprising against the Mongols then began among the Türkmen, Kurds and Arabs of Anatolia and Mesopotamia. The Türkmen of Kastamonu attacked Tokat, but Ruknuddin and Muineddin called in Mongol reinforcements to beat them back. The Ayyubids of Mayyafarikin and the Artukids of Mardin then took advantage of the confusion to take Diyarbakır.

At that point the Seljuk embassy to Möngke, the Great Khan of the Mongols, sent back a messenger with news that Alaeddin Keykubad II had died on the way to Karakorum. Nevertheless, the embassy continued to the Mongol court, where towards the end of 1257 Möngke agreed to a treaty that divided the Seljuk Sultanate of Rum into two parts, with the eastern provinces, including Kayseri and Sinop, going to Ruknuddin, and the rest to Izzeddin.

At the end of 1257 Hülagü led a campaign against Baghdad, which he captured on 15 February 1258. Hülagü ordered that the entire Muslim population of the city be put to the sword, and over the next forty days some 80,000 of them were executed, including Caliph al-Mustansir. Al-Mustansir was the thirty-seventh caliph of Baghdad, and with his death the Abbasid Caliphate came to an end. The Christian community took refuge in their churches and were spared by the intercession of Dokuz Hatun, a Nestorian Christian who was the highest-ranking of Hülagü's wives.

After his victory Hülagü received envoys from many states that sought friendship with him. Among them were the Seljuk sultans Izzeddin Keykavus II and Ruknuddin Kılıç Arslan IV, who were accompanied by the *pervane* Muineddin Süleyman and the vizier Baba Tüghra'i. The Seljuk delegation were seeking Hülagü's approval for the partition of the Sultanate of Rum that had been agreed to by Möngke. Hülagü approved the partition, but since the Seljuk sultans were his vassals he ordered Izzeddin and Ruknuddin to accompany him with their armies on his campaign into Syria in 1259–60, in which he captured Aleppo and Damascus.

The Mongol army entered Damascus on 1 March 1260 under the command of Kitbuqa, a Christian, who was accompanied by Izzeddin and Ruknuddin as well as Hethoum, the king of Armenian Cilicia, and his son-in-law Bohemund VI, prince of Antioch, a stunning sight for the populace of a city which had until then been the Ayyubid capital of Syria. At the conclusion of the campaign Hülagü allowed the two sultans to return to Anatolia, but he forced Izzeddin to hand over to Ruknuddin the *yarligh* that had been given to him by Möngke.

The Great Khan Möngke died on 11 August 1259 while campaigning with his brother Kubilai in China. This led to a war of succession between Kubilai and Möngke's youngest brother, Ariqboga. The conflict dragged on until the end of 1261, when Kubilai finally crushed Ariqboga. Meanwhile, Hülagü cautiously remained close to his eastern frontier, ready to move into Mongolia if it became necessary. This led to friction in the Caucasus, which was the frontier between the territory of Hülagü and that of Berke, Khan of the Golden Horde.

These preoccupations caused Hülagü to remove many of his troops from Syria after his conquest of Damascus. The Mongol advance into Palestine had provoked the only remaining undefeated Muslim power, the Mamluks. Early in 1260 Hülagü sent an embassy to Egypt to demand the submission of the Mamluk sultan Saif al-Din Qutuz, who had seized power in December the previous year. Qutuz put the ambassador to death and prepared to meet the Mongol army in Syria.

It was at this moment that the news of Möngke's death and the civil war in Mongolia forced Hülagü to remove the larger part of his army to the east. The force left in Syria under the Mongol commander Kitbuqa was considerably smaller than the army Qutuz now mustered to oppose him. On 26 July 1260 the Mamluk army crossed the frontier and marched on Gaza, with Rukn ad-Din Baibars leading the van. There was a small Mongol force at Gaza, whose commander, Baidar, who sent a courier to warn Kitbuqa of the invasion, but before help could arrive they were overwhelmed by the Mamluks.

The Mamluk force under Qutuz met the Mongol army of Kitbuqa at Ain Jalud near Nazareth on 3 September 1260. The more numerous Mamluks inflicted a crushing defeat on the Mongols, and Qutuz had Kitbuqa beheaded after his capture. Steven Runciman writes of the historic significance of this battle:

> The battle of Ain Jalud was one of the most decisive of history. The Mamluk victory saved Islam from the most dangerous threat it ever had to face. Had the Mongols penetrated into Egypt there would have been no great Moslem state left in the world east of Morocco. The Moslems in Asia were far too numerous ever to be eliminated but they no longer would have been the ruling race... Ain Jalud made the Mamluk Sultanate of Egypt the chief power in the Near East for the next two centuries, till the rise of the Ottoman Empire. It completed the ruin of the Christians of Asia. By strengthening the Moslem and weakening the Christian element it was soon to induce the Mongols that remained in western Asia to embrace Islam. And it hastened the extinction of the Crusade States; for,... the victorious Moslems would now be eager to finish off the enemies of the Faith.

So far as the Seljuks were concerned, the Mamluk victory gave them a little breathing room, though, as events would show, they squandered their opportunity.

Less than two months after his great victory Qutuz was assassinated by Baibars, who was immediately chosen to succeed as Mamluk sultan. Thus began the remarkable reign of Baibars, a Kipchak Turk who had been bought as a slave by a Mamluk emir.

Meanwhile, there had been a change of regime in the Empire of Nicaea, where Theodore II died on 16 August 1258, to be succeeded by his son John IV Lascaris, who was only seven and a half years old. Just before he died Theodore appointed George Muzalon, the Grand Domestic, or prime minister, to act as regent for his son. But nine days later the nobles of Nicaea assassinated Muzalon and replaced him with Michael Palaeologus, their acknowledged leader. Three months later Michael was given the royal title of despot, and then in December he was proclaimed co-emperor. Early the following year the patriarch performed the double coronation of Michael VIII Palaeologus and John IV Lascaris. Michael was crowned first, for there was no doubt in anyone's mind that he was the emperor, and the young John soon disappeared from sight as a virtual prisoner of his co-ruler.

The following year Michael won a great victory over a coalition of Latin forces at the Battle of Pelagonia in northern Greece. This victory eliminated all but one of the obstacles in the way of the Greek recovery of Constantinople, and that was the Republic of Venice. Michael thus sought the aid of Genoa, which had long been the principal rival of Venice. He signed a treaty of alliance with the Genoese at Nymphaeum (Kemalpaşa) on 13 March 1261, giving them extensive commercial privileges in return for their support, particularly the use of their formidable navy.

The recapture of Constantinople in the end occurred quite by chance, coming almost as an anticlimax. A one-year truce had been agreed between the Greeks and Latins in August 1260, and towards the end of that period Michael sent a small force to Thrace under the command of Alexius Strategopoulos, who had orders to reconnoitre the environs of Constantinople. When Strategopoulos reached Selymbria (Silivri) he was told that Constantinople was virtually undefended, since the Venetian fleet had left with most of the Latin garrison on a raid in the Black Sea. Strategopoulos approached the city under the cover of night, and some of his men made their way through a secret passageway under the walls by the Gate of the Pege. They surprised the guards inside the gate, which they forced open to allow their comrades in before the alarm was raised. Early the following day, 25 July 1261, Strategopoulos gained control of the city after some street fighting with the remnants of the Latin garrison. The noise awakened Emperor Baldwin II, who had been sleeping in the Blachernae Palace, whereupon he rushed aboard a Venetian ship in the port and ordered it to sail away at once.

Strategopoulos, acting on the advice of the Greek populace, set fire to the buildings in the Venetian quarter on the Golden Horn. When the Venetian fleet returned from the Black Sea the mariners found their homes and warehouses along the Golden Horn in flames and their families milling about on the shore of the Golden Horn like 'smoked out bees', according to one chronicler. All that the Venetians could do was load their families aboard the galleys, after which they sailed away, ending the Latin occupation of Constantinople, which had lasted for fifty-seven years.

The emperor Michael was in Greece when the great news arrived, whereupon he immediately struck camp and headed for Constantinople. He arrived at the walls of the city on 14 August and made his triumphal entry into Constantinople the next day, the feast of the Assumption of the Virgin. The procession ended at Haghia Sophia, where Michael escorted the patriarch, Arsenius, to the patriarchal throne. A service of thanksgiving was then held to mark the restoration of Byzantium to its ancient capital on the Bosphorus, beginning the last two centuries of the empire's long history.

The quarter-century that began with the reign of Keyhüsrev II and continued through the first fifteen years of the reigns of his sons had been disastrous for the Sultanate of Rum, which never recovered from the triumph of the Mongols at Kösedağ. Nevertheless, the Seljuk Sultanate of Rum continued in existence through the first quarter of the fourteenth century, though only a shadow of its former self, soon to vanish from the earth.

– 8 –

The Collapse of the Sultanate of Rum

I zzeddin Keykavus II and Ruknuddin Kılıç Arslan IV had returned to their respective courts in 1260, after having accompanied the Mongol khan Hülagü on his victorious campaign into Syria. Both of them had obtained loans from the Mongol treasury, the repayment of which proved to be a great burden, particularly when added to the heavy tribute which they had to pay to Hülagü. Hülagü, it will be recalled, had forced Izzeddin to hand over to Ruknuddin the *yarligh* he had obtained from the Great Khan Möngke. This added to the tension between the two brothers, indicating that the unity of the sultanate could not be maintained for long.

Izzeddin chose Sahip Ata Fahrettin Ali as his *naib*, while Ruknuddin added the vezierate to the other offices held by Muineddin Süleyman, the *pervane*, on the strength of the *yarligh* he had been given by Hülagü. The two halves of the Seljuk sultanate each had a different relationship to their Mongol protector, in that Ruknuddin was far more directly controlled by Hülagü than was Izzeddin. The Mongols sent agents to Ruknuddin to supervise the collection of the tribute and the repayment of loans made to the Seljuks. Izzeddin had done nothing about paying the tribute and loans, and was accused by the Mongols of acting in bad faith. He was also accused of preparing for a revolt against the Mongols with the aid of the local Türkmen tribes, despite the fact that he was fighting a difficult campaign against Mehmet Bey, the chief of the Türkmen tribe near Ladık in the upper Menderes valley.

Izzeddin tried in vain to negotiate with Ruknuddin, who felt secure under the Mongol protectorate and knew that he would win out over his brother. This led Izzeddin to seek an alliance with the Mamluk sultan Baibars, with whom he was able to communicate easily via Antalya, which was part of his share of the sultanate. After the Mamluk victory over the Mongols at Ain Jalud in 1260, Baibars appeared to Izzeddin to be his best hope. But events moved so rapidly that Izzeddin was unable to establish a Mamluk alliance in time to avert defeat in the struggle with his brother.

Backed by a Mongol army, Ruknuddin marched on Konya. Muineddin won over Fahrettin Ali by offering him the vizierate of the combined sultanate. Izzeddin thus found himself abandoned by his chief minister with the enemy at the gates, and so he had no recourse but to flee from Konya to Antalya. Meanwhile, Ruknuddin entered Konya on 13 August 1261, becoming undisputed ruler of the entire Seljuk Sultanate of Rum.

Izzeddin made his way by ship from Antalya to Constantinople, arriving soon after Michael VIII Palaeologus had re-established the city as capital of the Byzantine Empire. Izzeddin had given refuge to Michael when he fled from Nicaea to Konya, and now the emperor gave refuge to the displaced sultan.

Izzeddin's hopes of having Byzantine help in restoring him to his throne were soon to be disappointed. Michael's foreign policy was directed towards Europe and he was desirous of marshalling all his forces against the Latins in Greece and the Mongols of the Golden Horde in Russia. He sought an alliance with Hülagü, who had just broken off relations with the Mongols of the Golden Horde, and so it was out of the question for the emperor to support Izzeddin's claim to the throne.

Thus Michael confined Izzeddin and his family in the Thracian seaside town of Aenos (Enez). Izzeddin managed to get word to Berke, khan of the Mongols of the Golden Horde, informing him that he was being held at Aenos and asking for deliverance. Berke then led a daring raid in Thrace and put Aenos under siege, forcing the garrison to surrender Izzeddin to them. Izzeddin was forced to leave behind part of his family, who then converted to Christianity, joining the Byzantine service. One of them was Izzeddin's son Melik, who became a Christian and married a Greek girl in Constantinople, changing his name to Melik Konstantine.

Izzeddin's eldest son, Mesut, remained with his father as Berke took them to the town of Serai in the Crimea, his capital. Izzeddin lived there until his death in 1279, after which Mesut made his way back to Anatolia, seeking to press his claim on the Seljuk throne. A number of Izzeddin's followers resettled in Dobruja, the area on the Black Sea coast south of the Danube and north of the Balkan range, in what is now Romania and Bulgaria. These are believed to be the ancestors of the Gagauz, the Christian Turks of Romania, whose name is an obvious corruption of Keykavus. Still others moved on to Serbia, where in 1309 King Milutin gave them a grant of land on which to settle.

Izzeddin's flight had left Ruknuddin as the sole ruler of the Sultanate of Rum. But he was merely a puppet of the Mongols, and the little autonomous power of the sultanate actually rested in the hands of Muinnedin Süleyman, the *pervane*, who in an inscription proudly refers to himself as 'King of the emirs and the viziers'. These lofty titles were rejected by those Türkmen chieftains who opposed Mongol rule, as well as those who still supported the exiled Izzeddin.

The principal opponent to Mongol rule in western Anatolia was Mehmet Bey, the Türkmen ruler of Ladık, Honaz and other places in the upper Maeander valley. Mehmet Bey had made an attempt to have his authority recognised by Hülagü, who accepted on condition that the Türkman chief would come to pay obeisance to him at the Mongol court. Mehmet refused to do so, whereupon Hülagü sent a combined force of Mongols and Türkmen that defeated him in 1262. Mehmet's son-in-law, Ali Bey, who had supported the Mongols in this dispute, was then invested by Hülagü with authority over Ladık and the surrounding area, which thus became an autonomous Türkmen principality.

South of Konya, in the region known to the Byzantines as Isauria, another independent Türkmen chieftain emerged in the person of Karaman, founder of the Karamanid dynasty, one that would last for two centuries. The Karamanid supported Izzeddin, and after he had been forced out by Ruknuddin they attacked Konya. The Mongol–Turkish force that put down Mehmet Bey of Ladık in 1262 also defeated the Karamanid, but it by no means destroyed them. The Karamanid also fought on the south side of the Taurus Mountains in Cilicia, where that same year Karaman was defeated and killed by the Armenian king Hethoum. But the Karamanid continued to be a significant force under Karaman's son and successor, Mehmet Bey.

As a result of these Türkmen uprisings, detachments of Mongol troops were stationed throughout most of central and eastern Anatolia. By 1262 the Mongols had established security in those regions from which they were deriving profit, though in other areas the Türkmen remained a threat.

Another development that became evident after the Mongol conquest was the granting of certain towns as fiefs to the viziers and their favourites or members of their families. Fahrettin Ali, supposedly to defray the cost of his vizierate, gave his sons possession of Kütahya, Sandıklı, Gurgurum, Akşehir and Afyon. Baha al-Din, a relative of Muineddin, was given autonomous control of Antalya and the other provinces along the Mediterranean coast, with the title *malik al-sawahil*, or King of the Shores. Masud ibn Kathir, a long-standing follower of Muineddin, was awarded the title of *beylerbey* and was given Niğde as a fief, thus obtaining control of the Cilician Taurus. Muineddin himself held Tokat and other former possessions of the Danışmendid, along with Sinop. Taj al-Din Mu'taz, the Seljuk official primarily responsible for the Mongol loan, was given Kastamonu, Aksaray and Develi Karahisar.

Meanwhile, Sinop had been recovered by the Empire of Trebizond in the late 1250s and then recaptured by the Seljuks in the early 1260s. When Hülagü died in 1265 Muineddin went to pay his respects to the new Ilkhan, Abagha. Abagha granted Sinop to Muineddin as his personal possession, and on his return the *pervane* rebuilt it as a Muslim town, erecting a mosque and a *medrese*. The *pervane*'s possession of Sinop was passed on to his descendants, a dynasty that lasted for several generations.

Ruknuddin was angered by the granting of Sinop to Muineddin, who as a result felt that the sultan was plotting against him. Abagha authorised Muineddin to use force to back up his authority, and later in 1265 the *pervane* led an army against the sultan, who was at Akşehir. An attempt was made to settle the dispute, but at a banquet Ruknuddin had a violent confrontation with Muineddin, who had the sultan strangled.

Ruknuddin was succeeded by his young son Giyaseddin Keyhüsrev III, who was about three years old at the time. Muineddin immediately assumed the roles of tutor and regent to the young sultan, as well as retaining his position as *pervane*.

The situation in Anatolia remained stable for the next decade, as Muineddin ruled the Seljuk Sultanate of Rum under the aegis of the Ilkhan Mongols. Seljuk troops assisted the Mongols in the Caucasus region against the Mongols of the Golden Horde, and also against the Mamluks, who were making inroads in Mesopotamia. On their southern frontier the Seljuks cooperated with the Armenians of Cilicia, who were also allies of the Mongols and enemies of the Mamluks.

Meanwhile, the Mamluk sultan Baibars had mounted a great expedition against the Latins, which left Cairo in January 1265. His first conquest was the port of Caesarea in Palestine, which surrendered to him on 27 February of that year, followed by the fortress of Arsuf on 29 April.

In the early summer of 1266, while Abagha and his Seljuk allies were fighting off an invasion in Iran by Khan Berke and the Mongols of the Golden Horde, two Mamluk armies set out from Egypt. One, under Baibars himself, appeared before Acre on 1 June, but the sultan found the city so strongly defended that he went on to Safed, which surrendered at the end of July, giving the Mamluks control of Galilee.

The second Mamluk army, commanded by the emir Qalawun, captured a number of fortresses in Palestine before joining with the army of al-Mansur of Hama, after which their combined force marched to Aleppo and then headed into Cilicia. King Hethoum sent an army to stop them at the Syrian Gates but the outnumbered Armenians were routed by the Mamluks. The Mamluks then swept through Cilicia, sacking the Armenian capital at Sis and slaughtering thousands of its inhabitants. The Armenian Kingdom of Cilicia never recovered from this disaster, and thenceforth it played only a minor and passive part in the power politics of the region.

Two years later Baibars mounted another expedition, which on 7 March led to the capture of the Templar castle of Athlit, followed on 15 April by the taking of the crusader castle of Beaufort. Then on 14 May Baibars appeared before Antioch, his main objective, which four days later fell to the Mamluks, who enslaved all of the populace they did not massacre.

This effectively ended the history of the Latin Principality of Antioch, the first of the states founded in the Levant by the crusaders, after 171 years. Antioch, the 'Fair Crown of the Orient', never recovered from the Mamluk sack, for the Muslim conquerors had no interest in repopulating or rebuilding the city, which diminished to the status of a frontier fortress, known in Turkish as Antakya.

Abagha, the khan of the Ilkhanid Mongols, sent Muineddin on an embassy to Baibars in 1271, seeking for a peace settlement that would allow for the rebuilding and reorganisation of the war-ravaged territories he governed. No settlement could be reached, and so the following year a Seljuk–Mongol force, accompanied by Muineddin, attacked Birecik, a fortress on the middle Euphrates guarding one of the passages from Syria into Upper Mesopotamia. But the expedition proved to be a failure.

Muineddin was frustrated by the interference posed by the Mongol administrators who were overseeing Seljuk affairs, one of them being Prince Ajay, brother of the Ilkhan Abagha. He asked Abagha to recall Ajay, and when this was not done the *pervane* began negotiating secretly with

Baibars to initiate a campaign in Anatolia, promising that the Seljuks would accept vassalage to the Mamluks. But when Ajay was finally recalled Muineddin abruptly broke off negotiations with Baibars. The administrator who replaced Ajay proved easier to deal with; nevertheless, Muineddin knew that he and the other Mongol representatives in the sultanate were keeping a very close watch on his conduct of government affairs.

Ajay was brought back to Anatolia in 1275, which led Muineddin to reopen negotiations with Baibars. Ajay was now obviously out to eliminate Muineddin, who was trying to do the same with him, while at the same time the *pervane* was trying to allay the suspicions of Abagha. A new joint Seljuk–Mongol expedition against Birecik was mounted in 1276, but because of the mutual suspicion and disagreement it had to be abandoned.

Muineddin's clandestine plot to bring Baibars in to aid the Seljuks against the Mongols came out into the open in 1276. One of his co-conspirators in this plot was Masud ibn Kathir, the Seljuk governor of Niğde, who called in a Mamluk force without waiting for Muineddin's approval. This led to a violent internal struggle in Niğde, from which ibn Kathir emerged triumphant by killing all his opponents and seizing Sultan Giyaseddin Keyhüsrev III as a hostage. While ibn Kathir held the sultan in Niğde, Muineddin withdrew to his family seat at Tokat to await developments.

The Mongols took Niğde and executed Masud ibn Kathir and his supporters, while the sultan was excused from any complicity in the revolt. Although ibn Kathir had denounced Muineddin as a traitor, the Mongols made no move against the *pervane* at that time.

As part of his revolt, Masud ibn Kathir had given a free hand to the local Türkmen tribes. Thus Mehmet Bey, the Karamanid emir, not only attacked the Mongol troops who were occupying Isauria, but he also defeated a Seljuk–Mongol force sent against him by the governor who had been appointed in Niğde after the fall of Masud ibn Kathir. Reinforcements sent against him by the sons of Fahrettin Ali from Afyon and by Baha al-Din from Antalya had only limited success, and the Karamanid were able to waylay a Franco-Armenian trade caravan and make off with all its goods.

At that point Baibars launched his long-awaited invasion of Anatolia, for which he was counting on the help of the Türkmen tribes, some Seljuk emirs and possibly Muineddin, although the wily *pervane* continued to keep his hand secret as long as possible.

The first battle was fought near Elbistan on 16 April 1277, when Baibars routed the Mongols, nearly all of whose commanders were killed or captured. Among the captives was a contingent under a son of Muineddin, whom the Mongols had left out of their order of battle because of their suspicions that the *pervane* had been plotting with Baibars.

Five days later Baibars entered Konya, while Muineddin, along with the sultan and Fahrettin Ali, took refuge in Tokat. A number of emirs surrendered to Baibars, who was then elevated to the royal Seljuk throne and proclaimed sultan of Rum. Baibars' secretary, Muhyi al-Din ibn'Abd al Zahir, writes in the *Life* of his master that the Mamluks admired the splendid public buildings of Konya, as well as the wealth of the *pervane* and his associates, much of which had now fallen into their hands.

A week later Baibars left Konya, although he had received a letter from Muineddin asking him to wait. Baibars knew that there were not enough supplies in Konya to support his army, and he planned his homeward march through areas that could provide sufficient food for his men. Thus the Mamluk expedition ended up by being a demonstration of force rather than an invasion, limited by the inability to obtain widespread support from the Seljuk emirs and the Türkmen tribes, a failure that Baibars attributed to the duplicity of Muineddin. In any event, the expedition into Anatolia was to be Baibars' last campaign, for he died on 1 July 1277. According to some chroniclers, he succumbed to wounds suffered on the Anatolian campaign, but the dominant theory is that he died from drinking poisoned *kumiz*, the fermented mare's milk favoured by the Turks and Mongols.

Meanwhile, the Karmamanid emir Mehmet Bey launched a wide-spread offensive. Reinforced by the Eşref and Menteşe tribes, the Karamanid attacked and captured Konya. The Türkmen then set up as sultan a pretender named Jimri, who claimed to be Prince Siyavuş, a son of the ex-sultan Izzeddin, still living in exile in the Crimea. Negotiations had in fact been entered into with Izzeddin Keykavus II, but the Crimea was too far away for him or one of his sons to return to Konya in time to take the throne. So the Türkmen made do with the pretender Jimri, who was proclaimed sultan with the royal insignia taken from the tomb of Alaeddin Keykubad I, after which he married a daughter of Ruknuddin Kılıç Arslan IV who was in Konya at the time.

The pretender appointed the Karamanid emir Mehmet Bey as his vizier, and distributed honours and titles to the other Türkmen chieftains.

Claude Cahen makes an interesting observation about these appointments in his *Pre-Ottoman Turkey*; referring to the Türkmen emirs, he writes, 'Remarkably enough, as these latter knew neither Arabic or even Persian, a chancellery using the Turkish language was established, something never before seen in Seljukid Asia Minor.'

Somewhat earlier a tribe known as the Germiyan, comprised of a mixture of Kurds and Turks, made their appearance east of Malatya. The Germiyan were moved from there by the Seljuks and established in western Anatolia as a counterforce against the Türkmen. Baha al-Din, the Seljuk governor of Antalya, and the sons of Fahrettin Ali at Afyon joined forces with the Germiyan to fight the Türkmen rebels at Konya. The two forces met north-west of Konya at a place called Altuntaş, where the Türkmen rebels defeated the Seljuks, killing Baha al-Din and the sons of Fahrettin Ali. Their victory led many others to join the ranks of the rebels, and a Türkman chieftain seized Aksaray as his own possession.

These uprisings led the Mongol Ilkhan Abagha to mount an expedition into Anatolia, taking command himself. After surveying the site of the Battle of Elbistan and remarking indignantly that there were no Turkish corpses there, only Mongols and Egyptians, he marched on to enter Kayseri. There he executed numerous Türkmen suspected of being rebels and had Christian captives held to ransom.

After this show of force Abagha withdrew to the east. He stopped at Kemah, west of Erzincan, where Muineddin came to pay his respects. Abagha asked him to hand over the fortress of Kughuniya, the *pervane*'s personal possession, and Muineddin gave orders to the governor that it should be surrendered to the Mongols. But the governor refused to comply, and Abagha concluded that he had been secretly ordered to do this by Muineddin.

Abagha then held a court of enquiry to review the various charges against Muineddin, most notably that the *pervane* had murdered Sultan Ruknuddin, and that he had conspired with Baibars to invade Anatolia and drive out the Mongols. After hearing the evidence, Abagha condemned Muineddin to death, and on 2 August 1277 the *pervane* was executed, after having governed the Seljuk Sultanate of Rum almost single-handedly for nearly twenty years. According to Steven Runciman, rumour had it that the *pervane*'s 'flesh was served in a stew at the Ilkhan's next state banquet'.

Abagha then set out to put down the Türkmen rebellions. He mounted an expedition in 1278 under the command of his brother Kangirtay, assisted by his own vizier, Shams al-Din Juwayni, as well as the Seljuk vizier Fahrettin Ali and the young sultan Giyaseddin Keyhüsrev III, who had come at once to put himself under the Ilkhan's protection. After capturing Kughuniya, the Seljuk–Mongol force went on to take Tokat and Aksaray, where they killed or enslaved 6,000 of the inhabitants. They then took Konya without a struggle, for the Karamanid had withdrawn to their own territory around Ermenek. The Seljuk–Mongol army withdrew for the summer to Kayseri, whereupon the Karamanid reappeared to besiege Konya. The Seljuk–Mongol army then rushed back to Konya and succeeded in surrounding the Karamanid in the mountains, and in the ensuing battle Mehmet Bey and two of his brothers were killed.

The pretender Jimri escaped from Konya and succeeded in establishing himself as a force in the Afyon region. Rather than have a Mongol force ravage the region, Fahrettin Ali persuaded the Ilkhan to empower him to put down the rebels. Enlisting the support of the Germiyan and Türkmen contingents from Ankara, Fahrettin Ali succeeded in defeating and capturing Jimri. Jimri was then flayed to death, after which his remains were stuffed with straw and paraded through all the towns of Rum, mounted on an ass.

Fahrettin Ali then went on to attack the Türkmen of Denizli and Burghlu, even though they had not taken part in Jimri's rebellion. Their chieftain Ali Bey, son-in-law of the late Karamanid emir Mehmet Bey, was captured and executed. Fahrettin Ali's grandsons were then granted possession of Afyon and the surrounding region.

The Mongol military campaign of 1278 was accompanied by an administrative reorganisation of the Ilkhanid protectorate over the Seljuk Sultanate of Rum. The reorganisation was headed by the Ilkhan's vizier, Shams al-Din Juwayni, and included not only measures of restoration, principally financial, but also the introduction of specifically Mongol institutions. After Shams al-Din had completed his reorganisation and departed, Abagha gave control of the government to Fahrettin Ali, who served not only as vizier but also as the Ilkhan's deputy. A friend of Fahrettin Ali served as deputy for the young Keyhüsrev III, which effectively made him the sultan's authorised representative.

The Mamluks again became a threat under Baibars' second successor, Kalaun (r. 1279–89). When Kalaun took Rum Qal'a on the Euphrates from the Armenians he was aided by the Karamanid, showing that the Türkmen tribe had recovered from their recent defeat at the hands of the Mongols.

Giyaseddin Mesut II, eldest son of the former Sultan Izzeddin Keykavus II, appeared in Sinop in the summer of 1280 and proclaimed himself sultan. Mesut paid his respects to the Seljuk emir of Kastamonu and than went to submit his imperial claim to the Ilkhan Abagha. Abagha left the sultanate in the hands of Giyaseddin Keyhüsrev III, but he mollified Mesut by giving him the territory of the Karamanid. But a nephew of Mesut, Alaeddin Keykubad, had stolen a march on him and obtained recognition by the Karamanid. Fahrettin Ali and Mesut led a force against Alaeddin Keykubad and forced him to flee to Cilicia, though he reappeared years later.

In any event, Mesut abandoned his plans to govern Karamania. Sultan Giyaseddin Keyhüsrev III in his turn went to visit Abagha, to request that the Ilkhan stop Mesut's intrigues against him, and at the same time to obtain reinforcements against the Karamanid. Abagha complied with his second request, and, with the aid of a Mongol contingent, Keyhüsrev succeeded in driving the Karamanid back almost as far as Ermenek, freeing Konya from their threat.

Abagha sent a Mongol army into Syria in 1280, and after sacking Aleppo it withdrew. The following year the Ilkhan appointed his inexperienced younger brother Mangutimur to command a Mongol–Seljuk expedition into Syria, but it was defeated by the Mamluks near Homs in October 1281.

The following year both Abagha and Mangutimur died. Abagha had bequeathed the throne to his son Arghun, but the youth's uncle, originally known as Tegüdar, usurped the throne. Tegüdar, born to a Nestorian mother and baptised as a Christian, had in his youth converted to Islam and changed his name to Ahmet, taking the title of sultan rather than Ilkhan when he was raised to the throne.

In 1283 Ahmet decided to confer the undivided Sultanate of Rum on Giyaseddin Mesut II. Fahrettin Ali acquiesced in this decision, since it was really of little importance, given the Seljuk sultan's lack of any real authority. Ahmet then brought Giyaseddin Keyhüsrev III to Kayseri, where he had him executed.

A Mongol civil war then erupted between the forces of Ahmet and his nephew Arghun. Finally, in August 1284, Arghun triumphed and succeeded as Ilkhan, as his forces defeated and killed Ahmet.

Soon afterwards Keyhüsrev's widow petitioned Arghun on behalf of her young sons. She asked that they be given the western half of the Seljuk sultanate, with Konya as their capital, while Mesut would have the eastern half, with Kayseri as his capital. Arghun agreed to the partition, whereupon the two young princes established themselves in Konya.

Their mother conferred the title of *naib* on Güneri Bey, the new Karamanid emir, and that of *beylerbey* on Süleyman Bey, chieftain of the Eşref Türkmen tribe – appointments that were resented by Fahrettin Ali and by the people of Konya.

The princess then went to visit Arghun, and while she was away Mesut's supporters, secretly aided by Fahrettin Ali and others in the Mongol government, put the two young princes to death. Mesut did not establish himself in Konya until the following year, 1286, when he accompanied a Mongol expedition let by Gaykhatu, Arghun's only remaining representative in Anatolia.

Meanwhile, the Byzantine emperor Michael VIII Palaeologus had passed away on 11 December 1282, to be succeeded by his son Andronicus II. Andronicus continued the main thrust of his late father's foreign policy, which was to concentrate his efforts towards the West and Europe, thus neglecting Anatolia, where all but the north-western part of the subcontinent had now been taken by the Turks, who themselves were now largely under a Mongol protectorate.

The Turkish tribe later to be known as the Osmanlı had *c.* 1275 settled around Söğüt, a small town in the hills of Bithynia. Their chieftain was Ertuğrul, a vassal of the Seljuk sultan, who died *c.* 1281 and was succeeded by his son Osman, from whom the Osmanlı dynasty subsequently took their name. Richard Knolles writes of Ertuğrul in his *Lives of the Ottoman Kings and Emperors*, published at London in 1609:

> Thus is Ertogrul, the Oguzian Turk, with his homely heardsmen, become a petty lord of a country village, and in good favour with the Sultan; whose followers, as sturdy heardsmen with their families, lived in Winter with him in Sogut, but in Summer in tents with their cattle upon the mountains. Having thus lived certain yeares, and brought great peace with his neighbours, as well the Christians as the Turks... Ertugrul kept himself close in his house in Sogut, as well contented there as with a kingdom.

The Seljuk Sultanate of Rum was now in the final stages of its collapse, its power sapped by the Mongol protectorate and its central authority all but destroyed by the rise of independent Türkmen emirates such as the Karamanid. The thirteenth-century Turkish chronicler Karim al-Din Mahmud, reflecting on the sad state of the Seljuk Sultanate of Rum, remarked that 'thorns replaced the rose in the gardens of excellence and prosperity, and the period of justice and security in the kingdom came to an end'.

– 9 –

The End of the Seljuks

When Giyaseddin Mesut II became sultan in 1283 he ruled over the undivided territory of the Seljuk Sultanate of Rum, though with no real power, since he was merely a puppet and vassal of the Mongol Ilkhan Arghun. What little power the Seljuks had was held by the Sultan's vizier, Sahip Ata Fahrettin Ali, who was effectively a deputy of the Mongol Ilkhan.

Soon after he established himself in Konya, Mesut, together with Fahrettin Ali, led a Seljuk–Mongol force again the Germiyan tribe. The Germiyan, although they had been settled in western Anatolia to help the Seljuks put down the Türkmen, soon proved to be just as much of a problem themselves. The Germiyan retreated before the sultan's army, but as soon as he withdrew they returned, and in one of their attacks Fahrettin Ali's grandson was killed. Fahrettin Ali did manage to save Afyon from their attacks, but in the end he was not able to put down the Germiyan. After the conclusion of the campaign, Sultan Mesut and Fahrettin Ali set out together to explain the situation to Arghun.

Arghun added to the difficulties of Mesut and Fahrettin Ali by ordering them to put down the Karamanid, which they were unable to do. The Karamanid then petitioned the Mongol Ilkhan for peace, as did the Germiyan and Eşref tribes. Arghun granted all of them peace, which settled nothing, though it added to the frustration of the Seljuk sultan and his vizier. Fahrettin Ali died in November 1288, after a career of more than forty years in Seljuk government, which never saw his like again.

He was succeeded by Fahrettin Qazwini, who had previously been *mustawfi*, or chief auditor, of the Ilkhan Mongol government. Sultan

Mesut had not been consulted about this appointment, which was a very unpopular one, since Fahrettin Qazwini was not a Seljuk official and knew nothing of local Anatolian conditions, besides which he surrounded himself with other outsiders who were often interested only in enriching themselves. Furthermore, his authority extended only to the western half of the sultanate, while the eastern half was administered by Mujir al-Din, the representative of the Mongol treasury, who had been an enemy of Fahrettin Ali.

Mesut's ties to the Mongols were strengthened by his marriage to an Ilkhanid princess, a dynastic union arranged by Arghun. Mesut tried to arrange a marriage between his brother Siyavuş and the daughter of an Eşref chieftain. But the chieftain captured Siyavuş and held him for ransom, until the Karaman emir Güneri Bey intervened and arranged for his release.

At the end of 1290 the Ilkhan Arghun mounted another campaign against the Türkmen, sending a large Mongol army into Anatolia under the command of his brother Gaykhatu. When the army entered Konya the Karamanid emir Güneri Bey hastened to pay his respects to Gaykhatu, as did the emir of the Germiyan tribe.

Arghun died on 9 March 1291 and was succeeded by his son Ghazan. As soon as Gaykhatu heard the news he rushed back to challenge the succession, taking with him the entire Mongol army from Anatolia. Gaykhatu easily pushed aside Ghazan and was proclaimed Ilkhan later that same year.

Gaykhatu had established Mesut in Ankara and appointed the sultan's brother Siyavuş to govern as deputy in Konya. Gaykhatu's withdrawal from Anatolia provided an opportunity for the Türkmen tribes to renew their raids. The Germiyan attacked and looted Konya, nearly capturing the *kale*, or citadel. Siyavuş called for aid from his brother, but Mesut was unable to send him reinforcements because of his fear that the other Türkmen tribes would attack Kayseri. Siyavuş was finally able to get help from a grandson of Fahrettin Ali who was ruling Ladık, and with his aid the Germiyan were driven out of Konya.

At this point the Ilkhan Gaykhatu reappeared in Anatolia with an even more powerful army than before, determined to crush the Türkmen for all time to come. His aim was to terrify the rebels by destroying everything in his path and massacring all who stood in his way, which led him to leave a swathe of destruction across the country of the Karamanid and the Eşref as well as the Menteşe. The Mongol army returned to

Konya to spend the winter of 1291–92, bringing with them hordes of prisoners to be sold into slavery. Gaykhatu's campaign had no positive results, for it created such hatred among the Türkmen and other Anatolians that it only laid the foundations for subsequent revolts against the Mongols and their Seljuk vassals.

Meanwhile, the Karamanid had recaptured Alanya, which had been held briefly by Latins from Cyprus. Sultan Mesut went off to battle the Türkmen of Kastamonu and was nearly captured in the fighting. While he was on campaign his brother Siyavuş tried to usurp the throne, which led to a brief civil war, whose events and chronology are difficult to follow. The two brothers were reconciled, only to renew the conflict two years later before again coming to terms. All this gave renewed opportunities for the Türkmen to resume their raids, withdrawing only on the rare occasion when a Mongol army was sent into Anatolia.

Gaykhatu was deposed and executed in April 1295 by his cousin Baidu, who thus succeeded him as Ilkhan. In June that same year Baidu was deposed and executed in a military coup, whose leaders replaced him with Ghazan, son of the late Ilkhan Arghun.

Shortly after Ghazan became Ilkhan, a Mongol chief named Tugachar tried to establish himself as an independent ruler in Anatolia, aided by descendants of Muineddin Süleyman, the *pervane*. His revolt was put down by another Mongol chief, named Baltu, who then began his own attempt to form an independent state in Anatolia. Baltu was defeated by still another Mongol chief, named Sülemiş, and fled for refuge to the Armenians of Cilicia. But the Armenians, fearing the wrath of the Ilkhan, turned Baltu over to Sülemiş, who in 1297 beheaded him.

The powerless Sultan Mesut had been drawn into Baltu's revolt. Though he was given a personal pardon by the Ilkhan Ghazan, Mesut was exiled to Tabriz in 1298, and he was replaced as sultan of Rum by his nephew Alaeddin Keykubad III, who had fled to Cilicia in 1280.

Then in 1299 Sülemiş himself revolted, with the help of the Karamanid, but he was defeated by an Ilkhanid army near Sivas. Sülemiş then fled to Syria, but when he returned to Anatolia the following year he was captured and executed.

Alaeddin Keykubad III went to pay court to Ghazan in 1302, but the Ilkhan had him beheaded. Ghazan then ordered that Giyaseddin Mesut II be restored as sultan of Rum, and in 1303 he returned to Konya to begin his second reign. Real power was at first exercised by the Mongol commander Chupan, one of those who had defeated Sülemiş.

The Mongol occupation was for the most part confined to central and eastern Anatolia, and thus it had much less of an effect in the western part of the subcontinent, where the Byzantine Empire was bordered by a number of Türkmen emirates that were by then effectively independent of the Seljuk Sultanate of Rum. The smallest and least significant of these was that of the Osmanlı, the followers of Osman Gazi, son of Ertuğrul, whose tiny emirate was in the Bithynian hills just eastward of the Byzantine cities of Nicomedia, Nicaea and Prusa.

The only contemporary Byzantine reference to Osman Gazi is by the chronicler George Pachymeres, writing during the reign of Andronicus II Palaeologus (r. 1282–1328), son and successor of Michael VIII Palaeologus, who says that he was living in a time when 'troubles confused the Emperor on all sides'. Pachymeres first mentions Osman in connection with an offensive mounted against the Turks by Andronicus in the spring of 1302. One detachment of the Byzantine force, numbering about 2,000 men under a commander named Muzalon, was driven back by a force of 5,000 Turks under a *gazi* emir whom Pachymeres calls Atman, actually Osman. According to Pachymeres, this success attracted other Turks to join Osman Gazi from 'the region of the Maeander' and from Paphlagonia. With these reinforcements, Osman decisively defeated Muzalon's army in a second battle, which took place at Bapaeus near Nicomedia in 1302. Pachymeres goes on to say that some time later Osman captured the fortified Byzantine town of Belakoma (Bilecik), and implied that he also captured other fortresses, which he used to store the loot he had accumulated.

According to Pachymeres, after Osman's victory in 1302 the country-side around Nicomedia was 'subjected to uncoordinated attacks from different quarters, mostly people finding easy foraging in the area, through grave lack of anyone to stop them... Some of the inhabitants were taken prisoner, others butchered, while some even deserted.' Only the fortified Byzantine towns could withstand the Turkish attacks. Pachymeres tells of how Osman's forces attacked Nicaea, 'uprooting vineyards, destroying crops, and finally attacking... the citadel'. But the walls of Nicaea proved too strong for Osman, as did those of Prusa and Pegai, on the Asian shore of the Marmara. Pachymeres describes the ordeal endured by the people of Pegai during the Osmanlı siege, when 'the surrounding population were confined within the city. Those who had escaped the sword suffered famine, and these bad conditions caused an epidemic of the plague.'

These Turkish attacks led to a mass exodus of the Greeks from Bithynia, and Pachymeres describes how many of them made their way across the Bosphorus to Constantinople:

You saw at that time a pitiful sight, namely those who were carrying away their possessions and crossing over to the city [Constantinople], who had despaired of their salvation. And the strait received a throng of people and animals daily who had not been freed without the greatest of tragedies. There was no one who did not lament the privation of the members of his family, one recalling her husband, another her son or daughter, another a brother and sister, and another one some name of a relation.

Andronicus was desperate for help, and in 1303 he hired a mercenary army of Catalans under the command of Roger de Flor. The Catalan Grand Company, as they were called, were described by Pachymeres as 'men who died hard in battle and were ready to gamble with their lives'. Roger de Flor drove a hard bargain with the emperor, but Andronicus was ready to pay the price, for he felt that he had no other hope. The Catalans were to be paid double the salary ordinarily given to mercenaries in the Byzantine service, and it was to be paid to them for four months in advance. In addition, Roger was to marry the emperor's niece, Maria, and to be honoured with the title of grand duke.

Roger de Flor arrived at Constantinople in September 1303 aboard a flotilla that carried the Catalan Grand Company, 6,500 in number, along with their wives and children. Despite the name, the company included Aragonese as well as Catalans. The chronicler Francisco de Moncada describes the company at the time of its arrival in Constantinople:

They took with them their women and children, witnesses of their glory or defeat, and... dressed in animal skins with sandals and leggings of the same hide. Their weapons included an iron network worn on the head like a helmet, a pointed staff somewhat like those used today in companies of harquebus fighters, and usually three or four throwing darts. They handled these darts with such speed and violence that they challenged armed men and horses...

Some of the ships belonged to Roger himself, others were hired from the Genoese, allies of the Byzantines. Soon after they arrived Roger married the princess Maria Palaeologina, and was for a time the honoured guest of the emperor. But Andronicus was anxious for Roger to move his men out of Constantinople, for soon after their arrival the Catalans got into violent street battles with the Genoese, who had not been paid for the hire of their ships. The emperor persuaded Roger to move his men over to Cyzicus on the Asian shore of the Marmara for the winter. There too they spent their time rioting and looting, and Roger was forced to pay for the damage they had done.

Early in 1304 the Catalans went into action against the Turks around Cyzicus, and succeeded in driving them back, 'leaving the camp strewn with three thousand dead horsemen and ten thousand men', according to Moncada. Moncada, in the introduction to his account of this action, gives a fascinating description of the way of life of these frontier Turks at the time:

> When Roger had definite information that the Turks had attacked the cape ramparts, he realised that they could not be far off and hastily unloaded his men, sending spies to scout the enemy camp. In a few hours he found that the Turks were lodged six miles away between two streams with their women, children and households. At that time they had not yet abandoned the customs of the Scythians, from whom they claim descent, living mostly as warlike tribes in tents and sheds in the field, moving with the change of season and produce of the land. Their main strength was their horsemen, who were governed by captains and princes, men of courage rather than blood. They waged perpetual war without military order against their neighbours, like the Arabians who now possess Africa.

At the beginning of May Roger marched the Catalan Grand Company, reinforced by 1,000 Alan mercenaries and a contingent of Greeks, to the relief of Philadelphia, where they routed a Turkish army that had been besieging the city.

Later that year the Catalans, reinforced by a new contingent of 200 cavalry and 1,000 infantrymen under Berenguer de Rocafort, began an invasion that would take them deep into Anatolia. Their first action was against a Turkish chieftain whom Moncada calls Sarkan, who must be Saruhan, eponymous founder of the Saruhan Türkmen tribe. The battle seems to have been fought outside Tire, where the Catalans routed the Turks, according to Moncada, 'leaving a thousand enemy horsemen and two thousand foot soldiers dead on the field'.

The Catalans then moved on to the foothills of the Taurus Mountains, where they came upon another Turkish force, which Moncada estimated to number 10,000 cavalry and 2,000 foot soldiers. Once again the Catalans were victorious, killing 6,000 of the Turkish cavalry and 1,200 foot soldiers, according to the testimony of Ramon Muntaner, another Catalan chronicler quoted by Moncada. Moncada concludes his account by describing the scene on the battlefield the following morning, when the victorious Catalans felt that nothing could stop them:

> The sun came out, revealing the extent of their victory, and a vast silence hung over the blood-soaked earth, piled here and there with the bodies of men and animals... The Company was so elated with this victory that its men forgot their fears of all major difficulties and began to clamor for crossing the mountains and invading Armenia. They wanted to go to the farthest boundaries of the Roman Empire, and recover in a short time what the Emperors had taken centuries to lose. But their captains calmed this daring determination, and proceeded with the prudence worthy of the difficulty of such an undertaking.

This was the last major battle fought in Anatolia by the Catalans, who soon afterwards became involved in a violent dispute with the Byzantines. Then in 1305 Roger de Flor was assassinated by one of the Alan mercenaries of Andronicus, whereupon the Catalans set themselves up as an independent power at Gallipoli (Gelibolu) on the European shore of the Dardanelles.

By now the Turks, despite their defeats at the hands of the Catalans, had made their way across the Dardanelles into Europe. One group of them offered their services to King Stephen Milutin of Serbia and were gladly accepted. Another, headed by a chieftain named Halil, pillaged the countryside throughout Thrace, making land communication impossible between Constantinople and Thessalonica. Andronicus came to terms with Halil in 1310. According to their agreement, Halil and his men, numbering 1,300 cavalry and 800 foot soldiers, were to be given free passage in Genoese ships across the Dardanelles, along with all their loot, so that they could return to Anatolia.

The agreement broke down when one of the emperor's officials tried to relieve the Turks of their booty. Halil then summoned reinforcements to join him, and for the next two years most of Thrace was in Turkish hands. Andronicus, calling for help from the Genoese and the Serbs, was finally able to trap Halil and his men on the Gallipoli peninsula, where in 1312 the Turks were annihilated, fighting to the last man.

Meanwhile, the last major Mongol invasion of Syria ended in the spring of 1303, when its commander Kutluk-Shah was defeated by the Mamluks near Damascus. That same year Andronicus appealed to Ghazan for help against the Turks. The emperor offered him the hand in marriage of his illegitimate daughter, and the Ilkhan was pleased to accept.

But Ghazan died in May the following year, before the marriage could be arranged. He was succeeded by his brother Oljaytu, whom the Byzantines knew as Charbadas. In the spring of 1305 Andronicus sent an embassy to Oljaytu with the same proposal he had made to Ghazan. Oljaytu accepted the proposal and promised to send Andronicus 40,000 men, 20,000 of whom were reported to be already in the region of Konya.

At that time Nicaea was being besieged by Osman Gazi, who had almost cut off the city from outside help. Andronicus sent his sister Maria to Nicaea to rally the populace, telling them of the help that the Mongols were going to send the Byzantines. The news only spurred on Osman Gazi, who in 1307 captured the fortress of Trikokkia, thus cutting off Nicaea from Nicomedia. The proposed alliance with the Mongols never came to pass, and the Byzantines were left to fight a losing battle against the rising power of Osman Gazi.

Meanwhile, Oljaytu had in 1306 sent the Mongol prince Erenjen to govern the Seljuk Sultanate of Rum. Two years later the second reign of Sultan Giyaseddin Mesut II came to an end when he was murdered in Kayseri. The circumstances of his death are unclear, and it is uncertain as to who if anyone succeeded him, a measure of how low the status of the Seljuk Sultanate of Rum had declined at the end of its history.

The last Seljuk ruler in Anatolia, though he may not have had the title of sultan, was an intriguing character known as Gazi Çelebi. The Ottoman chroniclers make him a son of Sultan Giyaseddin Mesut II, but he was more likely a grandson of Muineddin Süleyman, the famous *pervane*. Gazi Çelebi ruled in Sinop up to *c.* 1324, and won fame in his battles on land and sea against the Byzantines of Trebizond as well as the Genoese traders on the Black Sea. The Arab traveller Ibn Battutah tells the story of Gazi Çelebi's most famous exploit, which would seem to make him the world's first frogman:

> This Gazi Çelebi was a brave and audacious man, endowed by God with
> a special gift of endurance under water and power of swimming. He used
> to make expeditions in war galleys to fight the Greeks, and when the fleets
> met and everybody was occupied by fighting, he would dive under the
> water, carrying in his hand an iron tool with which to hole the enemy's
> galleys, and they would know nothing of what had befallen them until
> the foundering of their ship took them unaware. On one occasion a fleet
> of galleys belonging to the enemy made a surprise attack on the harbour
> and he holed them and captured all the men who were on board. He

possessed indeed a talent that was unmatched, but they relate that he used to consume an excessive quantity of hashish, and it was because of this that he died.

Such was the last ruler of the Seljuks, who thenceforth were supplanted by the *beyliks* into which Anatolia was divided after the fall of the Sultanate of Rum.

– 10 –

The Rise of the Beyliks

The collapse of the Seljuk Sultanate of Rum coincided with the rise of the Türkmen and other *beyliks*, which by the end of the fourteenth century extended their control through virtually the whole of Anatolia in a mosaic of independent emirates, some of which survived well into the fifteenth century.

These *beyliks*, usually named for an eponymous founder, included the Aydınid, Dülgadır, Eretnid, Eşref, Germiyan, Hamidid, Isfendiyarid (also called the Candarid), Karamanid, Karası, Menteşe, Ramazanoğlu, Saruhan, Teke and Osmanlı.

The oldest, most powerful and longest-lived of the Anatolian emirates was that of the Karamanid, founded during the reign of Sultan Alaeddin Keykubad I by Karaman Bey. According to tradition, Keykubad settled the Karamanid south of Konya in a region extending from Larende on the north to Anamur, Silifke and Corycus on the Mediterranean coast. The Karamanid established their capital at Larende, whose name they changed to Karaman. By the end of the thirteenth century the Karamanid *beylik* extended from its old centres of Karaman, Ermenek and Mut down to the Mediterranean coast, where it held Alanya, Anamur, Silifke and Corycus. Around 1300 the emir Mahmut extended Karamanid influence as far eastward as Niğde. Then in 1311 Mahmut's successor, Musa Bey, briefly occupied Konya, before being driven out by the Mongol commander Chupan.

The Eşref tribe, who were perhaps a mixture of Turks and Kurds, had aided the Karamanid on the two occasions when they occupied Konya. But after the 1311 occupation the Eşref split with the Karamanid, because they felt they had not received a fair share of the loot. As a result, the Eşref moved westward to the region around Beyşehir, which their emir Süleyman ibn Eşref had occupied as early as *c.* 1290, as evidenced by an inscription on the town gates. Süleyman's son Mubariz al-Din Mehmet extended the territory of the Eşref by taking Akşehir and Bolvadin.

After the death of Oljaytu in 1313, Chupan returned to take over the Mongol protectorate of Rum. Chupan remained only long enough to turn over the government to his son Timurtaş. Then in 1321 Timurtaş revolted and attempted to set up his own state in Anatolia, proclaiming that he was the mahdi, or messiah. Chupan was sent to put down the rebellion, which he did with ease, though sparing his son and putting the blame on his accomplices, whom he executed. Chupan then took his son to the Ilkhan, Abu Sa'id, who pardoned Timurtaş and reappointed him as Mongol governor of Rum. After the death of Chupan in 1326 Timurtaş revolted again, taking Beyşehir and executing the Eşref emir Mubariz al-Din Mehmet. Timurtaş was then defeated and fled to Egypt, where the following year he was executed.

The death of Mubariz al-Din Mehmet ended the short history of the Eşref dynasty, whose *beylik* was divided between the Karamanid and the Hamidid, who here make their first appearance in history. Texts at the end of the thirteenth century and the beginning of the fourteenth mention that the Hamidid were then in possession of Eğirdir, Isparta, Uluborlu and Antalya. The Hamidid split into three parts, the most prominent of which was the Teke *beylik*, which centred on Antalya.

The principal power opposing the Karamanid in the last quarter of the thirteenth century and the beginning of the fourteenth was the Germiyan. As noted earlier, the Germiyan were a tribe of mixed Kurds and Turks who *c.* 1275 were moved from their original home east of Malatya to western Anatolia, where they were supposed to help the Seljuk–Mongol government against the marauding Türkmen. With the collapse of the Seljuk state they were often at war with the government and evolved as an independent *beylik.* Their capital was Kütahya, and their emir, a descendant of 'Alişir, the founder of the Germiyan tribe, achieved some degree of dominance over the Türkmen chiefs in the surrounding area, who had freed themselves from government control as they migrated westward. At the end of the thirteenth century the Germiyan emir Ya'qub, a descendant of 'Alişir, is recorded in an inscription as ruling Ankara, Tripoli on the Maeander, Gümüşar, Sivriköy, Simaw and Kula, while his relatives or vassals held Ladık, Aydın and Afyon.

The eponymous founder of the Menteşe first appears in 1277 as the chieftain of a Türkmen tribe that had established itself in the region around Sivas. As a result of the conflict between the Karamanid and the Eşref, Menteşe moved his tribe westward 'beyond Ladık', where chroniclers record him waging war against other Türkmen tribes *c.* 1282. At the beginning of the fourteenth century Menteşe's territory included Aydın, Sultanhisar, Miletus, Milas and Muğla.

According to tradition, the Aydınid tribe was founded by Muhammad ibn Aydın, who is first mentioned *c.* 1300. The dynasty first emerged into prominence under Muhammad's grandson, Umur, who ruled over Birge, Ayasuluk (Ephesus), Tire and Izmir.

Both the Menteşe and the Aydınid built ships and ventured out into the Aegean, where their corsair raids against the Greek isles brought them up against the navies of the Byzantine Empire, Genoa and the Knights Hospitallers of St John, who had built fortresses on Rhodes and some of the other isles along the coast of Anatolia, as well as on the mainland itself.

North of the Aydınid were the Saruhan, and north of them were the Karası. At the beginning of the fourteenth century the Saruhan controlled Manisa, Foça, Saruhan and Demirce, while the Karası held Assos, Edremit, Bergama and Balıkesir. Although the Catalan chroniclers do not mention the Karası by name, it was probably they who were defeated early in 1302 outside the walls of Cyzicus by Roger de Flor and his men. In their third major battle, later in 1302, we have seen that the Catalans defeated the Saruhan outside Tire.

West of the Karası were the Osmanlı, who would soon burst into prominence and sweep all before them, on their way to becoming a world empire.

The *beylik* that developed around Kastamonu has a history that is at the same time complicated and obscure, the latter because of its relative remoteness from the main political centres. Under Sultan Alaeddin Keykubad I, the Seljuk governor of Kastamonu was Husam al-Din Chupan, whose son and grandson in turn controlled the region through inheritance from him. The next dynasty to control Kastamonu were the Candarid, sometimes known as the Isfendiyarid, from a later member of the dynasty. The eponymous founder of the dynasty was Candar Bey, probably a descendant of Muineddin Süleyman, the *pervane*, who was originally established in Aflani, to the west of Kastamonu. Candar went on to capture Kastamonu, which in 1314 is recorded to be in the hands of his son Süleyman Paşa, who ten years later took Sinop.

After the death of the Ilkhan Abu Sa'id in 1335, another rebellion broke out in Anatolia under the leadership of the Mongol commander Eretna, a former lieutenant of Timurtaş. Eretna gained control of a territory which included Kayseri, Sivas and Tokat, and which under his heirs during the next half-century at times extended eastward as far as Erzincan and Erzurum, and westward as far as Aksaray and Ankara. Then in 1381 the Eretnid *beylik* came under the control of Kadı Burhaneddin of Sivas, who claimed descent on his mother's side from the Seljuk royal family. His heirs remained in possession of the *beylik* for about half a century. Kadı Burhaneddin, who was also an accomplished poet, writing in Turkish as well as Persian and Arabic, did not change the system of government instituted by the Eretnid, and under his rule the Kastamonu *beylik* surpassed all other states in Anatolia in its cultural level.

The Dülgadır tribe made its appearance in south-eastern Anatolia in the mid-fourteenth century, principally in the region around Maraş and Ainteb. East of the Dülgadır were the Akkoyunlu, and east of them were the Karakoyunlu, two tribes that would come into prominence in the fifteenth century. West of the Dulgadır were the Ramazanoğlu, who held sway along the Mediterranean coast from Tarsus to Adana.

Meanwhile, the Osmanlı were beginning what proved to be an almost uninterrupted expansion. Ahmedi's *History of the Ottoman Kings*, written *c.* 1390, lists Osman's conquests as Bilecik, Inegöl and Köprühisar, to which two other lists compiled in the mid-1440s add Yarhisar and Yenişehir, all towns in the valleys of the river Sakarya and its tributary, the Göksu.

Osman Gazi died in 1324 and was succeeded by his son, Orhan Gazi. Two years later Orhan Gazi won a major victory, when he captured the Bithynian city of Prusa, which the Turks called Bursa. Orhan seems to have made Bursa his capital almost immediately, since an extant specimen indicates that he was minting coins in the city as early as 1327.

Andronicus III Palaeologus, who had succeeded to the throne in May 1328, mounted an expedition against Orhan in the spring of the following year. The emperor, together with his Grand Domestic John Cantacuzenus, collected a force of 4,000–5,000 veterans and ferried them across the Bosphorus from Constantinople to Scutari (Üsküdar), where they began to march along the shore of the Gulf of Nicomedia.

On the third day of their march they came to a place called Pelekanon, where they sighted Orhan's force of about 8,000 men encamped above the coast. On 10 June the Byzantines challenged the Turks to attack, but at the end of the day's action neither side had gained an advantage. John Cantacuzenus advised Andronicus to begin an orderly retreat to Constantinople the following morning. During the withdrawal the Turks attacked the rear of the Byzantine force and Andronicus was wounded in the knee. A rumour spread that the emperor had been killed, causing the Byzantine troops to panic and flee for their lives, as Cantacuzenus vainly tried to restore order. The emperor was carried on a stretcher to the port of Philokrene, where he was put on a ship for Constantinople, arriving there safely on 11 June. Cantacuzenus led the Byzantine army in its retreat, fighting off an attack by the Turks at Philokrene, and finally crossing the Bosphorus from Scutari to Constantinople.

Thus the emperor's offensive against the Turks was completely ineffective, and his army had failed to relieve Nicaea, which finally fell to the Osmanlı on 1 March 1331. After the fall of Nicaea, which the Turks called Iznik, Orhan laid siege to Nicomedia. According to the chronicle of John Cantacuzenus, when Andronicus learned of this he loaded infantry and cavalry onto ships and set sail for Nicomedia. As his flotilla approached the city he received envoys from Orhan, and they concluded a treaty. According to Cantacuzenus, the treaty was made 'on condition that Orhan was to be the Emperor's friend and that the Sultan would not harm the cities which obeyed the Byzantines'. But Cantacuzenus omits the humiliating terms that Orhan imposed on Andronicus as the price of peace. These terms appear in a Byzantine source known as the *Short Chronicle*: 'On...August 1333 the Emperor went to Nicomedia by ship and made a peace treaty with Orhan. The Emperor agreed to pay him twelve thousand hyperpera for the fortified places between Nicomedia and Constantinople.'

Orhan did not long honour the terms of the peace treaty, for four years later he captured Nicomedia. As Nicephorus Gregoras writes of the events in the year 1337: 'When the Emperor was occupied with other things, Nicomedia, the chief city of Bithynia, was captured, reduced by great famine brought on by the obstinate siege of the enemy.'

Orhan's treatment of the captured cities was so lenient that he gained the confidence of the conquered Greeks, many of whom converted to Islam.

The capture of Nicaea and Nicomedia all but completed the Osmanlı conquest of Bithynia, the north-western corner of Anatolia. By 1336 Orhan had also absorbed the Karası *beylik*, thus extending his territory along the south shore of the Sea of Marmara up to the Dardanelles and as far south as Bergama.

Andronicus died on 15 June 1341 and was succeeded by his son, John V Palaeologus, who was barely nine at the time. Because of the emperor's youth, John Cantacuzenus was appointed regent. Supporters of Cantacuzenus proclaimed him emperor later that year, beginning a civil war that lasted for six years. The civil war ended on 8 February 1347, when Cantacuzenus was crowned as John VI, the agreement being that he and John VI would rule as co-emperors, he himself being the senior emperor.

Meanwhile, Cantacuzenus and Orhan had signed a peace treaty in 1346. One of the terms of the treaty was that Orhan would marry· Princess Theodora, a daughter of Cantacuzenus. The wedding ceremony was held in Selymbria, some 65 kilometres west of Constantinople, where, according to Cantacuzenus, Orhan came with 'thirty galleys, many horsemen and the most eminent men of his realm' to join the emperor and his court. Cantacuzenus describes how he placed his daughter Theodora on a platform surrounded by curtains, and as he waited on horseback

> the tapestries of silk with gold thread were drawn back, and the bride was revealed. To her left and right were torches borne by kneeling eunuchs who were invisible. Trumpets, flutes, pan-pipes and all instruments invented for men's delight played… After the usual ceremonies for an emperor's daughter who is about to be married, the commanders and officials from both sides feasted together for some days. The [Canatacuzenos] handed over his daughter to Orhan, who received her with delight.

When Cantacuzenus became senior emperor in 1347, Orhan came to Scutari to offer his congratulations. Cantacuzenus records that he crossed the Bosphorus to Scutari to meet Orhan, and the two of 'them amused themselves for a number of days hunting and feasting'.

During the eight years that Cantacuzenus reigned he kept his alliance with Orhan, who on three occasions sent his son Süleyman with Turkish troops to aid the emperor on campaigns in Thrace. On the third occasion, in 1352, Süleyman had seized the fortress of Tzympe on the European shore of the Dardanelles and refused to return it to Cantacuzenus. Then on 2 March 1354 a violent earthquake destroyed Gallipoli and other towns on the European shore of the Dardanelles, whereupon Süleyman took advantage of the situation to seize all of them and garrison them with Turkish troops. An Italian source known as the

Florentine Chronicle records this incident, the establishment of the first permanent Turkish foothold in Europe, after which it goes on to mention the first Osmanlı attack on Constantinople, a brief and unsuccessful siege that would have taken place later in 1354.

> The Turks received a great army of their people and laid siege by land to Constantinople. But they [the Greeks] united in defence against the Turks, so that when they had spent some time without being able to capture the city, they attacked the towns and pillaged the countryside. Meeting with no resistance outside the walls, they returned to their country.

Orhan also extended his domain eastward, as evidenced by a notice in the chronicle of John Cantacuzenus for 1354, recording that 'Süleyman, the son of Orhan, led large forces against the Galatians of eastern Scythia [i.e. the Turks] and in the summer conquered two of their most important cities, Ancyra [Ankara] and Krateia [Sivrihisar?]'. Cantacuzenus is probably referring to the Eretnid dynasty of Sivas; his reference to the Osmanlı conquest of Ancyra is corroborated by an inscription in Ankara's Alaettin Camii, which records the name of the 'Most Mighty Sultan Orhan'.

The Osmanlı were on the march in both Europe and Asia, where the *beyliks* would eventually give way before them.

– 11 –

The Triumph of the Osmanlı

Orhan Gazi died in 1362 and was succeeded by his son, Murat. Around 1369 Murat captured Adrianople, Turkish Edirne, which soon replaced Bursa as the Osmanlı capital. During the next two decades Murat penetrated into Greece, Bulgaria, Macedonia, Albania, Serbia, Bosnia, Wallachia and Hungary, while at the same time his forces advanced eastward into Anatolia.

By then the Karası *beylik* had been conquered by the Osmanlı. The next *beylik* to fall was that of the Germiyan, which Murat had annexed by 1379. He then pushed back the Karamanid, after which he conquered both the Hamidid and Teke *beyliks*, taking Antalya to give the Osmanlı a port on the Mediterranean.

Murat then invaded Serbia and Bosnia, beginning in 1386. Three years later a Christian coalition led by Prince Lazar of Serbia tried to stop the Osmanlı. The two armies met on the plain of Kosovo on 15 June 1389, when the Osmanlı defeated the Christian allies with great slaughter. Murat was killed at the very moment of victory, whereupon his son and successor Beyazit took command and massacred Lazar and all of the other surviving Serbian nobles.

The new sultan came to be known as Yıldırım, or Lightning, from the speed with which he marched his armies between his European and Asian frontiers. According to the contemporary Iranian chronicler Aziz ibn Ardashir, Beyazit's initial goal in Anatolia 'was the reduction of the principality of Saruhan and the land of Aydın'. Then, after telling of how the Osmanlı annexed the Saruhan and Aydınid *beyliks*, he goes on to describe how Beyazit attacked Alaeddin, the emir of Karaman, forcing him to surrender the fortress of Beyşehir. A Turkish chronicle records that Beyazit captured Philadelphia, a town on the border of the Aydınid *beylik* that had remained in the hands of the 'infidels' i.e. – the Byzantines. Other Turkish sources mention Beyazit's conquest of the Menteşe *beylik* in south-western Anatolia.

Beyazit's next triumph in Anatolia came in 1391, when he defeated and killed Süleyman Paşa, the emir of Kastamonu and ruler of the Candarid *beylik*, later to be called the Isfendiyarid. This brought Beyazit up against Kadı Burhaneddin of Sivas, who later in 1391 defeated the Osmanlı in a battle near Çorum. This forced Beyazit to terminate his campaign in Anatolia, marching his army back to Europe after appointing his commander Kara Timurtaş as *beylerbey* of Anatolia, with his headquarters in Ankara.

The Karamanid emir Alaeddin took advantage of Beyazit's departure to attack and capture Kara Timurtaş, whom he imprisoned at Konya. Beyazit responded by marching his army back to Anatolia, where he captured Konya, beheading Alaeddin. Beyazit then went on to capture the town of Karaman, capital of the Karamanid *beylik*, which thereupon became an Osmanlı protectorate.

Then in 1398 Beyazit mounted a campaign against Kadı Burhaneddin of Sivas, who had seized Amasya from an Osmanlı vassal. Beyazit's son Mehmet recaptured Amasya from Kadı Burhaneddin, while the sultan himself took Sinop, installing another of his vassals there as ruler. Beyazit went on to take Sivas and the other possessions of Kadı Burhaneddin, who was killed in the conflict. The sultan appointed his son Mehmet as Osmanlı governor of Sivas and Amasya and the surrounding area. Using Sivas as a forward base, Beyazit attacked and conquered Malatya, which had been a northerly outpost of the Mamluk sultan of Syria, Barkük. Thus by the end of the fourteenth century Beyazit had extended his dominions deep into Anatolia, though his control was anything but stable, as events would soon show.

During the last years of the fourteenth century Beyazit was also active in Europe. In May 1394 he put Constantinople under siege, building the fortress of Anadolu Hisarı on the Asian shore of the Bosphorus to cut off the Byzantine capital from the Black Sea.

While the siege continued, Beyazit invaded Hungary and Wallachia. The rapid Ottoman advance alarmed the Christian powers of Europe, and King Sigismund of Hungary led the call for a crusade against the Turks. A Christian army of nearly 100,000 mustered at Buda in July

1396 under the leadership of Sigismund, with contingents from Hungary, Wallachia, Germany, Poland, Italy, France, Spain and England, while an allied fleet with ships from Genoa, Venice and the knights of Rhodes patrolled the straits and the Black Sea coast. The Christian army headed down along the Danube valley to Nicopolis, where they put the Turkish-occupied fortress under siege. Beyazit caught up with them there, and on 25 September 1396 he totally routed the Christian army. This victory established Beyazit's control over the lands south of the Danube, so that no help could now reach Constantinople overland from Europe.

The siege of Constantinople was lifted in the spring of 1402, when Beyazit was forced to march his army back to Anatolia to deal with an invasion by the Mongols under Tamerlane. The two armies met on the plain outside Ankara on 28 July 1402, when Tamerlane's forces defeated Beyazit's army, most of whom fled from the battlefield. Beyazit himself was captured by Tamerlane and died soon afterwards in captivity. His sons Mustafa and Musa were also captured. Musa was later freed by Tamerlane, while Mustafa seems to have died in captivity, though later a pretender appeared using his name, referred to in the Osmanlı chronicles as Düzme (False) Mustafa.

Meanwhile, Tamerlane went on to capture and sack Bursa, Konya, Tire, Ephesus, Izmir, Foça, Uluborlu and Üçhisar, slaughtering the inhabitants. He then departed from Anatolia in the summer of 1403, never to return, extracting tribute from the places he had subjugated. The Spanish diplomat Ruy Gonzales de Clavijo, who passed through Anatolia in 1404 on his way to see Tamerlane in Samarkand, reported that everywhere he saw piles of human skulls erected by the Mongol conqueror as monuments to create terror among those who might think to oppose him.

After the Battle of Ankara the Osmanlı lost most of the territory that Beyazit had conquered in Anatolia, which Tamerlane gave back to the beylik emirs who had previously ruled them, on condition that they served as his vassals. Thus the Saruhan beylik was given to Orhan Bey, son of Ishak, who was restored to his capital, Manisa, on 17 August 1402. Tamerlane divided the Aydınid beylik between Umur II and Musa, though their relatives Hasan Ağa and Cüneyd disputed the succession, the latter emerging as sole ruler in 1405. The Menteşe beylik was returned to Ilyas Bey, whose name appears on a coin of 1402–3, though without the name of his suzerain, Tamerlane. The Germiyan beylik was returned to Yakub Çelebi, though the earliest coins of the restored emirate, dated 1402–14, bear only the name of Tamerlane. The Karamanid *beylik* was restored to the two sons of the late emir Alaeddin, Mehmet Bey and Ali Bey, whom Tamerlane released from captivity in Ankara. The Isfendiyarid *beylik* was returned to Süleyman Paşa's brother Isfendiyaroğlu Mübarizeddin, who held power in Sinop and Kastamonu.

Beyazit's death led to a war of succession between his four surviving sons, a struggle that finally ended when the youngest of them, Mehmet I, emerged victorious on 5 July 1413, ending an interregnum that had lasted eleven years, leaving the Ottoman Empire a shambles in both Europe and Asia.

Even before Mehmet's final victory over Musa, the old Osmanlı capital of Bursa had come under siege. The Karamanid emir had in June 1413 set fire to the town of Bursa and besieged the citadel, which was defended by Hacı Ivaz Paşa. The siege continued until the end of July, when the arrival of Mehmet and his army forced the Karamanid emir to withdraw.

Mehmet spent the rest of the year negotiating peace with the Byzantine emperor Manuel II Palaeologus and the Balkan princes. Mehmet signed a treaty with Manuel, whom he referred to as 'my father the Emperor of the Romans', ceding to him 'all the fortresses along the Black Sea, the villages and fortresses of Thessaly, and everything along the Sea of Marmara'.

Mehmet then turned his attention to Anatolia, where in 1415 he waged a campaign against the Karamanid, calling on his vassals, the emirs of the Germiyan and Isfendiyarid, to supply him troops. The chronicles report that he captured Akşehir and won a victory on the plain of Konya, capturing the Karamanid emir Mehmet and his son Mustafa. According to one chronicle, the Karamanid sued for peace and were forced to give the Osmanlı Beyşehir and 'the land of Hamid', the old *beylik* around Isparta, while another source records that Mehmet also annexed Akşehir, Seydişehir and Sivrihisar.

Later in 1415 Mehmet waged another campaign, this time in western Anatolia against the emir Cüneyd of Aydın, who was holding the citadel of Izmir. Mehmet besieged and captured the citadel, forcing Cüneyd to cede to him the *beyliks* of Aydın and Saruhan, which he gave over to the rule of a vassal.

The following year revolts against Osmanlı rule broke out in both Europe and Asia, both of which were put down by Mehmet. Mehmet led two campaigns into Anatolia in 1417. In the first of these he captured the town of Karaman, which he then returned to the emir Mehmet, who agreed to accept the status of an Osmanlı vassal. In his second campaign that year Mehmet took Çankırı, Bafra and Samsun, reducing the Isfendiyarid *beylik* to a small region around Sinop.

Mehmet spent the next four years campaigning in Europe, his deepest penetration coming in 1421, when he crossed the Danube and raided Wallachia. That was to be his last campaign, for he suffered a riding accident which led to his death later in 1421. He was succeeded by his son Murat II, who was only seventeen at the time, though already a seasoned warrior.

At the beginning of Murat's reign he had to fight two wars of succession, the first of them against a pretender and the second against his younger brother Mustafa, both of whom he defeated.

During the two wars of succession, the enemies of the Osmanlı took advantage of the situation to seize territory in both Anatolia and Europe. The Isfendiyarid emir Mübarizeddin of Sinop had enlarged his *beylik* at the expense of the Osmanlı, and so in the spring of 1423 Murat launched a campaign against him. Murat defeated and wounded Mübarizeddin, who fled to Sinop. Murat pursued him, capturing Kastamonu, finally forcing Mübarizeddin to agree to resume his status as an Osmanlı vassal. Within the following two years Murat also conquered the Aydınid, Menteşe and Germiyan *beyliks*, as well as extending Ottoman control along the western Anatolian coast of the Black Sea.

Then in 1437 Murat mounted a campaign against the Karamanid in which he conquered all of their territory north of the Taurus Mountains. The Karamanid emir Ibrahim Bey was forced to come to terms with Murat in May 1437, when he ceded Beyşehir and Akşehir to the Osmanlı.

The following year Murat returned to Europe and led his army across the Danube to invade Transylvania. In the two years following he first invaded Serbia and then Bosnia, after which, in April 1440, he put Belgrade under siege, though he was forced to withdraw in October of that year.

The relentless Osmanlı advance led Pope Eugenius IV to call for a crusade against the Turks. The crusade was finally launched in 1443 under the leadership of King Ladislas of Poland and Hungary and John Hunyadi, the Hungarian *voyvoda*, or princely governor, with contingents provided by the pope, the duke of Burgundy and the doge of Venice After two indecisive engagements the two armies met head-on at Varna on the Black Sea coast of Bulgaria on 10 November 1444, when the Osmanlı virtually annihilated the crusaders, with King Ladislas losing his life in the battle. John Hunyadi was one of the few Christian leaders to escape, and the following year he was elected regent of Hungary.

Shortly after the Battle of Varna Murat retired in favour of his son Mehmet, who was then not yet thirteen. But Mehmet's youth and inexperience led Murat to resume his reign in September 1446, whereupon Mehmet was made provincial governor in Manisa.

Meanwhile, John Hunyadi had mustered an army and tried to join forces with the Albanian leader Skanderbeg to fight against the Osmanlı. Murat caught up with Hunyadi's army at Kosovo, where the Serbs had gone down fighting against the Turks in 1389. The outcome of the second Battle of Kosovo, fought from 17–20 October 1448, was the same as that of the first, with the Osmanlı routing the Christians, Murat and his son Mehmet personally leading their troops in the fighting.

The Byzantine emperor John VIII Palaeologus died on 31 October 1448. He was succeeded by his brother Constantine XI Dragases, who had taken as his surname the Greek form of that of his mother, the empress Helena Dragas. Constantine was fated to be the last emperor of Byzantium, for the weak and fragmented empire he had inherited was no match for the rising power of the Osmanlı.

Murat II died at Edirne on 3 February 1451. His death was kept secret by the grand vizier Halil Çandarlı, so that Prince Mehmet could make his way from Manisa to Edirne to take control. He arrived on 18 February 1451, and that same day he was acclaimed by the army as Sultan Mehmet II.

Soon after Mehmet came to the throne he began making plans for the conquest of Constantinople. His first step was to order the construction of the great fortress of Rumeli Hisarı on the European shore of the Bosphorus, directly across the strait from Anadolu Hisarı, the fortress erected in 1394 by his ancestor Beyazit I.

Mehmet put Constantinople under siege on 2 April 1453, when he drew up his army outside the ancient Theodosian land walls of the city. Emperor Constantine personally led the defence of the city, which held out for nearly two months against the repeated attacks and constant bombardment by the Osmanlı. Constantinople finally fell to the Osmanlı early in the morning of Tuesday, 29 May, with the emperor killed in the final assault as the Turkish troops forced their way through the Theodosian walls and took the city by storm.

Mehmet entered the city in triumph later that same day, acclaimed by his troops as 'Fatih', or the 'Conqueror', the name by which he would thereafter be known. He rode directly to the ancient church of Haghia Sophia, ordering that it be converted into a mosque, where he presided over the noon prayer that Friday. This was the first step in the conversion of the Christian city of Constantinople into the Muslim city of Istanbul, which within the year supplanted Edirne as capital of what was now the Ottoman Empire.

The following year Fatih led a campaign into Serbia, which he invaded again in 1456, failing in his attempt to take Belgrade, defended by John Hunyadi. This was the only major defeat in Fatih's otherwise victorious career, which saw him extend the boundaries of the Ottoman Empire deeper into both Europe and Anatolia.

Fatih launched his first campaign into Anatolia in 1455, when he captured the towns now known as Eski and Yeni Foça on the Aegean coast north of Izmir, both of which had been held by the Genoese. Then in 1459 he captured the town of Amasra on the Black Sea, another Genoese possession. Two years later he captured Sinop from the emir Isfendiyaroğlu Ismail, effectively bringing the history of the Isfendiyarid *beylik* to an end.

Later that same year Fatih captured Trabzon (Trebizond) from the emperor David Comnenus, ending the history of the last fragment of the Byzantine Empire. David Comnenus was taken as a prisoner to Edirne, where two years later he and his sons were executed, ending the last dynasty of Byzantium.

Four years later King Mathias of Hungary signed an anti-Ottoman alliance with Venice, which for its part signed a similar pact with Fatih's two most powerful foes in Anatolia, the Karamamid emir Ishak Bey and the Akkoyunlu chieftain Uzun Hasan.

In the summer of 1472 Uzun Hasan launched a campaign against the Osmanlı under the command of his nephew Yusuf Mirzai and the Karamanid emir Pir Ahmet, along with a contingent of 500 Croatian cavalry supplied by Venice. The Akkoyunlu force sacked towns in the vicinity of Sivas and Tokat, after which they turned south-westward to capture Kayseri and other places in Karaman. The Akkoyunlu then headed westward towards Bursa, but they were defeated by an Osmanlı army led by Prince Mustafa. According to a contemporary Venetian source, 'Yusuf Mirzai...was taken prisoner by the Turk, and...Pir Ahmet...fled...with a great part of the army.' A Turkish source adds that the fleeing Akkoyunlu troops tried to take refuge in the Taurus Mountains with the Varsak Türkmen tribe, who killed all but 1,000 of them.

That same summer a Christian fleet sailed to attack Antalya, with forty-seven gallies from Venice, nineteen from the pope, seventeen from the king of Naples and three from the Knights of St John on Rhodes. The Christian allies sacked Antalya, but the Osmanlı garrison soon forced them to withdraw, inflicting heavy casualties.

Uzun Hasan launched another expedition in the autumn of 1472, estimated by a Venetian observer to comprise more than 300,000 troops. This time he headed towards the south-west, taking Malatya before going on to attack the Mamluk possessions in Anatolia and Syria. Fatih responded the following year by personally leading a huge army into Anatolia, estimated at more than 260,000 strong, with detachments led by his sons Mustafa and Beyazit as well as Daud Paşa, Mahmut Paşa and Hass Murat Paşa.

The first encounter between the two armies came on 2 August 1473 at a ford of the Euphrates near Erzincan, where a cavalry unit under Uzun Hasan's son Ughurlu Muhammad ambushed the contingent led by Hass Murat Paşa, who was killed along with 4,000 of his men.

The next encounter took place on 11 August at a place called Başkent in the mountains near Bayburt. The Akkoyunlu slightly outnumbered their opponents, but the Osmanlı had artillery and hand-guns, armaments that Uzun Hasan had never seen before. This seems to have demoralised Uzun Hasan, of whom the chronicler Neflri writes that 'having never seen a battle with handguns and cannon, he was powerless before the Osmanlı'. As a result the Akkoyunlu were defeated with heavy losses, after which Uzun Hasan abandoned his army and fled for his life.

Later that year the Karamanid emirs recaptured some of their former possessions within and to the south of the Taurus Mountains. The following year Fatih sent an army to Karaman under Gedik Ahmet Paşa, who recaptured the towns of Ermenek and Minyan within the Taurus, as well as Silifke and other fortresses to the south of the mountains and along the Mediterranean coast. This was the end of the Karamanid as an independent *beylik*, for although they continued to exist as a tribe after 1474 their territory was controlled by the Osmanlı. Karaman became an Ottoman province in 1475, and Pir Ahmet, the last Karamanid emir, died that same year.

By that time all the other independent emirates in Anatolia had been absorbed by the Osmanlı. And so the *beylik* period came to an end in 1475, 404 years after Alp Arslan's victory over the Byzantines at Manzikert, when the Seljuk period in Turkish history began.

– Part II –

The Seljuk Heritage:
a Traveller's Guide

– 12 –

Western Anatolia

T he Seljuk heritage is most evident in the beautiful buildings from their time that adorn the landscape of Anatolia, as well as in their art, music, dance and poetry, and even in their humour, as in the stories of Nasrettin Hoja, all of which are still part of Turkish life. The chapters that follow are a traveller's guide to this heritage, in a series of itineraries that will take us across Turkey through the places where the Seljuks and their immediate successors in the Beylik period flourished during the first Turkish centuries in Anatolia.

The first itinerary will take us across western Anatolia from Istanbul to Konya, capital of the Sultanate of Rum. Most of the early Turkish monuments in western Anatolia are from the Beylik period, including those of the Osmanlı, who would eventually conquer all of Anatolia in their march of conquest. In the itinerary that follows we will look only at the very earliest Osmanlı monuments, for the later ones are part of Ottoman architecture, which followed a different development from that of the Seljuks and their other successors in the *beyliks*.

The first rapid advance of the Seljuks after Manzikert took them as far as the Bosphorus in 1078, when they established their first capital in Nicaea, Turkish Iznik, which they held only until 1097, when they were driven out by the Byzantines and the knights of the First Crusade. The first stage of our itinerary will take us from Istanbul to Iznik. But before setting out we will visit two museums in Istanbul that have important Seljuk collections.

The first of these is the Çinili Köşkü, or Tiled Pavilion, a kiosk in a lower courtyard of Topkapı Sarayı, the great palace of the Ottoman

129

sultans. The kiosk was built in 1472 by Sultan Mehmet II as a hunting lodge, and early in the Turkish Republic it was converted into a museum of Turkish tiles, both Seljuk and Ottoman. The Seljuk collection includes some rare and beautiful exhibits, some of them from monuments in Anatolia.

The second is the Museum of Turkish and Islamic Art in the Ibrahim Paşa Sarayı, an Ottoman palace on the Hippodrome built *c.* 1520. The museum houses an extraordinary collection of objects from the Seljuk and Beylik periods, including kilims, manuscripts, calligraphy, miniatures, woodwork, metalwork, stonework, sculptures, ceramics and glassware, all superbly displayed.

The lower level of Ibrahim Paşa Sarayı houses the museum's ethnographical collection. This consists principally of objects belonging to the Yürük, the nomadic Turkish tribespeople of Anatolia, whose wandering way of life has not changed since the first Türkmen warriors swept across Anatolia nearly 1,000 years ago. The most fascinating exhibits here are the black goat-hair tents of the Yürük, furnished with objects that they use in their daily life, including their hand-carved musical instruments.

But in recent years the Yürük have to a large extent given up their nomadic ways, and it is only a matter of time before they will all be settled down. Then one will no longer see the black tents of the Türkmen on the Anatolian plateau, ending the last living vestige of the Seljuks and their successors, whose presence will then remain only in the heritage of art and architecture that they have left behind them, together with the Turkish way of life that they initiated in the land that is now called Turkey.

We leave Istanbul on the highway to Ankara, crossing the Bosphorus, and then turning off to take the car ferry at Darıca. This takes us across the Gulf of Iznik, after which we take the Bursa highway as far as Orhangazi. There we turn left to drive along the northern shore of Iznik Gölü, Lake Ascania. At the eastern end of the lake we come to the little town of Iznik, Greek Nicaea.

The first view of Iznik is very impressive, for the town is contained within a magnificent circuit of defence walls nearly 5 kilometres in circumference, studded with massive towers and with three of its four main gateways still intact. Most of the walls date from the Hellenistic and Roman periods, with repairs by both the Seljuks and the Ottomans.

Other than these repairs there is very little of the Seljuk presence in their first capital, although there is a ruined bath known as the Seljuk

Hamamı, dating from the last decade of the fifteenth century. Although extremely dilapidated, the *hamam* is a unique masterpiece, with each of its four domes, two of which have fallen in, decorated in a different style of brickwork, the most beautiful consisting of a dozen spiral arms radiating from the crown to the uppermost of a series of honeycomb bands that extend far down the walls.

On the street that leads eastward from the town centre we find Hacı Özbek Camii. This is the oldest Ottoman mosque in existence that still preserves most of its original structure, dated by an inscription to 1333, two years after Orhan Gazi captured Nicaea. The little building is a cube covered by a hemispherical dome, the basic plan for most subsequent Ottoman mosques, though later elaborated with semi-domes in the great imperial mosques of Istanbul.

The two most important Ottoman monuments in Iznik – Yeşil Cami and the Nilüfer Hatun Imareti – are near the eastern gateway of the town.

Yeşil Cami, the Green Mosque, took its name from the colour of the famous Iznik tiles that once revetted its minaret. These have now been replaced by much inferior Kütahya tiles, arranged in chevron patterns in various shades of green, blue and red. This beautiful mosque was built in the years 1382–87 by Çandarlı Kara Halil Hayrettin Paşa, who commanded the army that captured Nicaea for Orhan Gazi and who later served Murat I as grand vizier, the first to hold that office in the Ottoman Empire.

The second monument is an *imaret*, or refectory, founded in 1388 by Murat I and dedicated to his mother Nilüfer Hatun. (Hatun was a royal title meaning 'Lady'.) Nilüfer was born to an aristocratic Greek family in Bithynia and, after being captured by the Turks, she became the wife of Orhan Gazi and the mother of his son and successor Murat I. When Orhan Gazi was off on campaign Nilüfer acted as regent, which she did with great success. The Arab traveller Ibn Battutah, who visited Iznik in the 1330s, writes in his journal of Nilüfer, calling her Bayalun Katun and referring to Orhan as Urkhan:

> The town is now in a mouldering condition and uninhabited except for a few men in Sultan Urkhan's service. In it also lives his wife Bayalun Khatun, who is in command of them, a pious and excellent woman. I visited her and she treated me honourably, gave me hospitality, and sent gifts. Some days after our arrival the sultan came to this city...

Nilüfer's *imaret* was originally built as a hospice for the Ahi Brotherhood of Virtue, a religious and fraternal society formed by the craft guilds in Turkish Anatolia during the Seljuk era. Ibn Battutah writes of the Ahi brotherhood, praising the hospitality he received from them at one of their lodges:

They [the Akhi] exist in all the lands of the Turkmens of al-Rum, in every district, city, and village. Nowhere in the world are there to be found any to compare with them in solicitude for strangers, and in ardour to serve food and satisfy wants, to restrain the hands of the tyrranous, and to kill the agents of the police and those ruffians who join with them. An Akhi, in their idiom, is a man whom the assembled members of his trade, together with others of the young unmarried men and those who have adopted the celibate life, choose to be their leader. The Akhi builds a hospice and furnishes it with rugs, lamps, and what other equipment it requires. His associates work during the day to gain their livelihood, and after the afternoon prayer they bring him their collective earnings, with this they buy fruit, food, and the other things needed for consumption in the hospice. If, during that day, a traveller alights at the town, they give him lodging with them; what they have purchased serves for their hospitality to him and he remains with them until his departure. If no newcomer arrives, they assemble themselves to partake of the food, and after eating they sing and dance. On the morrow they disperse to their occupations, and after the afternoon prayer they bring their collective earnings to their leader. The members are called *fityan*, and their leader, as we have said, is the Akhi. Nowhere in the world have I seen men more chivalrous than they are.

The *imaret* now houses the Iznik Museum, where there are a few exhibits dating from the Seljuk period.

We now retrace our route to Orhangazi, from where we continue on to the beautiful and historic city of Bursa, the first capital of the Ottoman Empire. Bursa, Greek Prusa, is situated below Uludağ, the ancient Mount Olympus of Bithynia, its peak 2,543 metres above sea level. This is the loftiest mountain in western Turkey, although there are at least 150 peaks higher than it in eastern Anatolia, where the great plateau is itself some 1.6 kilometres high.

The Seljuks failed to take Bursa while they had their capital at Iznik, and thus the earliest Turkish monuments here are Ottoman. These include the tombs of five early Ottoman sultans: Osman Gazi (r. *c.* 1282–1326), Orhan Gazi (r. 1326–62), Murat I (r. 1362–89), Beyazit I (r. 1389–1402) and Murat II (r. 1421–51).

Ibn Battutah visited Bursa, which he describes as 'a great and important city, with fine bazaars, surrounded on all sides by gardens and running springs'. Bursa had just a few years beforehand been conquered by Osman Gazi, whose prowess is noted by Ibn Battutah:

> This sultan is the greatest of the kings of the Turkmens and the richest in wealth, lands and military forces. Of fortresses he possesses nearly a hundred, and for most of his time he is continually engaged in making the round of them, staying in each fortress for some days to put it in good order and examine its condition. It is said that he has never stayed for a whole month in any one town. He also fights with the infidels continually and keeps them under siege.

Bursa's principal monuments are the earliest imperial Ottoman mosques: Orhan Gazi Camii (1339); Hüdavendiğâr Camii, built by Murat I in the years 1365–85; Ulu Cami, the 'Great Mosque', founded in 1396–99 by Beyazit I; Yıldırım Beyazit Camii, built in the years 1391–95 by Beyazit I; Yeşil Cami, founded by Mehmet I in 1412 and completed in 1424; and the Muradiye, erected by Murat II in 1424–26. Bursa is particularly known for its thermal baths, the oldest of which is Eski Kaplıca, which tradition says was founded in the mid-sixth century by the emperor Justinian, and which in its present form dates to a rebuilding by Murat I. Bursa is also noted for its *hans*, or inner city caravanserais, most of which are in the old market quarter between Ulu Cami and Orhan Gazi Camii.

We now drive from Bursa to Izmir via Balıkesir and Manisa, taking us from Bithynia into the region known as Mysia. Balıkesir was capital of the Karası *beylik*, which comprised the north-western corner of Anatolia along the Marmara and the Dardanelles out to the Aegean. Ibn Battutah gives a very negative description of the ruler of Balıkesir at the time of his visit:

> Its sultan is named Dumur Khan, and is a worthless person. It was his father who built this city, and during the reign of this son of his it acquired a large population of good for nothings, for 'Like king like people'. I visited him and he sent me a silk robe. I bought in this city a Greek slave girl named Marghalitah.

We continue to Manisa, ancient Magnesia-ad-Sipylum, the latter part of its name due to its site under Mount Sipylos, on the Gediz Çayı, the river Hermus of the Greeks. The city was captured from the Byzantines in 1313 by the Saruhan tribe of Türkmen warriors, who made it the capital of their *beylik* until it was taken from them in 1390 by Beyazit I. The Saruhan emirs regained Manisa after Beyazit's defeat by Tamerlane in 1402, but Mehmet I recaptured it in 1415.

The principal monument of the Beylik period in Manisa is the Ulu Cami, built in 1376 by the Saruhan emir Ishak Bey, whose *medrese* (theological school) and *türbe* (tomb) are attached to the western side of the mosque and its courtyard. The mosque itself is preceded by a *şadırvan* (ablution fountain) court, with the minaret rising from the north-west corner. The central area around the octagonal *şadırvan* is surrounded on three sides by a portico of nineteen units covered by low domical vaults, with seven bays along the north and three pairs of two each on the sides. Many of the columns and capitals in the courtyard and within the mosque and *medrese* were taken from ancient buildings. The prayer hall of the mosque has the same number and arrangement of bays as the courtyard. The area in front of the *mihrap*, the niche indicating the *kible*, the direction of Mecca, is covered by a dome 10.8 metres in diameter. The dome rests on four pendentives, or spherical triangles, above the diagonals of the octagonal base formed by the *kible* wall and six free-standing piers. The carved wooden *mimber* (pulpit) is a fine piece of work in the Seljuk style.

A vaulted passage leads from the west side of the courtyard into the attached *medrese*. On the left side of the passage is the entrance to the domed *türbe* of Ishak Bey, who died in 1388. The *türbe* door is flanked by two pairs of 'knotted' columns of a red and yellow breccia, undoubtedly Byzantine in origin, as is the fluted column on the left at the entrance from the passage into the central courtyard of the *medrese*, which is in two storeys. The south side of the courtyard opens into the main *eyvan* (a vaulted space recessed from a central court). This is flanked by two chambers, the western one having collapsed. The student cells open off the west side of the courtyard in two storeys.

We finally reach the Aegean coast at Izmir, the Greek Smyrna. During the early Seljuk period Izmir was held by the emir Çaka, who in the last decade of the eleventh century was driven out by Alexius I Comnenus. The Turks later regained Izmir, which was part of the Aydınid *beylik* until it was finally absorbed by the Ottoman Empire.

Ibn Battutah writes of Izmir as 'a large city on the seacoast, mostly in ruins, with a citadel'. At the time Izmir was part of the Aydınid *beylik* and was ruled by Umur Bey, a son of Muhammed ibn Aydın, whom Ibn Battutah describes as 'a generous and pious prince, and continually in *jihad* [holy war] against the Christians'.

We now head south from Izmir on highway O-31, which takes us into the region known in antiquity as Ionia, where the first Greek cities on the

Aegean coast of Asia Minor were founded early in the first millennium BC. After crossing the Küçük Menderes, the river Cayster of the Greeks, we turn off highway O-31 for Selçuk, the modern town that has developed beside the ruins of ancient Ephesus, one of the most famous of the ancient Ionian Greek cities. Ephesus, known in the medieval era as Ayasuluk, was taken from the Byzantines in 1304 by the Aydınid emir Mehmet Bey. The principal Beylik monument is Isa Bey Camii, erected in 1374–75 by the Aydınid emir Isa Bey, grandson of Mehmet Bey. Isa Bey may have rebuilt or enlarged an earlier structure erected by Mehmet Bey, for the mosque is mentioned by Ibn Battutah, who visited Ephesus in the 1330s.

The mosque is adjoined to its north by a huge courtyard enclosed by a high wall, with a polygonal *şadırvan* at its centre. One of the two entrances to the mosque is on the southern side of the courtyard, where one enters the central area of the prayer hall through an arcade of three pointed arches carried on a pair of columns. Two domes along the longitudinal axis of the mosque cover the middle area of the prayer hall, which is flanked by long transepts with double shed roofs supported by colonnades along the transverse axis. The second entrance to the mosque is through an ornate portal in the Seljuk style at the end of the western transept.

We continue south from Selçuk via Söke, beyond which we turn off on to a secondary road that takes us to the site of ancient Miletus. Miletus was the greatest of all the Ionian Greek cities, which its proud citizens called 'the first settled in Ionia, and the mother of many and great cities in Pontus and Egypt, and in various other parts of the world'.

Miletus was known in Turkish as Balat, a variation of the Greek *palatia*, or palace, from the popular belief that its ruined monuments had been the palace of some great king in ancient times. During the late fourteenth and early fifteenth centuries Balat was part of the Menteşe *beylik*. The most important extant monument of this period is Ilyas Bey Camii, the handsome mosque that stands near the entrance to the archaeological site. The mosque was founded in 1404 by the Menteşe emir Ilyas Bey, who had been restored to his *beylik* two years beforehand by Tamerlane. Ilyas Bey Camii is one of the most impressive mosques of the Beylik period still standing in Anatolia, with a dome nearly 15 metres in diameter. The *külliye* (mosque complex) also includes a *medrese* and a *hamam* (Turkish bath).

We return to the main road, which now crosses the Büyük Menderes, the ancient Maeander. It then climbs up into the hills of Caria, the region that forms the south-western corner of Anatolia, where the Aegean merges with the Mediterranean. This brings us to Milas, ancient Mylas, which has been the principal city of the Carian highlands since antiquity.

Milas was one of the centres of the Menteşe *beylik*, which was finally taken by the Ottomans under Murat II in 1425. There are two monuments in the town dating from the Menteşe period, Ulu Cami (1378) and Firuz Bey Camii (1394). There are two more monuments of the Menteşe era in the nearby hilltop fortress of Peçin Kale, namely Ahmet Paşa Medresesi and Orhan Bey Camii, both founded in 1375.

Our itinerary now takes us eastward from Milas to Yatağan, where we turn north to drive to Aydın, crossing the Büyük Menderes once again. Aydın, ancient Tralles, was once an important town of the Aydınid *beylik*, of which no important monuments have survived.

We now drive eastward on highway E87 up the Menderes valley as far as Nazilli. There we turn north on a road signposted for Ödemiş, a short way before which we turn off for Birgi, the former capital of the Aydınid *beylik*.

The Ulu Cami of Birgi was founded in 1312 by the Aydınid emir Mehmet Bey. The building is preceded by a nineteenth-century porch supported by eight wooden pillars. The mosque itself is constructed with marble blocks taken from an ancient building. The minaret, unusually, rises from the south-west corner of the mosque; its shaft is decorated with glazed bricks in red and turquoise arranged in rows of lozenges and zigzags. At the south-west corner of the mosque exterior there is a Seljuk lion carved in high relief.

The prayer hall is the usual 'forest' of columns typical of an Ulu Cami of this period, with sixteen slender marble monoliths arranged in four rows of four each. This divides the hall into five north–south aisles, the central aisle being slightly wider than the others. The aisles are separated by arcades, in each of which the columns support a row of six arches of slightly ovoidal shape. The two southernmost columns of the central aisle are connected by a lateral arch, forming a square bay in front of the *mihrap* that is covered by a dome whose cornice is carried on straight triangular pendentives. The spandrels of the lateral arch in front of the *mihrap* are decorated with an inscription from the Kuran and geometrical patterns in bicoloured faience mosaic. The *mimber* is adorned with Seljuk faience mosaic in turquoise and manganese black; the stalactite niche in the rectangular frame is decorated with varying patterns in the same type of tiles, and below this is a panel with geometric interlacing. The walnut *mimber*, which is covered with calligraphic inscriptions, is a fine specimen of Seljuk carving, as are the shutters of the eight windows.

The *türbe* of Mehmet Bey, dated by an inscription to 1334, is attached to the north-west corner of the mosque. The dome, which is faced in red and turquoise bricks, rests on a drum carried by four pendentives decorated with faience mosaics. The graveyard surrounding the mosque has a number of beautiful carved Turkish tombstones of the fourteenth and fifteenth centuries.

When Ibn Battutah visited Birgi he and his companions were first lodged at the hospice of the local Ahi Brotherhood of Virtue, after which they stayed at the palatial mansion of a local scholar named Mufyi al-Din. They were then guests of the emir Muhammad ibn Aydın, founder of the Aydınid *beylik*, whom Ibn Battutah refers to as 'the sultan' in describing two of the emir's residences, one of them his mountain-top retreat and the other his palace in the lower town.

> Our stay on the mountain lasted so long that I began to weary and wished to take my leave. But at length he [the emir] went down to the city, and we with him. He called to us and bade us come into his palace with him. On our arrival at the vestibule of the palace, we found about twenty of his servants, of surpassingly beautiful appearance, wearing robes of silk, with their hair parted and hanging loose, and in colour of resplendent whiteness tinged with red. I said to the doctor [Muhyi al-Din], 'What are these beautiful figures?' and he replied, 'These are Greek pages.' We climbed a long flight of stairs with the sultan and came eventually into a fine audience hall, with an ornamental pool of water in the centre and the figure of a lion in bronze at each corner of it, spouting water from its mouth. Round this hall there was a succession of benches covered with rugs, on one of which was the sultan's cushion. When we came up to this bench, the sultan pushed away his cushion with his hand and sat down beside us on the rugs. The doctor sat on his right, the qadi next to him, and I next to the qadi. The Qur'an readers sat down below the bench, for there were always Qur'an readers in attendance on him in his audiences, wherever he may be. The servants then brought in gold and silver bowls filled with sherbet of raisins steeped in water, into which citron juice had been squeezed, with small pieces of biscuits in it, along with gold and silver spoons... I made a speech of thanks to the sultan and eulogised the doctor, sparing no efforts in doing so, and this gave much pleasure and satisfaction to the sultan...

We now retrace our route to Nazilli, where we continue eastward on highway E87 up the Menderes valley, which penetrates into the heart of Anatolia. This was the route taken by the Greeks when they settled on the Aegean coast in the first millennium BC, moving eastward up the Maeander valley into the interior of Asia Minor, and the same route was taken by the Türkmen tribes as they moved westward at the beginning of the second millennium AD.

Near the town of Sarayköy we come to the confluence of the Menderes and the Çürüsu, the river Lycus of antiquity. There we turn south from the E87 on a road signposted for Denizli, another city that was once an important centre of the Aydınid *beylik*.

Denizli was originally known as Ladık, a corruption of the Greek Laodiceia. It took this name from the fact that that the inhabitants of ancient Laodiceia, 16 kilometres to the north, were resettled here in the thirteenth century by the Seljuks. The earliest description of Ladık under Turkish rule is by Ibn Battutah, who visited the town in 1336. He writes that the town has 'splendid gardens, perennial streams and gushing springs. Its bazaars are very fine and in them are manufactured cotton fabrics edged with gold embroidery. Most of the artisans there are Greek women, who are subject to the Muslims and pay dues to the Sultan.' Ibn Battutah also notes that there was a slave market in the town where buyers could come 'to purchase Greek girls and put them out to prostitution and each girl has to pay a regular share to her master. The girls go into the bath houses with the men.'

At Denizli we turn eastward on the highway signposted for Dinar. About 9 kilometres along we come to the ruins of an old Seljuk caravanserai known as Ak Han. An inscription over the entryway records that it was dedicated on 19 July 1254 by the Seljuk sultan Izzeddin Kaykavus II. This is the westernmost of all the caravanserais founded in the Seljuk Sultanate of Rum, of which at least forty-six still stand along the highroads of central Anatolia, many of them in ruins, though still magnificent. They all date from the thirteenth century, their large number a testimony to the greatly increased trade and prosperity of the Seljuk Sultanate of Rum in its latter period. Known as *hans*, they gave free food and lodging to travellers for up to three days, also providing shelter for their animals, as well as a *hamam* for the merchants to bathe and a *mescit*, or small mosque, for their worship. These caravanserais look like miniature fortresses, since they had to provide protection from the raids of the lawless Türkmen tribes who preyed on the caravans crossing Anatolia.

At Dinar we turn north on the highway signposted for Afyon, ancient Akroenos, now officially known as Afyonkarahisar. As we approach Afyon we see the great spire of rock that rises dramatically in the centre of the town, its summit 226 metres above the surrounding plain. The rock is crowned with the ruins of a Byzantine fortress known in Turkish as Kara Hisar, 'Black Castle', whose name has now been attached to the town itself.

The oldest Turkish monument in Afyon is the Ulu Cami, built in 1272 by the famous Seljuk emir Sahip Ata Fahrettin Ali. This is built in the typical style of the 'great mosques' of pre-Ottoman Anatolia, with their 'forest' of wooden columns, in this case forty, all with capitals finely carved in the form of stylised stalactites.

The minaret is decorated with glazed tiles in lozenge-shaped segments, a rare example of a Seljuk type. There are also three monuments from the Beylik period, when Afyon was controlled by the Germiyanid emirs; these are Kubbeli Mescit (1331), Kaba Mescidi (1397) and Ak Mescit (1398).

We now head north-north-west on the highway to Kütahya, a route that brings us along the western side of the highland region known in antiquity as Phrygia.

Kütahya is built on the site of ancient Cotyaeum, which was captured by the Seljuks towards the end of the eleventh century, but after their defeat by the crusaders at Dorylaeum they were forced to abandon it. Kütahya was taken in 1302 by the Germiyan, a Kurdish–Turkish tribe that made it the capital of a *beylik* that included most of Phrygia. The Germiyan were eventually absorbed by the Ottomans in the late fourteenth century, although they regained their principality for a few years after Beyazit I was defeated by Tamerlane in 1402.

The principal mosque in Kütahya is the Ulu Camii, which was begun by Beyazit I in the late fourteenth century and completed in 1410 by his son Musa Çelebi. The original Ulu Cami was in wood with its roof supported by a veritable forest of wooden columns; the present structure is the result of a complete rebuilding in the years 1888–91.

On a corner beside Ulu Camii is the Vacidiye Medresesi, built in the years 1309–14 by the Germiyan emir Umarbin Savcı. Unlike most *medreses*, which were theological schools, the Vacidiye was an astronomical observatory and school of science, continuing a tradition that dated back to the medieval Islamic renaissance. The *medrese* now serves as the Kütahya Museum, with both archaeological and ethnographical collections.

Across the main street from the *medrese* is the ruined Dönemler Camii, a Germiyan foundation dating from the fourteenth century.

A short way up the street that passes in front of Ulu Cami is the *imaret*, or refectory, of the Germiyan emir Yakup Bey, founded in 1411 as a free soup-kitchen to feed the poor of Küthya. Beside the *imaret* is the *türbe* of Yakup Bey, dated 1427, the year of his death.

Elsewhere in Kütahya there are eight other monuments dating from the Seljuk and Beylik periods; these are: Ahi Arsan Camii (1219); Balıklı Cami (1237), Hıdırlık Mescidi (1243), Hezar Dinari Mescidi (1244), Pekmezpazarı Mescidi (1368), Kurşunlu Cami (1377), Süleyman Bey Mescidi (1381) and Demirtaş Paşa Camii (1389–1402).

From Kütahya we drive north-eastward to Eskişehir, ancient Dorylaeum. The ancient city gave its name to the Battle of Dorylaeum in June 1097, when the knights of the First Crusade defeated the Seljuk Turks, forcing them to retreat from western Asia Minor. The Seljuks soon returned and took Dorylaeum, which they renamed as Eskişehir, the 'Old City', retaining it until the Byzantines under Manuel I Comnenus recaptured it in 1175. The city was probably taken by the Osmanlı during the reign of Orhan Gazi, and after being lost after the defeat of Beyazit I in 1402 it was recaptured by the Ottomans a decade later.

The oldest monument in Eskişehir is the Ulu Cami, erected in 1277 by the Seljuk sultan Giyaseddin Keyhüsrev III. The principal Ottoman monument is Çoban Mustafa Paşa Camii, also known as Kurşunlu Cami, erected in 1525. Behind the mosque is the Yunus Emre Ethnographic Museum. This is named for the great Turkish poet Yunus Emre, who died in 1322, leaving a heritage of lyric poetry of the Seljuk era that is still recited by the people of Turkey.

From Eskişehir we take the road that leads south-east to the town of Seyitgazi, which takes us into the heart of ancient Phrygia, an out-of-the-way region that is still almost completely undeveloped.

The town is named for Seyit Battal (Giant) Gazi, whose supposed tomb on the acropolis hill, the site of ancient Nacolea, is one of the principal Islamic shrines in Anatolia. Seyit was a commander in the Arab army that invaded Asia Minor in 740, when he was killed in besieging Akroenos (Afyon). According to Turkish legend, a Byzantine princess, daughter of the Greek lord of Akroenos, had fallen in love with Seyit when she saw him during the siege. After seeing his corpse she killed herself, and the two of them, by her dying request, were buried in the same grave at Nacolea. The location of the grave was revealed in a dream to the mother of the Seljuk Sultan Alaeddin Keykubad I (r. 1219–36), who found them buried in a Greek monastery at Nacolea. She then reinterred them in a *türbe* and converted the monastery into an Islamic shrine. The *türbe* soon became a popular place of pilgrimage, particularly after a dervish *tekke* (lodge) was founded here in the second quarter of the fourteenth century by Hacı Bektaş Veli, founder of the Bektaşi dervishes. The shrine was rebuilt and enlarged by the Ottoman Sultan Selim II (r. 1512–20), at which time it took on the form we see today.

From Seyitgazi we head south on the road to Afyon, from which we turn left on to a secondary road signposted for the village of Kümbet, a drive of just two kilometres.

The village takes its name from a Seljuk *türbe* of the type known as a *kümbet*, which in this case is an octagonal structure surmounted by a pyramidal roof. It stands on a knoll above the mud-brick houses of the tiny village, the apex of its pyramidal roof surmounted by a stork's nest. The tomb, known to the locals as a *tekke*, is revered by them as the last resting place of a holy man named Kümbet Dede, the latter, meaning 'Grandfather', being one of the words used to designate a saint, the other being Baba, or 'Father', as in the *türbe* of other local saints known as Ahi Baba and Karababa. C. H. Emilie Haspels writes of these apocryphal saints and their tombs in *The Highlands of Phrygia* (1971):

> The tekkes, the graves of local holy men, continue to attract worship. The peasants do not even know who these dedes and babas may have been, but that is of no importance. The tombs are old holy places, and people go there to appeal to the healing power attributed to the saint... The tekkes in the highlands vary greatly... At some of them sacrificial animals are killed regularly, for example at the Tekke of the Ahibaba in the Karababa valley.

Haspels examined the old Turkish graveyards at Kümbet, Karababa and other *tekkes*, where she found interesting tombstones in the form of rams, some of them decorated with reliefs. Similar tombstones have been found as far afield as Central Asia, all of them belonging to the nomadic Türkmen tribespeople who followed the Seljuks in their march of conquest.

We now retrace our route to Seyitgazi and then continue in the same direction as far as highway E90, where we turn to head eastward for Sivrihisar.

About halfway to Sivrihisar we come to the village of Kurnaz, identified as the site of ancient Tricoma. All that remains of the ancient city is a Graeco-Roman sarcophagus built into the wall of the village mosque. This is the Ulu Cami, founded *c.* 1275 by the emir Mikail bin

Abdullah, a Greek who converted to Islam and rose to become regent for the Seljuk sultan Giyaseddin Keyhüsrev III.

Sivrihisar is a crossroads town set in a natural ampitheatre against the background of the jagged twin-peaked mountain behind it. The town has been identified as ancient Abrostola, which in the Byzantine period was called Justinianopolis, a strategic fortress on the borderland between Phrygia and Galatia. Its principal mosque is the Ulu Cami, built in 1275 by the Seljuk emir Mikail bin Abdullah. Across the side street from the Ulu Cami we see a handsome octagonal building with a pyramidal roof. This is the Alemşah Kümbeti, built in 1328 by the Ilkhanid Mongol emir Melikşah; it is in two storeys, with the founder's tomb on the ground floor and the upper floor housing a *mescit*.

Other monuments of the Seljuk and Beylik eras are the Gecek Medresesi (1174), Kılıç Mescidi (1175), Umurbey Mescidi (1175), Soğa Bey Medresesi (twelfth century), Eminettin Mikail Medresesi (thirteenth century), Nurettin Medresesi (1301), Alemşah Medresesi (1328) and Balaban Camii (*c.* 1348).

We now head south-west on highway E96 towards Afyon. About halfway to Afyon we turn off to the left to head south for the town of Çay. Here we pass from the borderland between Phrygia and Galatia into the region known in antiquity as Lycaonia, extending from the central Anatolian plateau to the mountains above the Mediterranean coast.

About 50 kilometres from the turn-off we pass through the village of Bolvadin, the ancient Polybotum. There we see the Esirüttin Ebheri Türbesi, a Seljuk tomb of the thirteenth century.

Thirteen kilometres farther along we come to Çay, identified as the site of ancient Julia Ipsus. This place gave its name to the Battle of Ipsus, fought here in 301 BC between three of the Diadochoi, the successors of Alexander the Great, in which Antigonus was defeated and killed by Lysimachus and Seleucus. Twenty years later Seleucus defeated and killed Lysimachus at Corupedium, giving him sole control of Asia Minor and Syria, beginning the Seleucid Empire.

Çay has two Seljuk monuments, both founded in 1278–79 by Ebül Mücahid Yusuf bin Yakub. One is the Taş Han, a large and well-preserved caravanserai with a *hamam*. The other is the Taş Medrese, one of the finest extant examples of a Seljuk *medrese*. The dedicatory inscription on the porch of the Taş Medrese mentions the founder's name and the date of the building, and it also identifies the architect as Oghulbek bin Muhammad. Besides the inscription, there is also a relief of a lion holding

a heraldic device. The large dome of the *medrese* is completely covered
with Seljuk tiles, and the smaller dome in the two-storeyed hospice is
also revetted in glazed brick. The *mihrap* of the great *eyvan*, now used as
a mosque, has lost most of its former tile decoration.

We now head eastward on the road to Konya, on the first stretch of
which we pass on the left a shallow lake known as Eber Gölü, while to the
south the landscape is dominated by Sultan Dağı, 'Sultan's Mountain',
its highest peak rising to an altitude of 2,610 metres.

Nineteen kilometres from Çay we come to the village of Sultandağı,
where on the right side of the road we see a ruined Seljuk caravanserai.
An inscription records that this was founded by the famous vizier
Sahip Ata Fahrettih Ali in 1249, during the reign of Sultan Alaeddin
Keykubad II.

Beyond the village of Sultandağı Eber Gölü gives way to another
and larger lake known as Akşehir Gölü. About 19 kilometres beyond
Sultandağı we come to the village of Nadir, where there are three
monuments of the Seljuk period: a mosque, a fountain and a tomb.
These are Nadir Camii (1222), Ay Çeşmesi (the Fountain of the Moon,
1253) and Ahi Şeker Türbesi (1302).

Seven kilometres farther along we come to Akşehir, which since
antiquity has been the principal town of this region, known to the Greeks
as Philomelium. The oldest mosque in town is the Ulu Cami, built in
1213, during the reign of the Seljuk sultan Izzeddin Keykavus I, but it
has lost much of its original character in subsequent repairs.

The most important Seljuk monument in Akşehir is the Taş Medrese,
founded in 1250 by the vizier Sahip Ata Fahrettin Ali. All that survives of
the original *külliye*, or building complex, are the *medrese* with a domed
mescit on the same façade, along with a *türbe* attached to the side *eyvan*.
The minaret rises up at the end of the monumental façade and its marble
porch. The *medrese* now houses the Museum of Stonework, including
examples from the Seljuk and Beylik periods.

Another notable building is the Seyit Mahmut Hayrani Kümbeti, a
Seljuk *türbe* set within a grove of pines on a hillside west of the town
centre. This is the tomb of Seyit Mahmut Hayrani, a friend and disciple
of Mevlana Celaleddin Rumi, the saintly mystic poet who founded the
Mevlevi order of dervishes in Konya. Seyit Mahmut died in 1208, and his
original *türbe* would have been erected at that time; the present tomb is
due to a reconstruction in 1410. The original carved wooden sarcophagus
is in the Museum of Turkish and Islamic Art at the Ibrahim Paşa Saray in

Istanbul. The *türbe* has a stone base supporting its fluted cylindrical drum, surmounted by a sixteen-sided pyramidal dome. The dome is adorned with glazed brick decoration in three colours, along with cruciform and star-shaped tiles inserted at a later date. The tile inscription records that the architect was Ahmed bin 'Abd Allah bin Aslı, who may have been the one who gave the famous *türbe* of Mevlana in Konya its final form.

There are two other Seljuk buildings in Akşehir with notable tile decoration. One of these is the Güdük Minare Mescidi, dated 1226, whose façade is articulated with pointed brick arches and faced with both cruciform and star-shaped tiles. The other is the Küçük Aya Sofya Mescidi, dated 1235. This has faience mosaic decoration on its drum and the interior of its dome, some of the designs being geometrical and others resembling plaited Kufic calligraphy.

There are three other dated monuments in Akşehir dating from the Seljuk and Beylik periods. These are Altın Kalem Mescidi (1223), Yağlı Dede Türbesi (1328) and Seyyit Yunus Tekkesi (1417).

Akşehir is renowned as the home of Nasrettin Hoja, the legendary Turkish sage who is thought to have lived here in the Seljuk or Beylik period. The supposed *türbe* of the Hoja is in a cemetery on the south bank of the stream known as Akşehir Deresi. The present *türbe* was built in 1905, but apparently it has the same form as the original tomb. The inscription on the tombstone bears the date 1284, but this is unsubstantiated, and one tradition dates the Hoja's life to at least a century later.

Everyone in Turkey can recite numerous Nasrettin Hoja stories, one of which I tell in my lectures on the history of Islamic science. It seems that a noted Muslim astrologer returned to his home one day and found his wife in bed with another man. When Nasrettin Hoja heard of this scandal he said of the astrologer, 'How can a man predict the motions of the celestial spheres if he doesn't know what's going on in his own house?'

Some 17 kilometres east of Akşehir we come to Yeşilköy, where we cross a stream on a bridge built in 1517, during the reign of Selim I. About 11 kilometres farther along we come to Argıthanı, where we cross another stream on a bridge built in 1437, during the reign of Murat II.

Eighteen kilometres farther along we come to Ilgın, renowned since antiquity for its hot springs. The principal monuments in Ilgın are the mosque and caravanserai of Lala Mustafa Paşa, built in 1577 by the great Ottoman architect Sinan. There is also a ruined Seljuk tomb at some distance from the town centre. This is the *türbe* of Şeyh Bedrettin, dated by an inscription to 1286. The only remarkable feature of the *türbe* is a sculpture over the lintel of the east window, where there is a relief of a human head with braided hair.

Eighteen kilometres beyond Ilgın we come to Kadınhanı. The village takes its name from the Kadın Hanı, a Seljuk caravanserai dated by an inscription to 1223. The inscription also records that the caravanserai was founded by the Seljuk princess Ruhiye Hatun. (Hatun and Kadın both mean 'Lady', hence the name of the caravanserai.) A number of ancient architectural members can be seen built into the caravanserai, apparently recycled from the ruins of a Graeco-Roman structure.

About 22 kilometres farther along we see on our right the ruined Dokuz Derbent Hanı, a Seljuk caravanserai dated 1210. Near the caravanserai there are the remains of a Seljuk bridge, probably of the same date.

Some 24 kilometres farther along we finally come to Konya, ending the long itinerary that has taken us from Istanbul across western Anatolia to the former capital of the Seljuk Sultanate of Rum.

– 13 –

Seljuk Konya

Konya the ancient Iconium, is one of the oldest cities in Anatolia, dating back to the third millennium BC. During the Graeco-Roman and Byzantine eras it was the principal city of Lycaonia. The Seljuks captured the city soon after their victory at Manzikert in 1071, renaming it Konya. After the Seljuks established their first capital at Nicaea in 1078 Konya was occupied by the Danışmendid Türkmen tribe. But then in 1134, during the reign of Ruknuddin Mesut I, the Seljuks captured Konya from the Danışmendid and established their capital there. Konya was the capital of the Seljuk Sultanate of Rum for most of the time from then until 1277, when it was occupied by the Mamluks. The city then went into a decline, held in turn by the Mamluks, the Karamanid, Tamerlane and the Karamanid once again, before it was taken by the Osmanlı under Mehmet II in 1457.

The citadel of ancient Iconium was on the low hill in what is now Alaeddin Parkı. During the Seljuk period the inner city within the citadel was refortified with a defence wall and towers, erected in 1220–21 by Sultan Alaeddin Keykubad I, of which only a single ruined fragment remains at the north end of the park. This is the Alaeddin Köşkü, a defence tower that was converted into an imperial pavilion by Kılıç Arslan II; it was later named after Alaeddin Keykubad I, who carried out extensive repairs on it. Both the exterior and interior were covered with rich and varied tile and stucco decoration, fragments of which are now preserved in various museums.

On the hilltop above the kiosk is Alaeddin Camii, the largest Seljuk edifice in Konya. Inscriptions record that the mosque was begun in 1155 by Mesut I and his son Kılıç Arslan II, and that it was completed in 1219 by Alaeddin Keykubad I, for whom it is named. Since it took so long to build, and also because of the several different reconstructions it has undergone, the layout and design of the mosque are irregular and unusual. The north side of the mosque is hidden behind a monumental façade, above which one can see the tops of two tombs. The present entrance to the mosque is on the east side, where one enters the main area of the prayer hall, covered by a flat timber roof supported by a façade of forty-two ancient stone columns forming seven aisles. The western end of the prayer hall is a smaller area, divided into three or four somewhat crooked aisles by fourteen stone columns.

The *mihrap* is at the centre of the south side, under a domed area preceded by an *eyvan*. The present *mihrap* is a modern work added during a restoration in 1891. The *mimber* is a magnificent structure of carved ebony; made in 1155, it is the oldest inscribed and dated work of Seljuk art in existence and one of the most beautiful.

North of the domed area and its *eyvan* are the two *türbes*. The eastern one is decagonal and has a conical roof, while the western one, only partially completed, is a domed octagon. Within the decagonal *türbe* are the remains of eight Seljuk sultans, the earliest being Kılıç Arslan II and the latest Giyaseddin Keyhüsrev III, while the octagonal *türbe* contains only the body of Alaeddin Keykubad I. The decagonal tomb is noted for its fine ceramic tiles.

Directly opposite the Alaeddin Köşkü is the Büyük Karatay Medresesi, founded in 1251 by the emir Celaleddin Karatay, whose *türbe* is in the main room. This and other Seljuk *medreses*, a few of which were medical schools, hospitals and astronomical observatories, were centres for the spread of Islamic learning in Anatolia, with Arabic as the language of instruction, though Persian was usually preferred by the poets who emerged in the Seljuk renaissance of the thirteenth century, just before the collapse of the Sultanate of Rum.

The monumental entryway of the Karatay Medresesi is decorated with elaborately carved designs and calligraphic inscriptions, one of the finest examples of Seljuk stonework in Turkey. The main room of the *medrese* is covered by a dome more than 12 metres in diameter, with a lantern oculus above and below the pool of a *şadırvan*, the four pendentives formed by quintuple Turkish triangles. The dome is adorned with brilliant tiles in deep blue and gold depicting a firmament of suns and stars; the circular drum below is decorated with a calligraphic design from the first verse of the Kuran; and the Turkish triangles of the pendentives are covered with an abstract pattern in which the names of the first four caliphs are repeated. The walls and vaults are also decorated with tiles, the predominant colours being turquoise, green and purple, while the *eyvan* is revetted in embossed tiles. The *medrese* now serves as a museum of Turkish tiles, ranging from Seljuk work of the thirteenth century to eighteenth-century Ottoman ceramics. Equally interesting are the early Seljuk tiles decorated with figures of humans, animals, birds and fabulous beasts.

On the west side of the main room is the *türbe* of the founder, one of the most distinguished men in Seljuk history. Celaleddin, a freedman of Greek origin, was the trusted adviser of Alaeddin Keykubad I. He twice acted as regent, first during the reign of Keyhüsrev II and then during the early years of the triumvirate of Keyhüsrev's three sons, Izzeddin Keykavus II, Kılıç Arslan IV and Alaeddin Keykubad II. Those were difficult times for the Seljuks, for the Mongols were threatening to sweep all before them after their victory at Kösedağ in 1242, but Celaleddin Karatay managed to hold the Sultanate of Rum together and administer its affairs wisely until his death in 1253.

On the west side of the park is Inceminare Medresesi. The *medrese* and its adjoining mosque, which is now in ruins, were founded in 1258 by the emir Sahip Ata Fahrettin Ali and built by the architect Kölük bin Abdullah.

Fahrettin Ali was the greatest builder of his time in the Sultanate of Rum, founding this and another *medrese* in Konya, two more in Sivas, one in Akşehir, a caravanserai in Ishaklı and a mosque in his home town of Afyon. After the death of Celaleddin Karatay in 1253, Fahrettin Ali succeeded him as vizier, acting as regent during the triumvirate of the three sons of Keyhüsrev II. He continued in that post until 1277, when he was executed by the Mongols after they took Konya. He and Celaleddin Karatay were the two greatest viziers in Seljuk history, and between them they effectively managed the affairs of the Sultanate of Rum during the last half-century of its independent existence

The entrance portal of the *medrese* façade, which is to the left of the mosque, is one of the grandest and most elaborately decorated in Turkey, an outstanding example of the baroque period in Seljuk architecture.

A fluted minaret with two balconies, decorated with glazed brick mosaic, was erected between the mosque and the *medrese*. The minaret was struck by lightning in 1901, destroying the section above the first balcony, and now it stands to less than a half of its original height. The main room is now a museum of Seljuk stonework, including some fascinating sculptural reliefs from Konya and Karaman.

Off to the south end of the park is the Sırçalı Medrese, now partially in ruins. The *medrese* was founded in 1242–43 by Bedrettin Muslih, tutor of Keykubad II. This was the first large-scale structure in Anatolia to be decorated throughout with ceramic tiles, some fine examples of which still adorn the *eyvan*. The *medrese* is now used to exhibit a collection of Islamic tombstones from the Seljuk, Karamanid and Ottoman periods, most of them decorated with fine calligraphic inscriptions and carvings. A Persian inscription on the *eyvan*, now in the Pergamon Museum in Berlin, read, according to the Turkish architectural historian Oktay Aslanapa, 'What I have created is unrivalled throughout the world. I shall pass away, but this shall remain forever and preserve my memory.'

The first alley to the left beyond the *medrese* leads to the handsome Hasbey Darülhadisi, a school for learning the Kuran. Founded in 1421, this is one of the very few examples of Karamanid architecture that has survived in Konya. Another example is the Nasuh Bey Darülhadisi in the Abdülaziz quarter of Konya, which is of about the same date.

One block south of the Sırçalı Medrese is the partially ruined mosque complex of Sahip Ata. The mosque was built in 1258 for Sahip Ata Fahrettin Ali by the architect Kölük bin Abdullah. According to Aslanapa, the roof was originally supported on wooden columns, which makes this the earliest wooden-columned mosque of the Seljuks in Anatolia.

The mosque originally had twin minarets, of which only the lower part of the one on the right has survived. Aslanapa points out that 'the porch of the mosque is the prototype of the twin minaret façades in Anatolia, and also presents the oldest example of the Seljuk ornamental *sebil* (fountain) in the form of a deep niche on the façade'. A *türbe* and a *hanikah*, or dervish oratory, were added in 1258, completing the complex. The six cenotaphs in the *türbe* cover the graves of Sahib Ata and members of his family. Aslanapa, in describing the superb decoration of the complex, writes: 'The *türbe* is the most spectacular work of its age, with the richest and most perfect tile mosaic that Seljuk art had yet produced.'

We now walk eastward from the park along Alaettin Bulvarı. On the left side of the street we pass the huge Şerafettin Camii, a Seljuk mosque originally erected in the thirteenth century, rebuilt in 1636 and restored in the mid-nineteenth century. On the right side of the avenue is Iplikçi Camii, founded by the Seljuk vizier Abu Said Altınapa in 1202, rebuilt by the Karamanid in 1332 and restored in the late Ottoman era.

Halfway along its course Alaettin Bulvarı passes through Hükümet Meydanı, and then at its end it brings us to Selimiye Cami, a classical Ottoman mosque built in the 1560s.

Behind the Selimiye is the Mevlana Tekkesi, the goal of pilgrims from all over Turkey and elsewhere in the Islamic world, for it is the tomb and shrine of the beloved Mevlana.

Mevlana Celaleddin Rumi, founder of the Mevlevi order of dervishes, was born at Balkh in the northern Persian province of Khorasan in 1207. His father, Bahaettin Walad, left Balkh in 1219 and moved to Anatolia, settling first in the town of Karaman, Greek Larende, where Mevlana was married and where his first son, Sultan Veled, was born. Presently Bahaettin moved his family to Konya, where he died in 1230, having won renown as a theologian and teacher.

After Bahaettin's death, Mevlana gathered his father's disciples around him and began preaching to an ever-widening circle of enraptured listeners. At the same time he fell under the influence of a mystic named Burhaneddin Muhaqqiq, a former student of his father in Balkh, who imbued him with enthusiasm for the doctrines and practices of the Sufis. This led Mevlana to found the order of dervishes known as the Mevlevi, famed in the West as the 'Whirling Dervishes'. Then in 1244 he met an itinerant dervish named Şemsettin, who, as Reynold A. Nicholson writes, made Mevlana believe that he had 'found in the stranger the perfect image of the Divine Beloved which he had long been seeking'. It was to Şemsettin that Mevlana devoted his greatest work, the *Mesnevi*, a collection of several thousand odes in which he sings of his mystical belief in the divinity and the doctrine of universal love. The first poem of the Mesnevi, known in English as 'The Song of the Reed', referring to the *ney*, or Turkish flute, the favourite instrument of the Mevlevi, is translated by Nicholson:

Hearken to this Reed forlorn,
Breathing, even since 'twas torn
From its rushy bed, a strain
Of impassioned love and pain.

'The secret of my song, though near,
None can see and none can hear.
Oh, for a friend to know the sign
And mingle all his soul with mine!

'Tis the flame of Love that fired me,
'Tis the wine of Love inspired me.
Would'st thou learn how lovers bleed,
Hearken, hearken to the Reed!'

Celaleddin died on 17 December 1273 and was buried beside his father in the garden of the Mevlevi *tekke*, or dervish lodge. Four years later a *türbe* was built over their graves, a structure designed by the architect Bedrettin Tabrizi and decorated by an artist named 'Abd al-Wahid. The original *türbe* is believed to have been in the form of a four-arched domed chamber with an *eyvan*. Around 1397 the Karamanid emir Alaeddin Ali heightened the structure by adding a fluted drum revetted with tiles and crowned with a conical roof. The other parts of the complex were added in Ottoman times, beginning with a restoration and rebuilding by Beyazit II (r. 1481–1512), Fatih's son and successor.

After Mevlana's death Hüsamettin Çelebi assumed the leadership of the Mevlevi order, and after his death he was succeeded by Mevlana's son, Sultan Veled. The Mevlevi subsequently established *tekkes* all over Anatolia and even beyond, as Mevlana's mystical teachings and poetry came to influence the whole Islamic world as well as people of other faiths. Mevlana's *türbe* was the revered shrine of this cult, and the pilgrims who flocked here made Konya a great religious centre, endowed with many mosques, *medreses*, *tekkes* and *türbes*.

The Mevlevi *tekke* in Konya functioned for more than six and a half centuries after Mevlana's death, a renowned centre of religion, art, music and literature, until it was finally closed in 1925 when the dervish orders were banned by the Turkish Republic. The following year the *tekke* was reopened as a museum, but for many of the multitudes who visit Mevlana's tomb, particularly Turks, it continues to be a religious shrine.

On entering the museum we come into a garden courtyard with a large *şadırvan*. The room to the left houses a fine collection of Seljuk, Karamanid and Ottoman fabrics dating from the thirteenth century to the eighteenth. Some of the cells in the *tekke* have been refurbished to show what they were like in the days of the dervishes.

To the right of the entrance there is a fountain called Şebi Arus, 'the Pool of Nuptial Night', named after the night on which Mevlana died, for as his death approached he referred to it as 'the night of union'. The tradition then began that on the anniversary of Mevlana's death the brethren of the Mevlevi would commemorate his passing by partaking of their evening meal around the pool and then performing the ethereal spinning dance that has made them famous in the West as the Whirling Dervishes.

At the far right-hand corner of the courtyard there are four tombs of the sixteenth century, all of them containing sarcophagi of Karamanid and Ottoman notables. There is a fifth *türbe* of the same period in the dervish graveyard to the south of the *tekke*, a place known as 'the Garden of Spirits'.

The door to the *tekke* opens to a small chamber once used as a reading room by the dervishes; this now houses a museum of Turkish calligraphy. From there we enter the *tekke* proper through Gümüşkapı, 'the Silver Door', a silver-encased portal made in 1599 and presented to the Mevlevi by Hasan Paşa, son of the grand vizier Sokollu Mehmet Paşa. The central hall of the *tekke* is called Huzuri Pir, 'the Presence of the Saint'. A raised platform on the left side of the hall supports the sarcophagi of the Men from Horosan, six dervishes who accompanied the family of Mevlana from Balkh to Konya. At the foot of the first pair of sarcophagi is a superb bronze urn known as the April Bowl, so called because it was used to collect the rainwater of that month, which was reputed to have miraculous healing power. An inscription records that the April Bowl was presented to the *tekke* in 1333 by Ebu Said, khan of the Ilkhanid Mongols. Two glass showcases in the central hall exhibit masterpieces of Seljuk calligraphy, as well as the oldest extant manuscripts of the *Mesnevi* and the *Divan Kebir*, a collection of Mevlevi poems, prose works, sermons and letters, both works dating from Mevlana's lifetime.

The northern end of the *tekke* is made up of two large domed chambers; the one on the west was used as a *mescit* and the eastern one as the *semahane*, the dancing room of the dervishes. The *mescit* is now used as an exhibition hall for ancient Islamic books, calligraphy and prayer rugs. The *semahane* has a fascinating collection of musical instruments used in their ceremonies, most notably the *ney*, the principal accompaniment to Mevlevi poetry and dance. Also exhibited here is one of the most precious treasures of Seljuk art, a beautifully carved Kuran lectern in walnut, dated 1278. The inner face of the lectern is decorated with a fabulous scene depicting lions and two-headed eagles, the only surviving example of Seljuk painting.

At the north end of the *semahane* are the musicians' quarters, with the visitors gallery to the west. The Mevlevi dance is performed here on special occasions, most notably the birthday of Mevlana. Mevlevi music is played on tape throughout the day, the haunting melodies on the *ney* accompanying verses from the *Mesnevi*. The atmosphere is much the same as when Gertrude Bell visited Mevlana's tomb more than a century ago, describing it in a letter she wrote on 13 May 1905:

> He lies under a dome filled with blue, bluer than heaven or the sea, and adorned inside with rich and sombre Persian enamel and lacquer and on either side are rows and rows of the Chelebis, the Dervish high priests and his direct descendants... So he lies, Jelal ed Din Rumi, and to my mind the whole quiet air was full of the music of his verses, 'Ah listen to the plaint of the reed/They reft me from the ashes of my home, my voice is sad with the longing, sad and low.' (But the Persian is the very pipe, the plaintive pipe of the reeds, put into words and there is nothing so invades the soul.)

On the right side of the central hall are the sarcophagi of Mevlana's successors as head of the *tekke*, as well as those of several members of his family. Farther on, directly under the Green Dome, are the marble sarcophagi of Mevlana and his son Sultan Veled, and beyond them are those of his father and other members of his immediate family. This is the most sacred part of the shrine, and the area before Mevlana's sarcophagus is always crowded with Anatolian pilgrims, many of whom weep unashamedly in a fervour of religious emotion as they pray to a holy man who for them transcends sainthood and approaches the divine. An inscription on the sarcophagus quotes the message that Mevlana left for the faithful: 'Do not search for our graves on the earth./ Our graves are in the hearts of enlightened men.'

Other monuments in Konya include *mescits*, *medreses* and tombs of the Seljuk and Karamanid eras, not to mention those of the Ottoman period. The most important of the Seljuk *mescits*, according to Aslanapa, is the Taş Mesci, which, he notes, 'is remarkable for possessing fan squinches and the first ornamented examples of a carved stone Seljuk porch at a date as early as 1215'.

Other dated Seljuk monuments in Konya, some of which are part of a *zaviye*, or shrine, include Altunaba (Iplekçi) Medresesi (1201), Mihmander Mescidi (1207), Akıncı Mescidi (1210), Beşarebek Mescidi (1213), Erdemşah Mescidi (1220), Karaarslan Mescidi and Türbesi (1236), Tercemen Mescidi (1236), Ateşbaz Türbesi and Zaviyesi (1237), Kemaliye (Küçük Karatay) Medresesi (1251), Pir Esad Türbesi (1263), Anber Reis Türbesi (1264), Şeyh Aliman Türbesi (1288), Molla-i Cedid Medresesi (late thirteenth century) and Süttekkesi Mescidi and Türbesi (1325).

Additional monuments from the Karamanid period include Kadı Mürsel (Hacı Hasan) Camii, Imareti and Türbesi (1409, rebuilt in 1907), Turgutluoğulları Türbesi and Darülhadisi (1431), Burhanettin Fakih Türbesi (1455) and Şeyh Vefa Mescidi (1459).

Before leaving Konya one might reflect once again on Mevlana, whose message of universal love is expressed sublimely in a verse of the *Mesnevi* quoted by John Ash in *A Byzantine Journey*:

Long nights have I passed with the priests,
And I have slept with pagans in the market places.
I am the green eye of jealousy, the fever of sickness.
I am cloud and rain, I have swept down over the meadows.
Yet the dust of mortality never touched the hem of my garment.
I have gathered a treasure of roses in the Field of Eternity.

– 14 –

Down to the Mediterranean Coast

We now set out on a long itinerary that will take us from Konya by a devious route down to the Mediterranean coast and back, the southern region of the Seljuk Sultanate of Rum.

The first stage of our itinerary will take us westward from Konya to Beyşehir, a town at the southern end of Beyşehir Gölü, the largest of the three Pisidian Lakes, which take their name from the region known in antiquity as Pisidia, south of Lycaonia in the mountains above the Mediterranean coast.

Beyşehir, ancient Karalia, first came into importance during the reign of Alaeddin Keykubad I, who rebuilt and fortified the town as a way-station on the highroad that linked Konya with Beyşehir.

The most notable monument in Beyşehir is Eşrefoğlu Camii. The mosque was built in the years 1297–99 by Süleyman Bey, emir of the Eşrefoğlu *beylik*, who is buried in the attached *türbe*. This is perhaps the most beautiful of the Seljuk 'forest mosques' of Anatolia, its tall wooden columns, forty-eight of them in six rows of eight each, surmounted by ornate stalactite capitals, its woodwork, stonework, painted decoration, and brick and tile mosaics all superbly executed. A unique feature is the *çeşme* set into the base of the minaret, with a Roman sarcophagus serving as the water tank.

The *türbe* is connected to the mosque through a window that opens into the prayer hall. It is an octagonal stone structure raised on a high square pedestal and surmounted by a conical outer dome. The dedicatory inscription over the door of the *türbe* gives the date of its foundation as 1302. Aslanapa describes the rich interior decoration of the tomb, which

157

is 'covered with 12-sided star patterns, combining with scrolls, palmettes and foliate arabesques (rumis) to form the richest and most spectacular composition of all Seljuk faience mosaic'.

Opposite Eşrefoğlu Camii we see the *bedesten*, or market hall, a rectangular structure with six domes in two rows of three each, with a series of domed shops around its exterior. This dates from the early fourteenth century and is another foundation of the Eşrefoğlu. The building has recently been restored and now houses the town museum.

Another monument from the Beylik period in Beyşehir is Ismail Aşa Medresesi, dated by an inscription to 1369–70. There are three other undated Beylik monuments in town: Taş Medrese, Demirli Mescid and Köşk Köyü Mescidi.

There is another mosque of the Beylik period in the nearby village of Bayındır. Dated 1310, this is a 'forest mosque' in the style of Eşrefoğlu Camii, its wooden columns surmounted by a variety of stalactite capitals, with much of its original painted decoration surviving.

We now drive along the southern shore of Beyşehir Gölü and then up its western side, with the landscape to the west dominated by the colossal peak of Dipoyraz Dağı (2,992 metres), the ancient Mount Anamas. Then at Kurucaova we make our way down to the lake shore to see the remains of the Seljuk palace of Keykubad Sarayı.

The palace took its name from Alaeddin Keykubad I, who built it as a retreat where he could escape the summer heat in his capital at Konya. The sultan had little time to enjoy his palace, for it was only completed in 1235, the year before he died. The palace comprised the royal apartments and a number of pavilions and kiosks surrounded by terraced gardens, baths, pools and fountains, all laid out on an idyllic site beside the lake. All are now in utter ruins, though recent excavations have at least laid clear the foundations and lower walls of some of the structures.

After passing the northern end of Beyşehir Gölü, we follow the road signs that direct us westward to Gelendost. After passing Gelendost we come to Eğirdir Gölü, the second largest of the Pisidian Lakes, ringed round with mountains rising to an elevation of 2,790 metres.

Driving south along the east shore of the lake, we come to a partially ruined Seljuk caravanserai known as Ertokuş Hanı, dated by an inscription to 1229. The main entryway is a double one, outer and inner, the latter gate flanked by two small chambers. This leads into the central aisle of a large court flanked by four pairs of vaulted chambers. At the inner end of the court another gateway leads into the central aisle of the caravanserai's main hall, flanked by two narrower side aisles, all three divisions covered with ogive-shaped vaults. The outer walls of this hall are reinforced with four angular bastions for defence.

At the southern end of the lake we come to the town of Eğirdir, crowned with the ruins of a Seljuk fortress, with the landscape to the south dominated by Davras Dağı (2,635 metres).

Eğirdir was taken from the Byzantines by the Seljuks in the early thirteenth century; subsequently it was part of the Hamidid *beylik*, before being absorbed by the Ottoman Empire in 1412. The fortress above the town was built by Alaeddin Keykubad I *c.* 1219. The restored *medrese*, now used as a market building, bears an inscription dating it to 1242–43. Another *medrese*, built by the Hamidid emir Dündar Bey, is dated 1302. The Hızır Bey Camii is also a Hamidid foundation, dating from the late fourteenth century or the early fifteenth.

We now drive westward to Isparta, which occupies the site of Byzantine Baris. Like Eğirdir, the town was captured by the Seljuks early in the thirteenth century, and a century later it became the capital of the small Hamidid *beylik*. The Hamidid retained the town until 1381, when their emir sold it to the Ottoman sultan Murat I. The Hamidid regained Isparta after Tamerlane defeated Beyazit I at Ankara in 1402. But then a decade later the Ottomans took back Isparta and it became a permanent part of their empire.

The only historic monument in the town is the ruined fortress of the Hamidid. The Isparta Museum houses antiquities from archaeological sites in the vicinity, as well as a small ethnographical collection that includes some exhibits from the Seljuk and Hamidid eras.

We now drive north-west and then south-west to Burdur, a town midway along the southern shore of Burdur Gölü, the smallest of the Pisidian Lakes.

Burdur is the ancient Arcaniae Limnae, which, like Isparta, was captured by the Seljuks early in the thirteenth century and then taken by the Hamitid emirs in the following century. Ibn Battutah, who visited Burdur in the 1330s, describes it as 'a small place with many orchards and streams, and a small fortress on a hilltop'.

The oldest monument in the town, apart from the ruins of the Seljuk fortress on the hilltop, is the Ulu Cami, built in the fourteenth century by the Hamidid emir Dündar Bey. The earliest Ottoman monument is the fifteenth-century Bulgurlu Medrese, which now houses the archaeological museum.

We now head southward for Antalya, and at Çeltikiçi our road joins
the highway leading south from Isparta, which takes us through the
mountains of Pisidia down to the region known as Pamphylia, on the
Mediterranean shore.

About nine kilometres south of the junction we come to the Incir Hanı,
a Seljuk caravanserai built in 1239 by Giyaseddin Keyhüsrev II. The
building is partly in ruins but nonetheless impressive, particularly its
ornately carved entryway, whose fluted outer arch is flanked by the small
figures in low relief of two confronted lions. The gateway leads to the
outer courtyard, a square area measuring 36 metres on a side. A second
gateway leads to the caravanserai proper, 28 metres wide and 40 metres
long, comprising a central aisle flanked by seven pairs of transverse
corridors. All the corridors are covered with ogive vaults, with a dome
raised on a drum over the central crossing, a circlet of windows providing
light and ventilation.

About 10 kilometres farther south we turn left on a secondary
road signposted for another Seljuk caravanserai, the Susuz Han, a
drive of about one kilometre. The caravanserai was built late in the
reign of Giyaseddin Keyhüsrev II, c. 1246. The building, which is
very well preserved, is square in plan, measuring 26.5 metres on a
side. The elaborately carved entryway leads to the central aisle,
from which five transverse aisles lead off on either side, all of
them covered with ogive vaults, with a dome on a drum over the
central crossing.

About 37 kilometres farther along we come to still another Seljuk
caravanserai, Kırkgöz Hanı, also dating from the reign of Giyassedin
Keyhüsrev II. Its overall dimensions are 45.7 by 10.6 metres, with its
entryway on the south side leading into a courtyard with rooms on either
side, and the main hall on the north side divided into six vaulted chambers.

The highway now passes through the Döşemaltı Gorge, taking us
through the Taurus Mountains and down into the Pamphylian plain,
finally bringing us to the Mediterranean coast at Antalya.

Antalya was originally called Attaleia, after Attalus II of Pergamum
(r. 159–138 BC), founder of the city. Attalus, who intended his city to be
the main Pergamene port on the Mediterranean coast, enclosed it with
a circuit of defence walls and towers. During the crusades, when it was
known as Adalia, it frequently served as a port for the Christian armies,
who often sailed from here to Syria to avoid the long and difficult march
across Asia Minor.

The city was captured in 1207 by the Seljuks under Giyaseddin Keyhüsrev I, and in Turkish it came to be called Antalya. Late in the thirteenth century Anatalya fell to the Hamidid Türkmen tribe, whose chieftain soon gave it over to his vassal, the emir of the Teke *beylik*. The Teke emirs held Antalya until 1361, when it was captured by Peter de Lusignan I, king of Cyprus, who kept it until he was assassinated eight years later. The city then reverted to the Hamidid, who held it until it was captured by Murat I in 1387, becoming a permanent part of the Ottoman Empire.

When Ibn Battutah visited Antalya in 1330 it was held by the Teke tribe. He noted that the Greeks and other non-Muslims lived in separate quarters apart from the Turks, as was the case in other cities in Anatolia under Turkish rule.

The oldest part of Antalya is the quarter around the port, with monuments from the Hellenistic, Byzantine, Seljuk, Beylik and Ottoman periods, the latter including many old houses that have been well restored. The port quarter is still partially enclosed by its ancient defence walls and towers. These were originally built in the Hellenistic period, though most of what survives dates from the imperial Roman era, along with considerable repairs by the Byzantines and some by the Seljuks.

The most prominent landmark in Antalya is Yivli Minare Camii. The fluted shaft of this striking minaret is built of pink-red bricks into which have been set small pieces of blue-green Seljuk tiles. The minaret was erected by Alaeddin Keykubad I in 1220. Originally the minaret was attached to a mosque that had been a Byzantine church before the Seljuk capture of the city in 1207. This edifice was replaced in 1373 by the present mosque, which was founded by Mehmet Bey, emir of the Hamidid *beylik*. The prayer hall is covered by three pairs of domes supported by twelve columns in three rows of four each, some of them surmounted by ancient capitals. Mehmet Bey also erected the *türbe* that stands in the courtyard above the mosque, a distinctive structure with a pyramidal roof. This was built in 1377 for Mehmet Bey's eldest son, who died before he could succeed his father as emir.

Directly across the courtyard from the mosque there are the ruins of two Seljuk *medreses*. The isolated portal to the right is all that remains of the Mübarizzedin Medresesi, founded in 1239. On the other side are the more substantial remains of a *medrese* founded *c.* 1220 by Alaeddin Keykubad I.

Along the winding streets in the upper part of the old quarter inside the ancient walls there are a number of interesting monuments. One of these is the Karatay Medresesi, founded in 1250 by the famous Seljuk vizier Celaleddin Karatay. Another is the Kesik Minare Camii, 'the Mosque with the Truncated Minaret'. This was originally a church dedicated to the Virgin, converted to a mosque after the Seljuk capture of the city. This once splendid basilica, now an utter ruin, was built in the fifth century and served as the cathedral of Attaleia until the Seljuks captured the city.

The Antalya Archaeological Museum is some two kilometres west of the city centre. This is perhaps the most outstanding local museum in Turkey, with exhibits from archaeological sites all over south-western Anatolia, dating from the palaeolithic period up through the Seljuk, Beylik and Ottoman periods. The museum's ethnographical collection is outstanding, particularly the objects belonging to the Yürük, the semi-nomadic people descended from the first Türkmen tribes who moved into Anatolia in the eleventh century.

An interesting excursion from Anatalya takes us out of the city along highway E87 towards Korkuteli. About seven kilometres along we come to a Seljuk caravanserai known as Evdir Hanı, built by Izzeddin Keykavus I. Between the caravanserai and the main road there are the scattered ruins of an unidentified ancient city, including a large number of sarcophagi. This site was first noted in 1847 by the British travellers Spratt and Forbes, who also describe a miserable night they spent in the Evdir Hanı, dispelling some of the romance associated with medieval caravanserais.

> The entrance to the khan is a magnificent gateway of Saracenic architecture, highly ornamented, and in part constructed of white marble. The marble slabs have inscriptions, probably sentences from the Koran. Within a great court, surrounded by lofty, vaulted cloisters, now partly in ruins; here we lodged, lighting our fire under the arches, and picketing our horses in the quadrangle. The lodging was snug enough, but had the disadvantage of being the camp of a mighty army of fleas, who forthwith, regarding us as natural enemies, proceeded to the attack, and though each of the party literally slew hundreds, did not seem in the least diminished by the morning. During the night they made incessant efforts to destroy us, and we arose in a very uncomfortable state and much wounded.

We now head eastward from Antalya on the coastal highway, with the Mediterranean to our right and to our left the Taurus Mountains looming above the Pamphylian plain.

Up until recent years one still saw camel caravans of Yürük tribes strung out across the plain, moving in their seasonal treks between their winter encampments on the coast and the summer pastures of their goat herds in the highland meadows of the Taurus, their black goat-skin tents speckled among the groves of olives, oranges and bananas, a way of life unchanged since their ancestors first moved into Anatolia with the Seljuk armies nearly 1,000 years ago. Now most of them have settled down in permanent quarters on the coast, earning their living from tourism, though they have retained most of the customs that link them with their immemorial past, particularly the music and poetry of their *aşıklar*, or troubadours, though few tourists are ever privileged to hear these except in recordings.

About 48 kilometres from Antalya we turn left on a secondary road signposted for ancient Aspendos, which is five kilometres up the valley of the Köprü Çayı, the river Eurymedon of the Greeks. This was the site of the Battle of the Eurymedon in 467 BC, when Kimon of Athens defeated the Persians by land and sea on the same day. Afterwards the Greeks erected a monument to honour their fallen warriors, with an inscription recorded by Thucydides: 'These are the men who laid down the splendour of their manhood beside the Eurymedon: on land and on their swift-sailing ships they fought with their spears against the foremost of the bow-bearing Medes. They are no more, but they have left the fairest memorial of their valour.'

A short way along the road we pass a humpbacked Seljuk bridge of the thirteenth century that still spans the river. Just upstream from this we see in the riverbed the ruins of a Roman bridge of the second century AD. Then after passing the remains of a Roman bath and gymnasium complex we come to the great Roman theatre of Aspendus, with the acropolis hill of the ancient city rising up behind it.

Aspendos was taken by the Seljuks in 1078 and was part of the Hamidid and Teke *beyliks* until it was taken by the Osmanlı in 1392. By then Aspendos was little more than a village, and in the late Ottoman period it was abandoned altogether, all its ancient monuments in ruins except for the theatre, which is still remarkably well preserved, particularly the stage building.

The stage building is an imposing structure – some 25 metres high and 110 metres across its outer façade – with the five major tiers of its windows corresponding to the different levels of its interior. The tower-like entrance is not an original part of its structure, but was erected by the Seljuks *c.* 1220, when Alaeddin Keykubad I converted the stage building into an imperial residence.

We now continue driving eastward on the coastal highway, and about 24 kilometres farther along we come to the town of Manavgat on the river of the same name, the Melas of antiquity. Some 29 kilometres past Manavgat we turn left on a secondary road signposted for Alarahan, a drive of about nine kilometres.

Alarahan is a well-preserved Seljuk caravanserai, its overall dimensions 51 by 39 metres, its crenellated walls giving it the appearance of a fortress. An inscription over the entryway records that the caravanserai was built in 1229–30 by Alaeddin Keykubad I. The portal leads into a long corridor, with seven rooms opening off on either side, those on the left giving access to larger chambers behind. Beyond the rooms on the right are the stables, which were approached by a separate entryway on the right side of the front façade. One of the rooms inside the main door served as a *mescit*, while the other was the living quarters for the porters. The rooms at the far end included the kitchen, dining hall, *hamam* and toilets.

The caravanserai stands in a beautiful river valley near the remains of a Seljuk bridge. At the head of the valley we see a steep-sided conical hill ringed around with the walls of a thirteenth-century Seljuk fortress known as Alarakale. A path at the end of the road brings us to a tunnel that leads to the outer courtyard of the fortress. From there rock-hewn steps ascend to a second court and then to the citadel on the summit, where there are the remains of a residential quarter along with a *mescit* and a *hamam* once used by the garrison.

About six kilometres beyond the Alarahan turn-off we see on our left yet another Seljuk caravanserai, the Şarapsa Hanı. This is a long and narrow building measuring 70 by 15 metres, with its entrance in the middle of one of its long sides. An inscription over the entryway records that the caravanserai was founded by Giyaseddin Keyhüsrev II. The caravanserai comprises nine vaulted bays, whose interior divisions are extended as buttresses on the outside of the building, with slitted windows in each compartment and a chimney in the corner of every bay. There is also a *mescit* at the east end of the building.

Soon after passing the Şarapsa Hanı we come within view of Alanya, one of the grandest sights along the Mediterranean coast of Turkey, with the crenellated walls of its rose-pink Seljuk fortress crowning the great peninsular rock above the sea. This spectacular landmark, known in antiquity as Kalonoros, marked the boundary between Pamphylia and Cilicia, the region stretching eastward along the Mediterranean coast.

The port town beneath Kalonoros was known to the Greeks as Coracesium, which was taken by the Seljuks in 1221 under Alaeddin Keykubad I, after whom it was called Alaiye, later changed to Alanya. The town remained under Seljuk rule until *c.* 1330, when it passed to the Karamanid, who held it intermittently until it fell to the Ottomans in 1471.

The spectacular defence walls of Alanya were built by Alaeddin Keykubad I soon after he took the town in 1221, and at the same time he erected the harbour works as a base for the Seljuk fleet. The most conspicuous monument in the lower town is Kızıl Kule (a *kule* is a tower), an octagonal structure more than 30 metres in diameter and nearly 30 metres high. This was probably the first structure that Alaeddin built when he began to fortify the town, for it was the anchor of his defence works, not only guarding the harbour but also linking the land and sea walls. Across the harbour from Kızıl Kule stands the Tershane, or naval arsenal, the only one of its type extant in Turkey. It is a long building with five vaulted galleries opening directly on to the sea; within these the ships of the Seljuk fleet were built and repaired, and sheltered from the elements during the winter. Next to the Tershane is Tophane, built as a fortified ammunition storehouse.

The main line of the land walls climbs steeply uphill from Kızıl Kule, the most formidable stretch of the fortifications. The road from the lower town winds uphill and passes through Kale Kapısı, the main gate in the outer wall. This is a handsome double portal with two successive entrances at right angles to one another, the first dated 1226 and the second 1231.

Inside Kale Kapısı the road winds uphill to the gate of Içkale, the citadel. A path leads from there to Ehmediye, the inner citadel, where the Turkish quarter of the town was located in Seljuk and early Ottoman times. The Ehmediye still shelters a picturesque hamlet of old wooden houses of the late Ottoman era, along with the remains of a *bedesten* and a Seljuk caravanserai that now serves as a hotel, as well as a seventeenth-century Ottoman mosque known as Süleymaniye Camii.

The walls of Içkale enclose the almost flat summit of the acropolis hill, on which the only Turkish structures are cisterns and vaulted galleries that probably served as barracks for the garrison. The only other building on the summit is a pretty little Byzantine chapel dedicated to St George.

The view from the ramparts of the fortress is breathtaking, with the Pamphylian plain stretching off to the west between the mountains and the sea, while to the east we see the foothills of the Taurus coming right down to the Mediterranean, which is why this region was called Cilicia Tracheia, 'Rugged Cilicia'.

The coastal scenery changes dramatically as soon as we begin driving eastward from Alanya, as the road winds around a series of heavily wooded headlands and deeply indented bays, with savage cliffs plunging sheer into the sea. Our itinerary in Cilicia Tracheia will take us past a succession of ancient fortress towns, most of them dating from the Hellenistic and Roman periods, all of them now uninhabited ruins.

We reach the southernmost point of the Turkish coast at the town of Anamur, with the mountains of Cyprus visible to the south on clear days.

Seven kilometres east of the town we come to the magnificent castle of Anamur, known in Turkish as Mamure Kalesi, the largest and best-preserved fortress on the Mediterranean coast of Turkey, with all its curtain walls and thirty-six towers still standing to their original height. The fortress was originally erected in the twelfth century by the rulers of the Cilician Kingdom of Lesser Armenia; then early in the following century it was completely rebuilt by the Seljuks under Alaeddin Keykubad I, as recorded in an inscription over the main gateway. The fortress was subsequently held in turn by the Lusignan kings of Cyprus, the Karamanid emirs and the Ottomans.

A drive of 141 kilometres from Anamur brings us to Silifke, the largest town on the coast of Cilicia Tracheia. Silifke stands astride the Göksu, the river known to the Greeks as the Calycadnus. The city was founded c. 300 BC by Seleucus I, eponymous founder of the Seleucid Kingdom. It was known as Seleucia ad Calycadnus, to distinguish it from a dozen other places that Seleucus had founded and named after himself.

The Seljuks under Izzeddin Keykavus I unsuccessfully besieged Seleucia in 1216, when it was held by the Knights of St John under Armenian suzerainty. Eight years later control of the city reverted to the Armenians, who occupied it until the late thirteenth century, after which it was held in turn by the Seljuks, Mongols, Mamluks, Karamanid and finally the Ottomans, who took the city in 1471, by which time it was known as Silifke.

Silifke is dominated by its *kale*, the great medieval fortress that crowns the acropolis hill above the west side of the modern town. The fortress was built by the Byzantines, perhaps as early as the seventh century, and it was rebuilt and repaired in turn by the Armenians, Seljuks, Karamanid and Ottomans.

Silifke's principal Islamic monument is the Ulu Cami, built by the Seljuks toward the end of the thirteenth century. The mosque has been rebuilt to a large extent, the only parts remaining from the original structure being the elaborately carved Seljuk entryway and the *mihrab*.

We now head inland from Silifke on the Konya highway, following the course of the ancient Roman road from the Mediterranean coast through the Taurus Mountains up to the central Anatolian plateau.

The first part of the drive takes us up the dramatic gorge of the Göksu into the heart of the Taurus. Some seven kilometres from Silifke we pause at a car park beside the road. Beside the gorge there is a sign in Turkish recording the historic incident that took place here more than eight centuries ago, during the Third Crusade. It reads, in translation: 'The emperor Frederick Barbarossa, having agreed with the Seljuk sultan Kılıç Arslan II to cross his lands freely in peace, was drowned in the Göksu in this region on 10 June 1190 on his way to Palestine at the head of his army.'

We continue up the gorge, with spectacular cliffs and spires of rock rising hundreds of metres above the road. Then the valley begins to broaden out into a long highland corridor flanked by tiers of hills covered with wild olive trees.

Some 75 kilometres from Silifke we come to the town of Mut, the Roman Claudiopolis, set deep in the valley of a tributary of the Göksu. The most prominent monument in Mut is the medieval *kale*, a Byzantine fortress rebuilt in the fourteenth century by the Karamanid and taken by the Ottomans in the following century. Two monuments remaining from the Karamanid era are the fourteenth-century Hocaendi Türbesi and Lal Ağa Camii, built in 1444.

Those with time to spare might make an excursion westward from Mut to Ermenek, a drive of 87 kilometres. The most prominent monument in Ermenek is its *kale*, which in its present state dates from the Karamanid period, though it may well be Byzantine in foundation. Monuments in the town from the early Turkish period are Akça Mescit (1300); the Ulu Cami, built in 1302 by the Karamanid emir Mehmet Bey; and the Tol Medrese and Türbe, founded in 1339 by the Karamanid emir Burhanettin Musa, distinguished by its elaborately carved entryway in the Seljuk style.

About 74 kilometres north of Mut we come to Karaman. The town is just within the Taurus on the southern rim of the great Anatolian plateau at an altitude of 1,038 metres, set in a surprisingly green oasis on the otherwise barren steppes.

Karaman is the ancient Larande, which some scholars have identified with the city of Landa mentioned in a Hittite inscription from the first half of the second millennium BC. Larande was an important Byzantine stronghold until the Seljuk victory at Manzikert in 1071, after which it fell to the Danışmendid Türkmen tribe. It was then taken in turn by the Seljuks, crusaders, Armenians, the Seljuks again and then the Karamanid, who captured Larande in 1271 and later made it the capital of their *beylik*, after which it came to be called Karaman. Karaman continued to be the Karamanid capital until 1466, when it was taken by the Ottomans and became a permanent part of their empire.

The most prominent monument in Karaman is its medieval *kale*, which was originally built by the Byzantines and repaired in turn by the Seljuks and the Karamanid. The fortress has been completely restored in recent years. The picturesque quarter around the citadel has a number of monuments from the Seljuk and Karamanid periods, as well as later ones of the Ottoman era. One of the most interesting of the Beylik monuments is Akteke Camii, a mosque built in 1370 by the Karamanid emir Alaeddin Ali Bey, its *külliye* also including a Mevlevi dervish *tekke*. Within the mosque are the tombs of several members of the family of Mevlana Celaleddin Rumi, founder of the Mevlevi order.

Another notable Beylik monument is Yunus Emre Camii, built in 1349 and heavily restored in the twentieth century. The mosque is named for the Turkish poet Yunus Emre, who died in Karaman in 1322 and is buried here in a tomb that has always been a popular place of pilgrimage. Yunus Emre is generally recognised as the first and greatest poet in the Turkish language. One of his poems is a particular favourite, and in just two lines it catches the spirit of his poetry: 'I love you, so the hand of death can never touch me.'

There are at least twenty monuments in Karaman from the Seljuk and Karamanid periods, including Lal Hamamı (1219); Saadetin Ali Bey-Ebülfetih Mescidi (1247); Emir Musa Paşa Medresesi (early fourteenth century); Süleyman Bey Hamamı (1358); Arapzade Camii (1378); Dikbasan Camii (1378); Hacı Beyler Camii (fourteenth century); Hatuniye Medrese (1382); Alaettin Bey Türbesi (1388), Halil Efendi Mescidi (1409); Ibrahim Bey Imareti (1432); Imaret Camii (1437); Kızlar Türbesi (mid-fifteenth century); Karabaş Veli Türbesi (1465); and Siyahser Camii (1465).

The final stage of our itinerary takes us north-west from Karaman to Konya, a drive of some 89 kilometres, completing our circuit around the Mediterranean coast below the Taurus Mountains.

– 15 –

Central Anatolia

O ur next itinerary will take us from Konya to Ankara via Kayseri, a great semicircular arc following the course of some of the famous Seljuk caravan routes across the central Anatolian plateau. We leave Konya heading north-east on the Ankara highway, which we will soon leave to turn off on to the road for Aksaray and Kayseri. About seven kilometres along we see on our left a Seljuk caravanserai known as Horozlu Han, 'the Han with a Rooster'. An inscription records that this was built in 1248 by Esedüttin Ruz Apa, an emir of Seljuk Sultan Izzeddin Keykavus II. The Horozlu Han is one of about a dozen caravanserais that the Seljuks built during the thirteenth century along the Uluyol, or Great Road, the main caravan route between Konya and Kayseri, the second city of the Sultanate of Rum. The caravanserai here was in ruins but it was restored in the late 1960s. The impressive but unadorned entryway opens into the outer courtyard, which is flanked by five vaulted chambers that housed the merchants who put up at the han. At the far end of the courtyard another portal leads to the stables, a building of square plan with five aisles formed by four rows of four piers each, the central compartment covered by an eight-sided pyramidal roof on a high drum.

Three kilometres farther along we turn right on to the highway for Aksaray and Kayseri, which takes us across the great Anatolia plateau from Lycaonia into Cappadocia.

The countryside along the road from Konya to Aksaray is bleak and completely featureless, the only signs of human habitation being a few hamlets and, up until a few years ago, Yürük encampments. As Gertrude

Bell wrote of these mournful Anatolian steppes: 'It is Asia, with all of its vastness, with all its brutal disregard for life and comfort and the amenities of existence; it is the ancient East, returned, after so many millenniums of human endeavour, to its natural desolation.' And as she remarked on the interminability of the journey we are now taking, referring to a trip she took in the opposite direction at the beginning of the twentieth century, when Anatolian travel was far slower and more difficult than it is today: 'All things come to an end,' she wrote, 'even the road from Aksarai to Konya.'

About 113 kilometres from the junction a secondary road on the left leads to Sadettin Hanı, a drive of five kilometres. This is a large Seljuk caravanserai built in the years 1235–37, begun by Alaeddin Keykubad I and completed by his son and successor Giyaseddin Keyhüsrev II. The monumental entryway is made of alternate courses of rust-red and cream-coloured ashlar blocks. This opens into the great outer courtyard, which is in two contiguous square sections, the first measuring 25 metres on a side and the second 30 metres. The inner hall is 22 metres wide and 28 metres long, with five transverse aisles opening off from each side of the central aisle, all of them vaulted. The caravanserai has a fortress-like appearance, with square and semicircular turrets projecting at intervals from its outer walls.

Returning to the highway, we continue driving eastward across the plateau, which here has an altitude of over 1,000 metres. About 11 kilometres along we see on the right a ruined Seljuk carvanserai known as Akbaş Hanı. This was built c. 1250 by Seyfettin Karasungur, Seljuk emir of Ladık.

About 36 kilometres farther along we see on our left another very ruined Seljuk caravanserai, the Obruk Hanı, which also dates from the mid-thirteenth century.

After another 36 kilometres we see on our right, directly beside the road, the famous Sultan Hanı, the largest and most splendid of the Seljuk caravanserais in Anatolia. An inscription records that this royal caravanserai was founded in 1229 by Alaeddin Keykubad I. It is surrounded by massive walls, reinforced with turret towers at the corners, midpoints, and flanking the monumental entryway, which is recessed and elaborately carved with reliefs.

The gateway leads into the vast outer courtyard, 44 metres wide and 58 metres long, flanked by eleven vaulted chambers on either side. The first chamber on the left served as the kitchen and the others on that side were dormitories, while the rooms on the right were used as shops, dormitories, workrooms, toilets and baths. At the centre of the court is a *mescit* in the form of a kiosk carried on four open arches, the prayer room approached by staircases on either side, the open space below containing a *şadırvan*.

A second monumental portal leads into the somewhat smaller inner hall, which served as a stable for the camels, horses and donkeys of the caravans. This structure comprises a vaulted central aisle with nine slightly lower transversely vaulted chambers opening off on either side. The central compartment is covered by a pyramidal dome carried on a cylindrical drum, with slitted windows in the walls to provide light and ventilation.

The Sultan Hanı and other such hostels provided for the needs of those travelling on the caravan routes that were the main arteries of Seljuk trade and commerce. During Seljuk times all merchants in the Sultanate of Rum paid a yearly tax to the Sultan, and in return they were allowed to use these caravanserais free when travelling from town to town. Besides providing food and lodging for the merchants, drivers and animals, the royal caravanserais had refectories, clinics, baths and toilets and were staffed with a physician, veterinary surgeon, cooks, bakers, porters, watchmen and armed guards, as well as the various workers and artisans needed to service and maintain the caravans. There were also clerics for the *mescit*, an essential element in every caravanserai. Caravanserais were also used as military stations in times of war, and were used to feed and supply the Seljuk armies when they were on campaign.

Forty kilometres farther we come to highway E90, where we turn left, and then four kilometres along we turn right. This brings us to Aksaray, a large town in a green oasis of pines, cypresses and fruit orchards, a welcome sight after a long drive across the barren Anatolian plateau. Aksaray is a very ancient place, identified by some authorities with the Hittite Kursaura, mentioned as early as *c.* 2200 BC. The town was captured, sacked and then rebuilt by the Seljuks during the reign of Kılıç Arslan II (r. 1156–88). Known to the Turks as Aksaray, it was captured by the Mongols after their victory over the Seljuks at Kösedağ in 1248. After the subsequent collapse of the Sultanate of Rum Aksaray was held by the Karamanid, who lost it to the Osmanlı under Beyazit I in 1390, regained it after Tamerlane's victory at Ankara in 1402, then lost it permanently in 1468 when Mehmet II conquered Karamania, as south-central Anatolia was known at that time.

The medieval *kale* of Aksaray may be Byzantine in foundation, but its present structure dates from the Seljuk rebuilding of the town in the second half of the twelfth century.

The oldest Seljuk monument in Aksaray is Alaeddin Camii, founded in 1156 by Kılıç Arslan II, but now in ruins. The second oldest is a Seljuk mosque known as Kızıl Minare, which is dated 1221. The Ibrahim Kadiroğlu Medresesi is a Seljuk foundation restored by the Karamanid in the first half of the fifteenth century. There is also a Seljuk *türbe* that is identified as the tomb of Kılıç Arslan IV, but there is no evidence to support this tradition.

The Zinciriye Medresesi was built by the Karamanid in 1336. The Ulu Cami, built by the Karamanid in 1433, has a shallow rectangular prayer hall with five aisles perpendicular to the longitudinal axis. The space containing the *mihrap* and the area in front of it are surmounted by domes, while all the other sections are covered with transverse vaulting. The beautifully carved *mimber* is of Seljuk workmanship, removed from the ruined Alaeddin Camii.

We now continue eastward on the Nevşehir road. Some 17 kilometres along we see on our right the Ağızkara Hanı, one of the best-preserved and most impressive Seljuk caravanserais in Anatolia. This was built to the same general plan as the Sultan Hanı we have just seen on the Konya–Aksaray road. An inscription over the entryway records that the inner hall was erected in 1231 by Alaeddin Keykubad I, and that the rest of the structure was completed in 1242–43 by his son and successor Giyaseddin Keyhüsrev II.

A short way farther along we turn right on a road signposted for Güzelyurt and Niğde. The first stretch of this road takes us through the hauntingly beautiful Ihlara valley, where we see some of the rock-hewn Byzantine churches and monasteries, many of them decorated with paintings in fresco, that have made Cappadoceia world-famous. Near the village of Selime we see, in addition to the Byzantine rupestrine structures, an octagonal Seljuk *türbe* of the thirteenth century.

The ancient town of Niğde, situated at an altitude of 1,228 metres, clusters around an acropolis hill topped with the ruins of a medieval *kale*. The *kale* on the acropolis hill may be Byzantine in foundation, but it was probably rebuilt by the Seljuks *c.* 1230, during the reign of Keykubad I, and subsequently restored *c.* 1470 by the Ottomans.

The oldest Islamic monument in Niğde is the Müeddin Medresesi, built in 1218, during the reign of Izzeddin Keykavus I. The most important Seljuk monument is Alaeddin Camii, which stands on the acropolis hill to the east of the *kale*. An inscription over the porch records that the mosque was built in 1223 by Beşare Zeynettin, Seljuk governor of Niğde during the reign of Alaeddin Keykubad I. The mosque was subsequently rebuilt by the Karamanid in 1410. Aslanapa points out that beneath the dedicatory inscription on the magnificent porch there are 'two human portraits in high relief with long plaits of hair hanging down on each side of their faces'.

The largest and most important mosque in the lower town is Sungur Bey Camii, built in 1335 by the Mongol chieftain Seyfettin Sungur Bey, rebuilt after a fire in the sixteenth century. The founder is buried in an octagonal *türbe* to the left of the porch. The distinctive elements in the sculptural decoration of the mosque include the heads of lions and griffins as well as a double-headed eagle.

The very long market building just to the north of the mosque is the *bedesten*. This is a Karamanid foundation dated by an inscription to 1409. The building is 80 metres long and 6.7 metres wide, with entrances at its north and south ends and in the middle of its east side. Eight ogive arches divide the wide central aisle into nine compartments, with twenty-nine vaulted shops opening off on either side.

Just to the south of Sungur Bey Camii and the *bedesten* we see a street fountain and a small mosque. The former is known as Eskiciler Çeşmesi, 'the Fountain of Those Who Buy Old Things', dated by an inscription to 1421. The mosque is the Şah Mescidi, which an inscription dates to 1413.

About 100 metres west of Sungur Bey Camii we come to the strikingly handsome Ak Medrese. This was founded in 1409 by the Karamanid emir Ali Bey, a grandson of the Ottoman sultan Murat I. The *medrese* is in two storeys, with an open central courtyard centred on a well. The monumental entrance porch, which rises high above the top of the *medrese* façade, has an elaborately carved surface, with an ogive arch framing a triangular stalactite canopy. The second storey of the façade has a loggia opening through two pairs of ogive arches, giving the building the appearance of a Seljuk palace. There are *eyvans* on both storeys inside the entryway, while at the opposite end of the courtyard a single great *eyvan* rises to the full height of the building. The great *eyvan* serves as a *mescit*, with a *mihrap* in the centre of its inner wall. On either side of the great *eyvan* there are two large domed chambers that served as *dershanes*, or lecture halls. The two sides of the courtyard are flanked by double arcades, with the rooms of the students, four on either side, opening off from both the lower and upper porticoes. There are also two larger rooms on either side of the entryway on the ground floor. The *medrese* now serves as the local archaeological museum.

There is an interesting Beylik mosque in the quarter north-east of the acropolis. This is Hanım Camii, founded in 1442 by an unidentified Karamanid princess. The mosque is rectangular in plan, its flat roof supported an arcade carried by two reused ancient columns with stalactite capitals.

Also of note are two Seljuk *türbes* on the north-western outskirts of the town. The largest and most important of these is the *türbe* of Hüdavent Hatun, built in 1312 for a daughter of Kuknuddin Kılıç Arslan IV. The princess, who was probably married to a Mongol ruler, lived until 1331, so she may well have planned and supervised the construction of her tomb.

The *türbe*, the base on which it stands and its pyramidal roof are all octagonal. The sides of the building are separated from one another by slender engaged colonnettes. The elaborately carved door, approached by a flight of three steps, is on the east side, and there are windows on three alternate sides, each of them with a semicircular opening above and with grilles resembling half-rosette traceries of Gothic fenestrations. A protruding band in the form of a moulding marks the division between the shaft of the building and its lower area. Just below the roof a cornice-like section forms a sixteen-sided belt, the sides separated from one another by small colonnettes carved with floral and geometric arabesques. There are heraldic-like figural reliefs among the carvings in the spandrels of each of the three windows, including those of two sirens and a pair of eagles with outspread wings.

The second tomb is known as the Gündoğdu Türbesi, a square structure covered by a dodegonal roof carried on a twenty-four-sided drum. The dedicatory inscription over the doorway records that this is the tomb of 'Hakkı Rawwab, son of Gündoğdu', who died in the month of Safar 745 (May–June 1334), probably a Karamanid nobleman.

We now head north towards Kayseri, turning off to the left at Yeşilhisar for Ürgüp. Then, some 35 kilometres along, we stop at the village of Taşkınpaşa.

The village takes its name from Taşkın Paşa, a Karamanid emir who ruled here in the fourteenth century. The *külliye* that he founded here is still for the most part standing, including a mosque, a *medrese*, and the *türbe* where he is buried. The beautifully carved wooden *mihrap* and *mimber* of the mosque are now preserved in the Ankara Ethnographical Museum. Of the *medrese* only the gateway survives, a handsome work in the Seljuk style. Recent scholarship suggests that this was not a *medrese* but a palace.

We now continue into Ürgüp, the centre of the eroded hill country of central Cappadocia, an extraordinary landscape that is like no other place on earth, with its phallic cones known to the Turks as *peri bacaları*, many of which have been carved and hollowed out to create rupestrine churches, monasteries and houses.

The oldest Turkish monument in Ürgüp is a Seljuk *türbe* on the summit of the rocky crag that towers above the town. Tradition has it that this is the tomb of Ruknuddin Kılıç Arslan IV (r. 1246–65), who was murdered on the orders of his son Giyaseddin Keyhüsrev III (r. 1265–83) when he usurped the throne.

We now follow the road signs to Kayseri, Roman Caesarea, the principal city of central Anatolia, dominated to the south by the great peak of Erciyes Dağı (3,918 metres).

The Seljuks captured Kayseri in 1082, eleven years after their victory over the Byzantines at Manzikert. But then, after the Seljuks were defeated by the crusaders at Dorylaeum in 1097, they lost Kayseri to the Danışmendid Türkmen, who made it the capital of a *beylik* that included much of central and eastern Anatolia. Kayseri was taken from the Danışmendid in 1164 by Kılıç Arslan II, after which it became the second city in the Seljuk Sultanate of Rum after Konya. Kayseri was held by the Seljuks until their defeat by the Mongols at Kösedağ in 1242, after which the victors occupied the city and made it part of the Ilkhanid Empire.

The Ilkhanid Empire broke up in 1335, whereupon the Mongol governor of Kayseri, an Uighur Turk named Eretna, proclaimed himself ruler of a *beylik* in Cappadocia, with his capital in Sivas. He and his successors, the short-lived Eretnid dynasty, ruled until 1365, when Kadı Burhaneddin usurped power, taking Kayseri in 1378. Burhaneddin retained control until his death in 1398, having extended his rule over much of central Anatolia in alliance with the Karamanid. Kayseri was then captured by the Ottomans under Beyazit I in 1397. After Beyazit was defeated by Tamerlane at Ankara in 1402 the Karamanid regained control of Kayseri. Then in 1419 the Mamluks took the city, giving it over to their vassals, the Dulgadır Türkmen. The Dülgadır retained control of Kayseri until 1466, when it was taken by the Ottomans under Mehmet II, becoming a permanent part of the Ottoman Empire.

The impressive and remarkably well-preserved ancient city walls of Kayseri were rebuilt by the Seljuks, a project begun in 1210 by Izzeddin Keykavus I and completed in 1226 by Alaeddin Keykubad I.

The two oldest Turkish monuments in Kayseri are in the centre of the market quarter. The most notable of these is the Ulu Cami, founded in 1135 by the Danışmendid. It is typical of the 'Great Mosques' built during the Seljuk era, in which the roof of the prayer hall is supported by a multiplicity of columns or piers. The hall here is divided into five aisles by four rows of thick piers supporting pointed arches, with the bay in front of the *mihrap* covered by a large dome on squinches and the central bay by a smaller dome on pendentives. The minaret, a thick cylindrical drum on a square base and octagonal plinth, rises from the middle of the west wall of the building.

Just to the south of the Ulu Cami is the Melek Gazi Medresesi, also dating from 1135. The *medrese* was founded by the Danışmendid emir Mehmet Melik Gazi, who began work on the Ulu Cami, and was completed by Mahmud ibn Yağıbasan.

Near the southern end of the market quarter is the Hatuniye Medrese, built in 1431–32 by the Dulgadır emir Nasureddin Mehmet Bey. The Hatuniye is designed in the traditional style of the Seljuk *medrese*, with an ornate entryway leading into an open courtyard flanked by arcades, within which there are five cells on either side that housed the students. At the far end is the *dershane*, or lecture-hall, a great vaulted *eyvan* flanked by two domed chambers which were used as classrooms. One unusual feature of the *medrese* is its façade, the right side of which is occupied by a fountain. Another is the use of ancient Ionic and Corinthian capitals in the colonnades.

There is another group of early Turkish monuments just to the east of the citadel and south of the Kayseri Archaeological Museum. Several of these are part of the Huant Hatun Külliyesi, which includes a mosque, a *medrese*, a *türbe* and a *hamam*, or public bath. The complex was founded in 1237–38 by Mahperi Hatun, the Greek wife of Alaeddin Keykubad I and mother of Giyaseddin Keyhüsrev I. The mosque has the typical Ulu Cami plan, with fifty piers supporting the flat roof, the central bay open, and a large dome over the bay in front of the *mihrap*. The massive buttresses at the corners of the mosque give it the appearance of a fortress. The *medrese*, which also is typically Seljuk in its plan, is attached to the south-east corner of the mosque, where the *türbe* of the foundress, an octagonal structure with a pyramidal dome, stands in the centre of a little open court. The *hamam* of the foundation stands off-axis in the angle of the 'L' formed by the mosque and the *medrese*. The medrese now houses the Kayseri Ethnological Museum.

Just to the east of the museum there are two Seljuk monuments: the one to the north is the Ali Cafer Kümbedi and the other is the Köşk Medrese.

The Ali Cafer Kümbedi is an octagonal structure set on a high square pedestal, covered from inside with a high hemispherical dome and with an outer pyramidal roof. A flight of steps on its south side leads to a low flat-roofed porch and vestibule that has now almost vanished. The *türbe* is dated to the mid-fourteenth century, and was probably the tomb of an Eretnid emir.

The Köşk Medrese is a very unusual structure. It looks like a miniature fortress, with its high outer walls of cut stone, above which one can see the tall eight-sided pyramidal roof of a Seljuk-style *türbe*. An inscription records that the *medrese* was founded in 1339 by Emir Eretna, founder of the Eretnid dynasty, who dedicated it to his wife Suli Paşa.

The entrance *eyvan* is flanked by two large vaulted chambers; from here one passes into an open court, with the octagonal *türbe* in the centre and fifteen cells for students opening off the surrounding portico.

About 100 metres to the south is the Saracettin Medrese. This was founded in 1240 by Lalalı Saracettin, who served as vizier under Giyaseddin Keyhüsrev II.

There are a pair of interesting tombs in the south-eastern part of the old city, one on either side of Talas Caddesi. The better preserved of the two tombs is Döner Kümbet, built in 1276 for the Seljuk princess Şah Cihan. This is a cylindrical structure of cut stone, its surface divided into twelve parts by blind arcading, surmounted by a conical roof resting on stalactite cornices. The façade is decorated with a remarkable number of figurative reliefs, including palm trees, a pair of winged leopards, a griffin and a two-headed eagle, the Seljuk symbol of royalty. The second tomb is known as Sırçali Kümbet. This was built in the mid-fourteenth century, when Kayseri was ruled by the Eretnid. It is a plain cylindrical structure of regular hewn stone; its conical outer roof has disappeared, revealing the bare stone dome inside.

North of Cumhuriyet Meydanı along Istasyon Caddesi is the Sahibiye Medrese, with a particularly splendid entrance portal. The *medrese* was founded in 1267–68 by Sahip Ata Fahrettin Ali, the great Seljuk vizier.

The third turning to the left off Istasyon Caddesi leads to Çifte Medrese, which has a stone Seljuk lion on the right side of the porch. This institution consists of two *medreses* built side by side and connected by a corridor, the larger one on the left built as a hospital and the other as a medical school. This is the earliest Islamic hospital and medical school in Anatolia. The complex was built in 1205–10, with the hospital founded by Giyaseddin Keyhüsrev I and the medical school by his sister Gever Nesibe. In the far right-hand corner of the medical school is the *türbe* of Keyhüsrev I. The *medrese* now houses a museum of medical history, particularly that of the early Turkish period in Anatolia.

About 250 metres to the north is the Hacı Kılıç Külliyesi. This consists of a combined mosque and *medrese*, founded in 1249 by Abul Kasım of Tus, an emir under Keykubad I. The ornate entryways of both the mosque and *medrese* are in the east façade of the building. The entrance to the mosque is on the right side, with the minaret rising to its right. The cells of the *medrese* open off three sides of a courtyard, the fourth side of which opens into the mosque. The mosque is divided into five aisles by four colonnades of piers, with a dome over the bay in front of the *mihrap*.

There is an ancient mosque known as Külük Cami in the south-western part of the old city. An inscription records a repair in 1210 by the princess Atsız Elti, daughter of the Danışmendid emir Mahmut bin Yağıbasan, and so it is possible that the mosque was built at a somewhat earlier date by her father. The mosque is noted for the particularly fine ceramic tiles that decorate its *mihrap*.

Other early Turkish monuments in the city are Hoca Hasan Medresesi (1202); Sultan Hamam (1205); Selçuka Hatun Türbesi (1205); Afguniye Medresesi (1238); Köşk Kümbet (1241); Adiliye Hatun Türbesi (1247–48); Haydar Bey Köşkü (1251); and Beş Parmak Türbesi (fourteenth century).

The last stage of our itinerary will take us north-westward to Ankara, stopping enroute at Hacıbektaş, which is approached by a turn-off to the left some 70 kilometres from Kayseri, and then at Kırşehir, another 22 kilometres along the main highway.

The town of Hacıbektaş was formerly known as Sulucakaraören. It takes its name from Hacı Bektaş Veli, founder of the Bektaşi order of dervishes, who is buried here in a *türbe* attached to the former *tekke* of his brotherhood. He was born in Horosan in 1208 and eventually settled in Sulucakaraören, where he died in 1280. Little definite is known about his life, though there are numerous fables. The order he founded ranked with the Mevlevi as one of the two most influential dervish brotherhoods in the Ottoman Empire, its members including the janissaries and most of the Ottoman sultans. The *tekke* includes a mosque, infirmary, refectory, dormitory, baths, fountains and several tombs, the grandest being that of Hacı Bektaş. His feast day is celebrated on 16 August with folk dancing and other cultural events, in which the depth of feeling exhibited by the multitude who visit the saint's tomb shows that the Bektaşi movement is still very much alive in Turkey, although officially banned along with all other dervish orders in the early years of the Turkish Republic.

Kırşehir took its present name in the twelfth century when it was captured by the Seljuks, under whom it became an important centre of the Ahi movement. This was a brotherhood established among the Muslim craft guilds of Anatolia by Şeyh Nasreddin Ahi Evran, an itinerant leather-worker and holy man who settled in Kırşehir in the thirteenth century.

The oldest Seljuk monument in Kırşehir is the Karakund Hamamı, built c. 1135–40, which may be the earliest extant Turkish bath in Anatolia. The oldest Seljuk mosque is in the medieval *kale*, itself probably of Byzantine foundation. This is Alaeddin Camii, built in 1246. The *medrese* of Muzaferetti Muhammad in the lower town is also dated 1246. The *türbe* of Melik Gazi, an octagonal structure covered with a conical dome, is dated 1250.

The other early Islamic monuments in Kırşehir date from the Ilkhanid and Eretnid periods. The oldest of these is the Caca Bey Medresesi, dated 1272–73. This was founded by Cabrail ibn Caca Bey, the Ilkhanid Mongol governor of Kırşehir. The dome of the *dershane* of the *medrese* was left open, apparently because it was originally used as an astronomical observatory. The *medrese* was later converted into a mosque, at which time the present minaret was added. The *türbe* of the founder is attached to the building to the left of the ornate entryway.

The *türbe* of Süleyman-i Türkmani, dated 1287, is an octagonal structure with a pyramidal brick roof. The founder was a student of Mevlana; he is reported to have founded a Mevlevi *tekke* in Kırşehir, but no trace of this remains.

The *tekke* and *türbe* of Şeyh Nasrettin Ahi Evran appear to have been founded in the late thirteenth century or early in the fourteenth. The complex originally included a *mescit* and living quarters for the dervishes, but these have now vanished. What remains is an L-shaped complex, with two *türbes* flanking a prayer room. One of the *türbes* contains the grave of Ahi Evran, while the other is the tomb of some of his disciples.

The *türbe* of Aşık Paşa is an Eretnid foundation dated 1322. Aşık Paşa was a noted philosopher and poet who chose to compose his works in Turkish rather than the classical Persian that had been the literary language of the Seljuk court.

Another monument in Kırşehir from the early Turkish period is Meydan Camii, built in 1368.

After seeing Kırşehir we drive on to Ankara, completing our long round of the Seljuk monuments in central Anatolia.

– 16 –

From Ankara to Erzurum

The modern name of Ankara is essentially the same as its ancient name, Ancyra, which some scholars believe to be of Phrygian origin, though it is a Greek word, meaning 'anchor'.

Ankara was taken by the Seljuks early in the twelfth century, after which it was held in turn by the Danışmendid, Seljuks, crusaders, Eretnid, Mongols and Ottomans. The Ottomans first captured Ankara in 1354 under Orhan Gazi. Tamerlane defeated Beyazit I in a great battle on the plain west of Ankara on 28 July 1402. Mehmet I, Beyazit's son and eventual successor regained control of Ankara a decade later and thenceforth the city remained part of the Ottoman Empire until 1923, when it became the capital of the new Turkish Republic.

The oldest part of Ankara is the quarter that clusters in and around the Kale, the great fortress that crowns the acropolis hill of the ancient city. The fortress dates from the medieval Byzantine era, with extensive reconstruction in the early Turkish period.

A short way inside the main gate of the Kale we come to the earliest surviving monument of the Seljuk era in Ankara. This is Alaeddin Camii, built in 1197, when Ankara was ruled by Sultan Muhuddin Mesut Şah, and restored in Ottoman times. The beautifully carved wooden *mimber* remains from the original mosque, and is a fine example of the Seljuk woodwork of that period. Its equally fine doorway is now on exhibit in the Ankara Ethnographical Museum. An inscription in the mosque, dated 1361–62, records the name of the 'Most Mighty Sultan Orhan', here referring to Orhan Gazi, who had captured Ankara some seven years before.

There is another mosque of the Seljuk era in the old quarter immediately below the Kale. This is Ahi Şerafettin Camii, built by a member of the Ahi brotherhood in 1289–90, during the reign of Giyaseddin Mesut I. This is the only Seljuk mosque in Ankara that retains its original form. It is a 'forest mosque', with twenty-four columns in four rows of six each, most of them topped by ancient marble Corinthian columns taken from an unidentified Roman building. Sixteen of the columns support the roof and eight the women's section. The superb *mimber* is one of the last brilliant examples of Seljuk carved stonework, while the *mihrap* is a fine work of stucco decoration with turquoise and manganese-violet ceramic inlays in the rococo style. In the façade of the mosque there are embedded a number of architectural fragments from ancient buildings.

Across the narrow street beside the mosque is the *türbe* of the founder, Ahi Şerafettin, who died *c.* 1292. This is the only extant example in Ankara of a *türbe* in the Seljuk style, with its characteristic octagonal drum and pyramidal dome. There are two stone statues of Seljuk lions embedded in the walls of the *türbe*; these are what caused Ahi Şerafettin Camii to be known also as Aslanhane Camii, the Mosque of the Lion-house. The beautifully carved wooden sarcophagus of Ahi Şerafettin is now in the Ankara Ethnographical Museum.

Farther along the same street is Ahi Elvan Camii, another ancient mosque built by a member of the Ahi brotherhood. The mosque was originally built towards the end of the fourteenth century; it assumed its present form in 1413, when Mehmet I took control of Ankara after becoming sole ruler of the Ottoman Empire. During the interregnum in the years 1402–13 Ankara had been governed and defended by the Ahi sect. Ahi Elvan Camii is typical of the so-called 'forest mosques' of the Beylik period, where the flat wooden ceiling is supported by a veritable grove of wooden columns, in this case twelve in three rows of four each.

Other monuments of the Seljuk and Beylik periods in Ankara are Isaklı Han (1248); Kızıl Bey Camii (1299); Ahi Yakup Camii (1316); Molla Büyük Mescidi (fourteenth century); Kesikbaş Türbesi (late fourteenth century); Karanlik Mescit (late fourteenth century); Ortmeli Mescidi (*c.* 1400); and Hacı Ivaz Mescidi (early fifteenth century).

The Ankara Ethnographical Museum has a superb collection of carved woodwork of the Seljuk and Beylik periods, including *mimbers*, doors and window shutters. It also has a rich collection of early Turkish folk arts, including costumes, women's headdresses, embroideries, hand-painted scarves, carpets, kilims, jewellery, metalwork, copper, bronze and ceramic kitchenware, china and glassware, weapons, household items and furniture. Among them are works from two monuments we have visited, namely the sarcophagus of Ahi Şerafettin from his mosque in Ankara, and the *mihrap* and *mimber* from the *külliye* of Taşkın Paşa in Ürgüp.

We now drive north-eastward from Ankara to Çankırı, the first stage of an itinerary that will take us all the way to Erzurum, in north-eastern Anatolia.

Çankırı retains in corrupted form its ancient name of Gangra. The ruined *kale* on the acropolis hill is Byzantine in foundation and was rebuilt in the early Turkish period. Within the ruins of the fortress is the *türbe* of the twelfth-century Danışmendid emir Karatekin, which has recently been rebuilt.

Other monuments in Çankırı from the early Turkish period are the *medrese* and *türbe* of Atabey Cemalettin Ferruk (1235), the *medrese* of Emulbey ibn Muhammed (1258), and the Taş Medrese and Mescit (1258).

We now drive north from Çankırı through the Ilgaz Mountains, going over the highest pass at 1,775 metres, and then downward towards the Black Sea coast before stopping at Kastamonu, the principal city of the region known in antiquity as Paphlagonia.

Like all old cities in Anatolia, Kastamonu clusters around its ruined hilltop *kale*, built originally in the medieval Byzantine era and reconstructed in the early Turkish period. The earliest Seljuk foundation in Kastamonu is the Ali bin Pervane Medresesi, founded in 1273 as a hospital (*darüşşifa*), and orphanage (*darüşşafaka*), along with a *mescit*, approached by a monumental stone portal in the Seljuk style. The oldest of the Beylik mosques is Atabey Gazi Camii, founded in 1373 by an emir of the Çobanoğlulları Türkmen tribe, who is buried in a semi-cylindrical *türbe* within the precincts. Elsewhere in the town there are at least thirty Turkish monuments of the Seljuk and Beylik eras, dating from the twelfth century through to the fifteenth.

The village of Kasabaköy is 12 kilometres north of Kastamonu on the Inebolu highway. On the outskirts of the village is Candaroğlu Mahmut Bey Camii, founded in 1363 by a Candarid emir. This is one of the most beautiful of the wooden Seljuk mosques in Anatolia. Four wooden columns with stalactite capitals support the beamed ceiling, while four other columns support the gallery over the entrance. The beams of the ceiling are finely carved and richly painted, as is all the other woodwork in the mosque.

We now drive north-eastward down to the Black Sea at the port of Sinop, the northernmost point on the Anatolian coast.

Sinop is the ancient Sinope, founded by Miletus in the seventh century BC, one of several Greek colonies in the region known in antiquity as the Pontus. It became part of the Greek Empire of Trebizond in 1204, but ten years later it was captured by the Seljuks under Sultan Izzeddin Keykavus. The city was recaptured by the Byzantines *c.* 1255, but a decade later it fell to the Seljuk emir Muineddin Süleyman, the famous *pervane*. Then in 1324 it came under the control of the Isfendiyarid emirs, who made it the capital of their *beylik*, holding it until Mehmet II conquered Paphlagonia and the Pontus in 1261.

The ancient walls of Sinop are very impressive, some three kilometres in length, standing to a height of 25–30 metres and with forty-three of the original sixty towers surviving at least in part.

One of the two principal Islamic monuments in Sinop is the Ulu Cami, founded in 1267–68 by Muineddin Süleyman, the *pervane*. The other is the Alaeddin Medresesi, another foundation of Muineddin Süleyman, erected in 1262. Within a chamber of the Alaeddin Medresesi there is a *türbe* with a stone sarcophagus bearing the following inscription: 'This is the tomb of Gazi Çelebi, son of Mesut.' Gazi Çelebi, who may be a great-grandson of the *pervane*, ruled Sinop as emir of the Isfendiyarid in the years 1298–1324, and may have been the last of the Seljuk royal line. He is probably also the Gazi Çelebi described by Ibn Battutah, who writes of his prowess in underwater warfare.

Other early Turkish monuments are Fatih Baba Mescidi (1353), Saray Camii (1374), Cezayirli Ali Paşa Camii and Seyyit Bilal Camii, the latter two being Seljuk mosques mentioned by Ibn Battutah in his visit to Sinop in 1332. There are also a number of Islamic tombs dating from the early Turkish period, most notably Sultan Hatun Türbesi, built for a sister of Murat I (r. 1359–81).

We now drive eastward along the Black Sea coast to Samsun, known in antiquity, founded as a Greek colony in the sixth century BC. The oldest Islamic monument is Pazar Camii, a mosque built by the Ilkhanid Mongols in the thirteenth century.

The next stage of our itinerary takes us inland to Amasya, Greek Amaseia, capital of the Pontic Kingdom in the Hellenistic period. After the Seljuk victory at Manzikert Amasya was taken by the Danışmendid, becoming the capital of their *beylik*. Amasya was then held in turn by the Seljuks, Mongols and Eretnid before being taken in 1391 by Beyazit I, after which it became an important provincial capital in the Ottoman Empire.

Amasya stands astride the Yeşilırmak, the river Iris of antiquity, which is crossed by six bridges within the city, the oldest of them, Çağlayan Köprüsü, built by the Danışmendid in 1122.

The two principal monuments of the early Turkish period in Amasya are Gökmedrese Camii and the Yıldız Hatun Medresesi, better known as the Timarhane, or Insane Asylum. Other more minor monuments of this era include a mosque and several tombs as well as Çağlayan Köprüsü and two other bridges across the Yeşilırmak.

Gökmedrese Camii is a Seljuk mosque that also served as a *medrese*, with a *türbe* attached to its left side and another, larger free-standing tomb in front of it. An inscription identifies the founder as the Emir Şerafettin Torumtay, a slave of Keykubad II who became governor of Amasya. The mosque and its attached *türbe* were built in 1266–67, while the free-standing tomb, where Torumtay was buried, was erected in 1278.

The Timarhane was founded in 1308–9 by Oljaytu, khan of the Ilkhanid Mongols, who dedicated it to his wife Yıldız Hatun. The building was laid out on the plan of a typical Seljuk *medrese*, with an arcaded courtyard and two *eyvans*, and with arched windows flanking the ornately carved entryway, framed by towers at its corners. The *medrese* was actually a *darüşşifa*, or hospital, with a section for mental patients. Like other hospitals in Anatolia at the time it was a medical school, a function it continued to perform until the nineteenth century.

The structure at the rear of the garden beside the Archaeological Museum is the *türbe* of Ruknuddin Mesut I (r. 1116–56). The *türbe* was erected in 1278 by the Ilkanid Mongols, so Mesut's remains must have been reinterred here. Exhibited in the museum are the mummified remains of six Ilkhanid nobles.

Two other tombs of the early Turkish period stand together along the main avenue. One is the Şadgeldi Türbesi, dated to 1381. The other is the *türbe* of the Danışmendid emir Halifet Gazi, traditionally dated to 1145–46. Halifet Gazi is buried in a splendid marble sarcophagus decorated with the heads of rams and gorgons, undoubtedly taken from a Roman tomb.

There is another Seljuk mosque in the old market quarter. This is Burmalı Minare Camii, 'the Mosque with the Spiral Minaret'. The mosque was founded in 1243 by two brothers who were members of the cabinet of Keyhüsrev II. These were the vizier Ferruh and the treasurer Yusuf, both of whom are buried in the octagonal *türbe* attached to the mosque.

We now drive eastward from Amasya on highway E80, following the Kelkit Çayı, a tributary of the Yeşilırmak, turning off to the left after 98 kilometres for Niksar.

Niksar, the ancient Neocaesarea, was taken from the Byzantines in 1073 by Gümüştekin Melik Gazi Danışmend, founder of the Danışmendid *beylik*. Niksar has a number of monuments dating from the early Turkish period, the most prominent being its hilltop *kale*, built by the Danışmendid on Byzantine foundations. Beside the road leading up to the fortress is the *türbe* of the Danışmendid emir Melik Ahmet Gazi, who died of an arrow wound in 1104 while fighting the Byzantines. Within the citadel are the ruins of the Yağıbasan Medresesi, founded in 1158. This is another Danışmendid foundation, the oldest dated *medrese* in Anatolia. The oldest Danışmendid monument in the lower town is the Ulu Cami; there is no dedicatory inscription, but tradition dates its founding to 1145. There are also two monuments of the Ilkhanid Mongol period. These are the fourteenth-century Çoreğibüyük Camii and the *türbe* of the emir Sentimuroğlu Nurettin, dated 1313.

We now head south-west from Niksar to Tokat, a drive of 45 kilometres that brings us back to the Yeşilırmak.

Tokat had much the same history in the early Turkish period as Kayseri and Sivas. It was held in turn by the Danışmendid, Byzantines, Seljuks, Mongols, Eretnid, Kadı Burhaneddin, Mongols again, Mamluks, Ottomans and Tamerlane, and finally the Ottomans again when it was taken by Mehmet I in 1415.

The ruined *kale* on the acropolis hill is Byzantine in foundation, rebuilt by the Danışmendid, Seljuks and Ottomans.

One of the oldest and most prominent Turkish monuments in Tokat is Hıdırlık Köprüsü, a five-arched Seljuk bridge built in 1247, still carrying traffic over the Yeşilırmak at the northern end of town.

The most famous and beautiful of Tokat's monuments is the Gök Medrese. The *medrese* was built soon after 1270 by the Seljuk emir Muineddin Süleyman, the famous *pervane*, who is buried there. The usual elaborately carved Seljuk entryway leads into an open courtyard, with a large *eyvan* at the far end and the other rooms arrayed in two floors opening out in ogive arcades, with slender columns below and sturdy piers above. Only a few patches remain of the beautiful turquoise Seljuk tiles that gave the *medrese* its name (*gök* means 'sky-blue'). The *medrese* now serves as a museum, with both archaeological and ethnographical collections.

Some 200 metres north of the Gök Medrese on the same side of the avenue we come to the *türbe* of Nurettin ibn Sentimur. The calligraphic inscription above the tomb identifies the deceased as a Mongol emir and gives the date of foundation as 1314.

Other monuments of the early Turkish period in Tokat in the Ebulkasım Türbesi (1223); Safer Paşa Türbesi (1251); Pervane Hamamı (1277); Ahmet Paşa Camii (1297); Idahund Hatun Türbesi (1287); Halef Gazi Türbesi (1291); Abdülmuhabib Zaviyesi (1318); Bulga Hatun Türbesi (fourteenth century); and Rüstem Çelebi Camii (early fifteenth century).

There are also a number of *hans* in the picturesque old market quarter dating from the early Turkish era. The shops that particularly catch the eye here are those of the copper merchants, whose wares are celebrated in an old Tokat folk song:

> From Tokat I bought copper,
> My beauty's eyes are blue.
> To these blue eyes,
> Let this pauper be sacrificed.

We now make a diversion that will takes us westward along the Yeşilırmak to Turhal, then south-west to Zile, and then back to Tokat via Pazar. En route from Tokat to Turhal we cross the Yeşilırmak on Karaltan Köprü, a Seljuk bridge that has been in use since the twelfth century.

Turhal stands astride the Yeşilırmak, its houses clustered around the ruins of an ancient *kale* that was originally a fortress of the Pontic kings. One of the early Turkish monuments in the town is the undated Şeyh Mustafa Camii, whose *külliye* also includes a dervish *tekke*. There are also two tombs of Muslim saints from the Ilkhanid Mongol period; these are the Mehmet Dede Türbesi (1312) and Ahi Mustafa Türbesi (1314), the latter holy man being the patron saint of saddle pack makers.

Zile is a picturesque old town on a tributary of the Yeşilırmak, dominated by a remarkably well-preserved ancient fortress on the acropolis hill above. The town preserves in only slightly corrupted form its ancient name of Zela. The plain north of Zela was the scene of two great battles between the Romans and the Pontic kings. The Pontic army were victorious in the first battle, in 67 BC, and then in the second one, twenty years later, they were defeated by Julius Caesar, who in his triumphal procession in Rome had his attendants display signs with the laconic legend 'Veni, vidi, vici!,' – 'I came, I saw, I conquered!'.

Zile has a large number of monuments from the early Turkish period, which began when the Danışmendid emir Melik Ahmet Gazi captured the town in 1073. The oldest is Kubbe Camii, founded by Melik Ahmet Gazi soon after he captured Zile. The building was originally a Byzantine church, whose dome has long since been replaced by a flat roof.

The principal mosque in Zile is the Ulu Cami. An inscription records that it was built in 1267, during the reign of Giyaseddin Keyhüsrev III, by the architect Mehmet Zalüli bin Ebu Ali. The mosque was repaired in the seventeenth century and rebuilt in 1909. It is preceded by a three-bay porch supported by four ancient marble columns. The entryway to the mosque is elaborately decorated in the Seljuk style, with the wooden door carved in geometric patterns and verses from the Kuran. The square prayer hall is surmounted by a dome carried on an octagonal drum.

At Pazar there is a Seljuk caravanserai with a particularly fine entrance porch. This is the Hatun Hanı, founded in 1238–39 by Mahperi Hatun, wife of Alaeddin Keykubad I and mother of Giyaseddin Keyhüsrev II, the grandest of five caravanserais she built along the road between Amasya and Sivas.

We now drive south from Tokat, passing four ruined caravanserais en route to Sivas, three of them Seljuk and the other Ottoman. The road goes over the Çamlıbel Pass at 1,645 metres before coming to Yıldızeli, then it turns eastward as it approaches the Kızılırmak, the river Halys of antiquity, which we follow into Sivas.

Sivas, the Greek Sebasteia, was taken by the Seljuks soon after their victory over the Byzantines at Manzikert in 1071. After the Seljuks were defeated by the crusaders at Dorylaeum in 1097 Sivas was occupied by the Danışmendid, who held it until 1178. The Seljuks then regained Sivas, and under Keykubad I it became the most important commercial centre in Anatolia. After the Seljuks were defeated by the Mongols in 1242 Sivas became part of the Ilkhanid Empire. In the years 1365–98 it was capital of the *beylik* established by Kadı Burhaneddin, which ended with its capture by Beyazit I in 1399. Then in 1400 it fell to Tamerlane, who sacked the city and slaughtered its inhabitants. Sivas never fully recovered from this catastrophe, and thenceforth it was reduced to the status of a backward provincial town throughout most of the Ottoman period.

The park on the south side of Cumhuriyet Meydanı, the main square of modern Sivas, is laid out on the site of one of the two citadels of ancient and medieval Sebasteia, the other being on Toprak Tepe, an eminence a few hundred metres to the south. Three Turkish monuments of the thirteenth century are grouped together in the park: the Muzaffer Bürücirde Medresesi, Keykavus Darüşşifasi and Çifte Minare Medrese.

The Muzaffer Bürücirde Medresesi was founded in 1271 by the Ikhanid emir Muzaffer, a Persian from the town of Bürücird near Hamadan. Two minarets flank the usual elaborately carved entryway. The *medrese* is a two-storeyed structure with four *eyvans*, the flat-roofed arcades of the portico supported by four columns on each side. The *mescit* of the *medrese* is to the right of the entrance *eyvan* and the square *türbe* of the founder is to the left. The *medrese* now houses the Ethnographic Museum, mostly a collection of Seljuk fabrics and stonework.

Just to the south of the *medrese* is the Keykavus Darüşşifasi, the largest (48 by 68 metres) medical institution ever constructed by the Seljuks. Founded in 1217 by Izzeddin Keykavus I, the hospital remained in use until 1916. Like the Çifte Medrese in Kayseri, the Keykavus Darüşşifasi was a combined hospital and medical school, with a special ward for mental patients. The sultan's deed of foundation records that music and hypnosis were among the methods used to treat those suffering from mental illness. The *medrese* is a four-*eyvan* structure with an arcaded courtyard surrounded by the cells of the students, each with a fireplace, with other chambers used for the *dershane*, refectory and *mescit*. The *türbe* of the founder, behind the *eyvan* to the right, is adorned with superb brick and faience decorations. The inscription on the *türbe* façade, done in raised white lettering on a blue ground, is the epitaph of the sultan, who died a slow death from tuberculosis: 'My wealth was of no use to me. My sultanate is finished. The day of my journey from this transitory world to the next was the fourth of Shawwai 617 [AD 1219].'

Directly across from the *darüşşifa* is the Çifte Minare Medrese, of which only the façade remains. The building takes its name from the pair of minarets that flank the monumental porch; these are in brick with decorative tile-work, an almost universal feature in early Turkish *medreses*. The *medrese* was built in 1271, the same year as that of Muzaffer Bürücirde; its founder, Şemsettin Cuwani, was also a vizier of the Ilkhanid Mongols. Excavations have revealed that it too was a four-*eyvan* structure on two storeys; the long façade is articulated by fluted half-towers and by niches in symmetrical rows on each side.

The Ulu Cami of Sivas is a few hundred metres to the south. An inscription records that the mosque was erected in 1197 by Kuthuddin Melik Şah, eldest of the eleven sons of Izzeddin Kılıç Arslan II, to whom he bequeathed his throne in 1188. The mosque is preceded by a shallow outer courtyard that once had a portico along its façade. The most remarkable feature of the mosque interior is the minaret, a cylindrical structure of brick arranged in basket-work patterns and resting on an octagonal base; the shaft is encircled by a Kufic inscription in turquoise tiles, with a second inscribed band just below the *şerefe*, or balcony. The interior is the usual pillared hall of the Seljuk Great Mosques, the flat earthen-covered timber roof supported by fifty piers in ten rows of five each, the *mihrap* framed by the two middle rows.

The most famous Seljuk monument in Sivas, the Gök Medrese, is a short distance from Ulu Cami at the eastern foot of Toprak Tepe, the ancient acropolis hill of Sebasteia. The Gök Medrese was also erected in 1271, one of three *medreses* built in Sivas that year – a measure of the importance of the city at the time. The founder was the renowned Seljuk vizier Sahip Ata Fahrettin Ali, who was known in his time as 'Abdül Khayrat', 'the Father of Good Works', because of the many splendid buildings he founded, including those we have already seen in Konya and Kayseri. Like the other two *medreses* built in Sivas in 1271, this is a two-storeyed structure with four *eyvans*. It has the most splendid façade in Seljuk architecture, with a monumental entrance porch flanked by two minarets, and a pair of buttress towers at the corners decorated with reliefs. There is a relief boss on either side of the doorway representing a dozen different animal heads, a theme probably derived from the old Turkish animal calendar. An eagle and other birds are carved among the foliate reliefs and stars on either side of the porch. To the left of the entrance there is a *çeşme*, or fountain, the first to be incorporated into a building in Turkish architecture.

Within the porch of the *medrese*, which was originally in two storeys, there is a domed *mescit* on the right side of the entrance and a *dershane* on the left. The *eyvans* and the vaulted rooms of the students are arrayed around the courtyard, which had an hexagonal pool at its centre. The *mescit* and the two side *eyvans* are decorated with mixed brick and tile mosaics that constitute one of the highest achievements of Seljuk art.

Not far away we come to the monument known as Güdük Minare. This is actually a *türbe*, which originally had a pyramidal roof on a high drum. The roof has now vanished, giving the drum the appearance of a truncated though very broad minaret – hence the name. The *türbe* was built in 1347 as the mausoleum of Şeyh Hasan Bey, son of Eretna, founder of the Eretnid dynasty.

We now drive south and then east to Divriği, the ancient Tephriki, a remote town on the Çaltı Çayı, a tributary of the Euphrates.

Divriği was captured by the Seljuks soon after their victory at Manzikert. The Seljuks allotted the town to the emir Mengücek, whose descendants, the Mengücekid, ruled Divriği until 1252. It was then held in turn by the Ilkhanid Mongols, the Eretnid, and Kadı Burhaneddin, finally becoming a permanent part of the Ottoman Empire in 1516 when it was captured by Selim I.

The ruined hilltop *kale* above the town is a work of the Mengücekid, as evident by inscriptions on two of the gateways, one dated 1236 and the other 1242. One of the towers in the citadel of the *kale* is decorated with a relief of two lions in the Seljuk style.

The walls of the citadel enclose a small mosque known as Kale Camii, the oldest monument in Divriği. An inscription records that the mosque was built in 1180–81 by the Mengücekid emir Şahanşah by the architect Hasan bin Firuz, from Maragha in Azerbaijan. The mosque is rectangular in plan, with three vaulted aisles separated by two rows of three piers each, and with domes on pendentives covering the four chambers on either side. The stone, brick and tile decoration of the mosque is very striking.

The Sitte Melik Kümbeti is on the eastern edge of the town south of the citadel hill. The tomb is an octagon covered by a pyramidal roof, all built in dressed yellowish stone. The entrance façade and porch are elaborately decorated in geometrical motifs, as is the cornice-like area, which is made up of three friezes. The frieze immediately below the roof is epigraphical, giving the date of foundation as 1195 and the name of the founder, the Mengücekid emir Süleyman bin Sayf al-Din Şahanşah. The tomb is named for Sitte Melik, probably a Türkmen princess, who was buried here in the fourteenth century.

The most notable monument in Divriği is the Ulu Cami, which includes a hospital as well as the mosque. The dedicatory inscription on the mosque records that it was erected in 1228–29 by the Mengücekid emir Ahmad Şah, grandson of Şahanşah. The inscription also mentions that Ahmad Şah was a vassal of Alaeddin Keykubad I. An inscription on the hospital, which adjoins the mosque to the south, records that it was erected by Malika Turan Malik, wife of Ahmad Şah and daughter of the Mengücekid emir Bahram Şah of Erzincan. Inscriptions on both the mosque and the hospital record that the architect was Khurramşah of Ahlat.

The exterior of the building is dominated by the high pyramidal roof covering the *mihrap* dome. The main entrance to the mosque is on the north, with other portals on the west and east sides, the latter giving entrance to the royal gallery. The hospital has a separate entrance on its west side. All four entryways are beautifully decorated with stone carvings. The interior of the mosque is rectangular in plan, the broad central aisle separated from the two narrower side aisles on either side by four rows of four octagonal pillars each. The bay in front of the *mihrap* is covered by a segmented dome, with the pyramidal roof rising above this on the exterior. The central bay is covered by an intricate ellipsoidal vault with an octagonal oculus at its crown. The stone *mihrap* is set in a very large niche containing large baroque palmettes in high relief surrounded by mouldings.

The hospital is designed in the traditional style of a Seljuk *medrese*, with the rooms surrounding a central courtyard, its central dome opening in a lantern. The domed chamber in the north-east corner of the *medrese* is a *türbe*, which also opens into the mosque.

We now make our way eastward towards Erzincan via Kemah, driving on secondary roads that follow the upper Euphrates.

Kemah is the ancient Kamacha, a town on the south bank of the Euphrates. All that remains of the old town is the ruined fortress of Kemah Kalesi on the acropolis hill, whose citadel encloses a Seljuk mosque known as Bey Camii. There are several early Turkish tombs in the town. The most notable is the *türbe* of the Mengücekid emir Melik Gazi, which dates to no later than 1219, when the Seljuks took Kemah.

We now continue on to Erzincan, a town on the north bank of the Euphrates. The town is situated on a fertile plain at an altitude of 1,200 metres, surrounded by mountain ranges with peaks rising to nearly 3,500 metres. Erzincan has been shaken by numerous earthquakes, the most catastrophic in recent times being that of 1939. Thus all the historic monuments in the town have been destroyed, though some have been rebuilt in recent years. The oldest extant monument is the *kale*, which is Byzantine in foundation, rebuilt by the Seljuks and restored by their successors. Two particularly interesting antiquities are displayed near the town centre: a pair of tombstones in the form of rams, dating from the fifteenth century, when Erzincan was held in turn by the Karakoyunlu and Akkoyunlu Türkmen.

The last stage of our itinerary will take us eastward along the Euphrates from Erzincan to Erzurum, with mountains rising to over 3,000 metres to both north and south. About 70 kilometres along we cross a tributary of the Euphrates on a twelfth-century bridge known as the Mamahatun Köprüsü. Then after another 13 kilometres we come to Tercan, a town on a lake created by a dam on the Euphrates, at an altitude of 1,475 metres.

There are two Seljuk monuments in Tercan: a caravanserai known as the Mama Hatun Hanı and the Mama Hatun Türbesi, both dated to the early thirteenth century. Mama Hatun, who was probably a Seljuk princess, was also the foundress of the bridge we saw earlier.

The caravanserai, which has the usual ornately carved entryway, is of a somewhat unusual design, in that it is grouped around a single courtyard rather than two courts. The design of the stables is also unusual, for the structure housing the camels is higher than the one for the horses and donkeys. The refectory is also uncommonly large.

The tomb also has a most unusual design, and is noted for the exceedingly fine workmanship of its decoration. It is built entirely of cut stone, the tomb itself contained within a cylindrical structure with a fluted conical roof, surrounded by a circular precinct wall. An inscription identifies the architect as Abu'l-Ni'ma bin Mufaddal of Ahlat.

We now continue on to Erzurum, completing an itinerary that has brought us into easternmost Anatolia.

– 17 –

Eastern Anatolia

O ur last itinerary will take us from Erzurum to Kayseri via Lake Van, Diyarbakır and Urfa, a great arc that will traverse the whole of eastern Turkey and its borderlands, where the Seljuk warriors and Türkmen tribes first penetrated into Anatolia nearly 1,000 years ago.

Erzurum, the largest city in north-eastern Turkey, is 1,950 metres above sea level, set in a great bowl ringed with mountains in which several peaks rise to over 3,000 metres.

The name of the city, which has been occupied since the sixth millennium BC, probably derives from Arz er Rum, or 'the Land of Rome', as the Seljuks called the dominions of the Byzantine Empire. The city, which had been held by the Armenians under the aegis of the Byzantines, was taken in 1089 by the Saltukid emir Ahmad, who made it the capital of his *beylik*. Erzurum was held by the Saltukid until 1202, when it was taken by the Seljuks and became part of the Sultanate of Rum. Subsequently it was held by the Ilkhanid Mongols, Eretnid and Karakoyunlu before falling to the Ottomans under Selim I in 1516.

The city is dominated by the usual *kale*, which was built by the Byzantine emperor Theodosius II (r. 408–50), and restored a number of times in the early Turkish period. The clock tower in the *kale* was part of the Byzantine fortifications, and early in the twelfth century it became the minaret of a mosque known as Kale Camii.

The oldest mosque in the town itself is the Ulu Cami, originally built by the Saltukid in 1179, but spoiled in a number of reconstructions. The mosque is a huge but simple building in cut stone without an outer courtyard. It is rectangular in plan, divided into seven aisles longitudinally and six laterally by rectangular piers, with a wooden cupola over the *mihrap* bay.

One of the most notable monuments in Erzurum is the Çifte Minare Medrese, which takes its name from the pair (in Turkish, *çifte*) of elaborately tiled minarets that frame its intricately carved entrance porch. The *medrese* has been dated to 1253, and its founder was probably the Mongol princess Hüdavend Padişah Hatun, wife of the Ilkanid khan Keyhato. Her *türbe* is behind the main *eyvan* on the longitudinal axis of the building.

About 150 metres behind the *medrese* there is a group of three tombs known as Üç Kümbet. The largest and most interesting of these is the Emir Saltuk Türbesi. Its lower part is in the form of an octagon, each side of which terminates in a triangular lunette, while the upper section is a cylinder topped by a low conical roof somewhat resembling a dome. The inward-drawn drum area has an interesting variety of decorative elements. Tradition identifies the founder as one of the Saltukid emirs, and it is thought that the *türbe* was built in the mid-twelfth century. The other two tombs probably date from the late twelfth or early thirteenth century.

Another notable monument is the Yakutiye Medrese, built in 1310 by Kwaca Yakut, emir of Erzurum and Bayburt under the Ilkanid khan Ölceytü. The emir dedicated the *medrese* to Oljaytu and his wife Bulgan Hatun, while the conical-topped *türbe* at the rear was built as his own tomb. The *medrese* is distinguished by its unusual façade, with its superbly carved porch in the centre, flanked by curtain walls ending in towers at the corners. The sides of the doorway are decorated with a striking relief in which an eagle stands astride the top of a date palm, with symmetrical confronted lions below. Originally there were twin minarets rising from the towers, but the left one has vanished and the one on the right is standing only as high as the first balcony, its shaft revetted in glazed bricks with geometric and vegetal patterns. The central courtyard is covered by two vaults on four piers and an open transverse vault with an oculus. The student cells flank small *eyvans* on either side of the courtyard, the one on the right serving as a *mescit*. The great *eyvan* opens off the rear of the courtyard, with the *türbe* at its rear, entered from a small chamber annexed to the room on the left.

Other early Turkish monuments in Erzurum include three dated to the twelfth century – Gümüşlü Kümbet, Karanlık Kümbet and Emir Saltuk Türbesi – as well as Gümüşlü Kümbet (1308-9), Karanlık Kümbet

(1308–9), Muradiye Medrese (1312), Ahmediye Medrese (1314), and Cimcime Hatun Türbesi (early fourteenth century).

We now drive eastward from Erzurum on highway E80, which at Horosan turns south-eastward towards Ağrı, going over the Şaçdağı Pass at 2,210 metres. Then at Ağrı we turn south for Patnos, where we turn south-west to approach Malazgirt.

Malazgirt is the Greek Manzikert, which gave its name to the historic battle fought on the plain to its south on 26 August 1071, when the Seljuks under Sultan Alp Arslan defeated the Byzantine forces led by Emperor Romanus IV Diogenes, opening up all of Anatolia to the Turks. An enormous monument commemorates the Seljuk victory, re-enacted every year on the anniversary of the battle, which was actually fought somewhere along the road between Malazgirt and Ahlat, on the northern shore of Lake Van, 54 kilometres to the south.

We now drive south to the lake, which at first sight is just as the traveller H. F. B. Lynch described it a century ago, 'glittering in indigo and streaming with sunshine'. Van is by far the largest lake in Turkey, at 3,764 square kilometres about six times the area of Lake Geneva, its altitude 1,646 metres above sea level. The lake and its surroundings are surpassingly beautiful, an azure blue inland sea in the midst of a vast plain ringed round with the lordly mountains of eastern Anatolia. The highest of the neighbouring mountains is Süphan Dağı, which looms over the north-eastern shore of the lake, its peak 4,058 metres above sea level – the second highest in Turkey after Mount Ararat (5,137 metres), some 160 kilometres farther to the north-east as the eagle flies. As Lynch wrote of Süphan, referring to it as Sipan: 'Nature alone has made the most of exceptional opportunities; and Sipan with this plain on one flank and the lake of Van on the other, is worthy to rank among the most beautiful objects in the natural world.'

Ahlat, known in Greek as Chliat, is renowned for its ancient Islamic cemetery, in which a dozen tombs survive from the early Turkish period. The tombs are all in the Seljuk style, cylindrical structures in two storeys, with the burial crypt below and a cenotaph above, the interior dome capped with an outer cone or pyramid.

The largest and most splendid of the tombs is Ulu Kümbet, erected in 1273. This is a cylindrical structure nearly seven metres in diameter on a square base with cut-away corners, surmounted by a conical-capped dome resting on stalactite cornices. There is a door in one wall and windows on the other three sides, with round-arched niches between them.

Two other fine mausolea of the same period, the Çifte (Twin) Türbe, are smaller versions of the Ulu Kümbet, built in 1279 and 1281 for relatives of a Seljuk emir. The *türbe* on the east retains traces of the paintings that decorated the crypt; what remains are floral designs, but when Albert Gabriel examined the tomb in late 1930 he saw representations of a pair of confronted peacocks over the door.

The Erzun Harun Kümbeti is a handsome tomb built for a Karakoyunlu princess in 1396. Another tomb of a rather different type is the Bayındır Türbesi, built for an emir of the Karakoyunlu. Here the cylindrical body of the *türbe* opens on the south through a decorative portico of rather heavy but attractive columns.

Aside from the tombs, the cemetery in Ahlat is noted for its beautiful Seljuk tombstones, many hundreds of them, superbly carved with calligraphic and floral designs, altogether making this the most remarkable burial ground in eastern Anatolia.

We now drive eastward along the north shore of Lake Van to the town of Erciş, three kilometres from the northern end of the lake. During the medieval era the town was known as Arjesh, which Marco Polo refers to as one of the three great cities in Armenia. On the outskirts of the town there is a handsome Seljuk *türbe* known as Kadın Hatun Paşa Kümbeti, dated 1458, a dodecagonal structure with a twelve-sided pyramidal roof.

We now drive around the lake to its south-eastern corner, where we see the ancient fortified acropolis rock known as Van Kalesi looming like a gigantic sandcastle above the modern town on the plain below.

The old town of Van was utterly destroyed at the end of World War II, and afterwards a completely new city was built some five kilometres south of Van Kalesi. Van has been identified as ancient Tuspa, capital of the Kingdom of Urartu, founded *c.* 833 BC. The Urartians were succeeded by the Armenians, who in the ninth century AD established a kingdom with its capital at Van. The last Armenian king of Van ceded his kingdom to the Byzantines in 1021, just half a century before the Seljuk victory at Manzikert.

From the south side of the acropolis rock we look down on the ghost city of old Van. The only structures that remain are two restored mosques, two minarets of mosques that have been destroyed, and two tombs. The oldest of these monuments is the one directly below the south side of the acropolis rock, where we see the fragmentary remains of the Ulu Cami. All that remains are the lower shaft of the minaret and parts of the lower walls, but the plan and decoration of the mosque are known from excavations carried out by Turkish and German archaeologists. Aslanapa dates Ulu Cami to the first sultanate of the Karakoyunlu ruler Kara Yusuf, 1389–1400.

The Archaeological Museum has antiquities ranging in time from the Urartian period up to the end of the Ottoman era. In the garden there are some fascinating Akkoyunlu and Karakoyunlu tombstones of the fourteenth and fifteenth centuries in the form of sheep, horses and bulls, other examples of which have been found at sites ranging from central Anatolia to Turkestan.

We now drive on from Van around the southern shore of the lake, pausing 37 kilometres along at the village of Gevaş.

Just beside the road we see a beautiful Seljuk mausoleum in an old Turkish cemetery. This is the Halime Hatun Kümbeti, dated by an inscription to 1358. The tomb is dodecagonal in form with a pyramidal roof and square base, the corners of which are cut into triangular planes to make the transition. The *türbe* was built for Halime Hatun, who was probably a Karakoyunlu princess, the wife or daughter of Abdül Melik Izzeddin, the Türkmen emir who is mentioned with her in the dedicatory inscription.

About one kilometre beyond Gevaş we come to Gevaş Iskelesi. This is the landing stage for a boat that goes out to the isle of Akthamar and its famous Armenian church of the Holy Apostles, built in 915–21.

We now drive on to the town of Tatvan at the south-western end of Lake Van. There we head south-west on highway E99, which after 22 kilometres brings us to Bitlis.

Bitlis, the ancient Balaleon, is a very distinctive town whose houses, mosques and medieval *kale* are all made of black basaltic stone, spread out picturesquely along the deep valleys of four streams that here converge to form the Bitlis Çayı, a tributary of the Tigris (in Turkish, Dicle Nehri). Aside from the *kale*, the principal monument in Bitlis is Ulu Camii, one of the oldest of the Seljuk Great Mosques of Anatolia. Its date of foundation is unknown, but an inscription records that it was restored in 1150. The prayer room is covered by three transverse vaults supported internally by two rows of four piers each, while the *mihrap* niche is covered by a dome with a conical roof. The minaret is a later addition, dated 1492–93.

Continuing along highway E99, some 53 kilometres farther along we take a detour to the left on a road signposted for Siirt, a drive of 40 kilometres that takes us along the Bitlis Çayı to its confluence with the Tigris.

The principal monument of Siirt is the Ulu Cami, another of the very early Seljuk Great Mosques of Anatolia. An inscription records a restoration in 1129 by Mughit-al-Din Mahmud II, sultan of the Great Seljuks in the years 1118–31. The most distinctive feature of the mosque is its leaning minaret, which has become the symbol of Siirt. The minaret is adorned with turquoise tiles set in a geometric pattern, one of the earliest examples of this type of decoration in the Islamic architecture of Anatolia.

We return to the E99 for another 55 kilometres, at which point the highway turns south for Batman, a town on the Batman Çayı, another tributary of the Tigris. Then at Batman we take a road that leads southeast to Hasankeyf, a village on the north bank of the Tigris, which is there spanned by a modern bridge.

The village takes is name from the medieval Muslim town of Hisn Kayfa, whose extensive ruins can be seen atop the cliff on the north bank of the Tigris. The remains of the medieval town, all in ruins, include the Byzantine citadel, a palace of the Artukid *beylik*, three mosques of the early Turkish period, the tiled *türbe* of Hasankeyf Zeynal Bey, and four arches of an ancient bridge across the Tigris, restored in 1116 by the Artukid emir Fakhr al-Din Kara Arslan. Early travellers remarked that this was the grandest bridge in the whole of Anatolia, but now it is about to be covered over by the waters of a dam being built on the Tigris.

We retrace our route back to the point where we turned south for Batman, and now we turn left on the highway for Diyarbakır, crossing the Batman Çayı on a modern bridge. As we do so we see downstream to our left the beautiful Malabad Köprüsü, a hogbacked bridge built in 1146–47 by Husam al-Din Temur Taş, who reigned as the Artukid emir in Mayyafarikin in the years 1122–52. It is a single span 35 metres in length, the longest ancient bridge in Anatolia, and after a recent restoration it is once again in use.

About 20 kilometres beyond the bridge we come to Silvan, the medieval Mayyafarikin. The town was taken from the Byzantines in 1121 by the Artukid, becoming capital of one part of their *beylik*, others being centred in Diyarbakır and Mardin. The principal monument of the medieval Muslim town is the very grand Ulu Cami, built in 1152–57 by Necmettin Alpı, emir of the Mayyafarikin branch of the Artukid in the years 1152–76. We see here the earliest example in Anatolia of the plan that evolved in the mosques of the Great Seljuks in Iran, with the conical-topped *mihrap* dome, 3.5 metres in diameter, dominating the building, while the side aisles of the prayer room are each covered by a wooden roof supported internally by piers.

The next stage of our journey takes us from Silvan to Diyarbakır, a drive of 86 kilometres. About 20 kilometres before reaching the city we cross the Ambar Çayı, still another tributary of the Tigris, where there is a Seljuk bridge with an inscription recording a restoration in 1223. Then as we approach Diyarbakır we see its great ring of basalt walls and towers looming above the Tigris, which we cross as we enter the city.

Diyarbakır, the Roman Amida, is one of the oldest cities in south-east Anatolia, fought over by every conqueror who ever passed this way. Amida fell to the Arabs in 638 and was allotted to the Beni Bakr clan, after whom it was called Diyarbakır, 'the Realm of the Bakr'. Thenceforth the city remained in Muslim hands except for a brief period after it was recaptured in 974 by the Byzantine emperor John I Tzimisces, held in turn by the Arabs, Seljuks, Marwanid Kurds, Artukid, Mongols, Tamerlane, Akkoyunlu, Karakoyunlu, Persians and then finally the Ottomans, falling to Selim I in 1515. Today the city is predominately Kurdish.

The city walls of Diyarbakır are the oldest and most impressive fortifications of any city in Anatolia, standing more or less intact for almost their entire length of 5.5 kilometres. The original walls date back to the late Roman era, but after the city was captured by the Seljuk sultan Melikşah (r. 1107–16) they were completely rebuilt. The walls were restored in 1208 by the Artukid emir Malik al-Salih Mahmud.

The citadel, known as İç Kale, takes up the north-eastern corner of the old city within the Roman walls. The mosque within the citadel, Kale Camii, was used by the Turkish garrison; an inscription records that it was built in 1160 by the Artukid emir Abül Kasım Ali.

Excavations have revealed the foundations of an Artukid palace within the citadel, dating from the first half of the thirteenth century. One of the Artukid emirs who would have lived in this palace was Nasr al-Din, patron of the great Muslim scientist al-Jazzari, whose *Book of Knowledge of Ingenious Geometrical Devices*, written at Diyarbakır in the thirteenth century, became the definitive text on mechanics and automata (self-moving devices) in the Islamic world; one of his inventions, the conical valve, was mentioned by Leonardo da Vinci.

Diyarbakır's Ulu Cami is the oldest of the Seljuk Great Mosques in Anatolia, built by Melikşah in 1092, fifteen years before he succeeded his brother Kılıç Arslan as sultan. The precincts are entered through a great round-arched portal in the outer wall of the mosque courtyard. Above the arch of the entryway there are a pair of reliefs, each showing a lion attacking a bull. After passing through the gateway and the eastern arcade we enter a vast rectangular courtyard with two pyramidal-capped columnar *şadırvans*, one rectangular and the other hexagonal. The south side of the courtyard is formed by the façade of the prayer hall, its high central bay rather resembling that of a Gothic cathedral, particularly with its square campanile-like minaret. The other sides of the courtyard are bounded by porticoes. The east and west wings of the courtyard are formed by two-tiered arcades of engaged columns with Corinthian capitals, apparently taken from a Roman theatre. A frieze with a floriated inscription in Kufic characters extends along the length of the two levels of the galleries on both wings.

The prayer hall of the mosque consists of a high central bay with the *mihrap* in an apse in the south wall opposite the door. The *mihrap* bay is flanked east and west by three transverse bays supported internally by two rows of six pillars each, many of them and their capitals reused from an ancient edifice. The Kufic inscription on the prayer hall records its foundation by Sultan Melikşah.

At the eastern end of the north side of the courtyard an arcade of ancient columns opens into the Mesudiye Medrese. The *medrese* was begun by the Artukid emir Qutb al-Din Sökmen II (r. 1185–1201) and was completed by his successor, Nasr al-Din Mawdud (r. 1201–22).

Close by the Ulu Cami is the Zinciriye Medrese, another foundation of Sökmen II, founded in 1198. Aslanapa notes that this is the earliest of a group of *eyvan medreses* that have survived from the Seljuk period.

The next stage of our journey will take us south-east from Diyarbakır to Mardin, a drive of 91 kilometres. We leave Diyarbakır through the Mardin Gate, and two kilometres outside the city we see on our left an ancient bridge of ten arches spanning the Tigris. An inscription records that the bridge was built by the Marwanid in 1065. This may have been a reconstruction, since a Byzantine chronicle records that a bridge was built across the Tigris here in 512 by Emperor Anastasius I.

Mardin stands on the last line of hills leading down to the Syrian border, just 20 kilometres to the south, looking more like an Arab than a Turkish town. The town is spread out along the south slope of an acropolis hill overlooking the arid plain of northern Syria, its white houses and mosques extending some three kilometres in the level east–west direction and only about 500 metres north–south on the steep slope of the hill. The houses are all built of stone, with numerous arches and arcades, and they perch upon one another tier on tier, forming a maze penetrated by a labyrinth of narrow streets that turn into flights of steps as they go upward. Here one hears less Turkish than Arabic, Kurdish and Syriac, the language spoken by the Christians of south-eastern Anatolia, for whom Mardin is their centre.

Mardin has Islamic monuments ranging in date through the whole of the early Turkish period. The earliest dated mosque is Necmettin Camii. This was founded in 1122 by Necmettin Ilgazi I, founder of the Mardin and Mayyafarikin branches of the Artukid, who is buried there.

The Ulu Cami was built in 1176 by the Artukid emir Melik Kutbettin Ilgazi. The founder and the date of construction are recorded in an inscription on the richly decorated minaret that rises over the ornate entryway. One distinctive feature is the fluted dome over the *mihrap*, resting on six piers.

Isa Bey Medresesi was founded in 1385 by the Artukid emir Majd al-Din Isa al-Zahir. The *külliye* includes the two-storeyed *medrese*, which is built around its two courtyards, a Kuran school, a mosque, the *türbe* of the founder, and other elements. The mosque and *türbe* are covered by ribbed domes on either side of the façade, with the splendid entryway to the complex on on the right. The Mardin Museum is now housed in the Kuran school of the *medrese*.

The Kasımiye Medresesi complex was begun late in the Artukid period and completed in 1487 by the Akkoyunlu emir Kasım Padişah (Sultan). The medrese is in two storeys around an interior courtyard, with a cascade fountain under an *eyvan* connected by water channels to a central pool. The ribbed domes of a pair of tombs rise from either side of the façade. Adjoining the *medrese* on the left is the mosque of the *külliye*, a rectangular structure with a large ribbed dome. The ornate entryway is in the façade between the mosque and the *medrese*.

Other monuments of the Seljuk and Beylik periods include the Husamiye Cami (1123), Sıtrıziye Cami (1177), Nizamettin Begaş Camii (1186), Süleyman Paşa Camii (1195), Şehidiye Camii (1214), Hatuniye Medresesi (1257), Sahidiye Medresesi (1239–60), Muzefferiye Camii (1264), Kale Camii (1269), Şeyh Çabuk Camii (1337), Savur Kapı Camii (1364), Melik Mahmut Camii (1367), Latifiye Camii (1371), Küçük Sultan Hamsa Mescidi (1443), Sultan Hamza Türbesi (1444), Tekiye Cami (1445) and Cihangir Camii (1468).

The Firdeus Köşkü is the only surviving part of an Artukid palace, probably built by the emir Shams al-Din (1312–64). The oldest commercial building in Mardin is a *han* that was almost certainly erected by the Akkoyunlu emir Kasım in the years 1497–1514. There are also a number of early Turkish baths, the oldest of which is the Emir Necmettin Hamamı, dated 1112. Other early Islamic monuments include at least ten fountains, the oldest of which date back to the Artukid and Akkoyunlu periods.

We now head south for 11 kilometres to Kızıltepe, where we turn westward on to highway E90, which we then follow westward all the way to Urfa, a drive of 165 kilometres.

Urfa is a very Arab-looking city on the upper end of the Harran plain, which at its south merges imperceptibly into the great Mesopotamian desert. (The city's official name is Şanlı Urfa, or Illustrious Urfa, because of its heroic resistance to French occupation after World War I.)

The origins of Urfa go back to the Bronze Age, and it has been identified as the city of Urshe mentioned in Sumerian, Akkadian and Hittite texts. It has also been identified as the Biblical Ur of the Chaldees. It was refounded early in the fourth century BC by Seleucus I, one of Alexander's successors, who called it Edessa, after the city of that name in his native Macedonia. The city was taken by the knights of the First Crusade in 1098 and became capital of the County of Edessa, which lasted until it was captured in 1144 by Imad al-Din Zengi, the Seljuk governor of Mosul and founder of the Zengid dynasty. Two years later, after the crusaders had briefly regained Edessa, Zengi's son and successor, Nur al-Din Zengi, recaptured the city and slaughtered all the male Christians, selling the women and children into slavery. This led Pope Eugenius III to proclaim the Second Crusade, but Edessa remained in Muslim hands, and as Urfa it was held in turn by Saladin, the Ayyubids, Seljuks, Mongols, Mamluks and finally the Ottomans, falling to Murat IV in 1637.

The most prominent of the city's monuments is Urfa Kalesi, the medieval fortress on the acropolis hill in the south-western corner of the old town. The fortress dates from the period of the crusader County of Edessa, although it was undoubtedly rebuilt and repaired by its subsequent Muslim conquerors.

The most famous site in Urfa is at the foot of the acropolis hill, a complex of monuments surrounding a pool known as Balıklı Gölü, 'the Fishy Lake', from the sacred carp that swim there. It is known in English as the 'Pool of Abraham', from a Muslim legend that Abraham camped here beside a sacred spring while on his way to the Promised Land. The triple-domed mosque on the northern side of the pool is Ridvaniye Cami, built in 1716 by Ahmet Ridvan Paşa, the Ottoman governor of Urfa. The smaller mosque at the north-western end of the pool is Abdurrahman Camii. This is the *mescit* of a Seljuk foundation, the Halil ur-Rahman Medresesi, founded in 1211–12 and subsequently restored several times.

The principal monument in the town centre is the Ulu Cami, whose campanile-like octagonal minaret is one of Urfa's landmarks. The mosque is dated to the third quarter of the twelfth century and was probably founded by Nur al-Din Zengi, since it closely resembles the Ulu Cami of Aleppo that he built at that time. On the eastern side of the mosque precincts there is a *medrese* built in 1192 by Melik Selahattin Yusuf.

Hasan Padişah Camii is one of the last monuments of the Beylik period to be erected in Anatolia, built by Sheikh Yakup (r. 1479–90), the last emir of the Akkoyunlu dynasty. The mosque was dedicated to the memory of Hasan's father, Uzun Hasan, sultan of the Akkoyunlu at the height of their power, the last of the *beyliks* to fall to the Ottomans.

We now make an excursion south of Urfa to Harran, which takes us to within about 15 kilometres of the Syrian border and the edge of the great Mesopotamian plain.

Harran is first mentioned in a Syrian tablet dated *c.* 2000 BC, which records the signing of a peace treaty here in the temple of the moon good Sin. It is also mentioned in connection with the story of Abraham's journey to the Promised Land told in *Genesis* 12,5: 'So Abram took Sarai his wife, and Lot his brother's son, and all their substance they had gathered, and the souls they had gotten in Harran; and they went forward into the land of Canaan; and into the land of Canaan they came.'

Harran is now a village of mud-brick houses, each of them surmounted by several conical domes that give them the appearance of giant beehives. The villagers all speak Arabic as a first language, and up until a generation ago their way of life was a semi-nomadic existence that had not changed in its essentials since the time of Abraham, but now there are television antennae protruding from the conical domes of their houses.

Most of the ancient walls of Harran have disappeared except for a few fragmentary ruins, including those of the principal gateways. The best preserved of the entryways is the Aleppo Gate; this bears an inscription recording the name of Saladin and the date 1192, the year before the great Kurdish warrior's death.

The largest monument in Harran is Qal'at, a ruined fortress at the south-eastern angle of the defence walls. Another prominent landmark is the square minaret of the ruined Ulu Cami, just north of the mound at the centre of the ancient city. The original mosque on this site was Cami al-Firdaeus, founded by Marwan II (r. 744–50), the last Umayyad caliph, who towards the end of his life made Harran the capital of his caliphate. The mosque was enlarged in 830 and rebuilt by Saladin in 1171–84.

We now return to Urfa, from where we set out on the last stages of our itinerary, which will bring us back to Kayseri via Malatya and Harput, through a region seldom visited by foreign travellers.

The present Malatya is a new city, founded in the mid-nineteenth century after the old town had been destroyed in 1838 by the Egyptian army of Ibrahim Paşa. The old town, known as Battalgazi, is 12 kilometres to the north.

Battalgazi is the Roman Melitene, which came to be known as Malatya after its capture by the Seljuks soon after their victory at Manzikert. The village is surrounded by the ruins of the Byzantine defence walls of ancient Melitene, one Roman mile in circumference. The principal monument remaining within the walls is the Seljuk Ulu Cami, built in 1224 by Sultan Alaeddin Keykubad I. The mosque is now largely in ruins, though still very impressive.

Harput is six kilometres north of Elazığ. Elazığ is a new city created in the mid-nineteenth century, when the Ottoman authorities decided that its site was more suitable than that of the old town of Harput, whose inhabitants were for the most part resettled here.

Harput, which fell to the Seljuks in 1090, and was then occupied by the Artukid, is dominated by the ruins of its medieval *kale*. The oldest monument in the lower town is the Ulu Cami, built by the Artukid in 1156–57. The finely carved wooden *mimber* of the Ulu Cami is now in Sara Hatun Camii, a fourteenth-century Beylik mosque rebuilt in the Ottoman period. Another notable early mosque in Harput is the Alaca Mescid, dated 1279, which is noted for its tile decoration, particularly in its *mihrap*.

There are a number of other monuments in Harput dating from the early Turkish period, the oldest dated ones being Balak Gazi Mescidi and Türbesi (1112) and Ahi Mustafa Mescidi (1185). There are also three undated monuments from the Artukid period: Araba Baba Mescidi and Türbesi, Esediye Cami, and Mansur Baba Türbesi.

The last stage of our itinerary takes us back to Malatya and then eastward across the mountains towards Kayseri, going over two passes 1,800 metres high and a third at 1,900 metres.

About 109 kilometres west of Kayseri we turn north on a road signposted for Şarkışla, a drive of 83 kilometres.

Şarkışla, the ancient Malandar, is renowned as the birthplace and lifelong home of Aşık Veysel, the most famous folk poet of modern Turkey, who is commemorated here in a small museum that contains memorabilia of his life as well as recordings of his songs. Veysel was born here of a poor peasant family in 1894 and lost his sight in early childhood. Early in his youth he learned to play the saz, the stringed instrument used by all folk musicians in Anatolia. Soon he began to compose the folk songs that make up the repertoire of the Turkish *aşık*, or bard (the word actually means 'lover'), a tradition that goes back to the wandering Turkish minstrels of Seljuk Anatolia. The songs of Aşık Veysel were about the world of the humble Anatolian peasants among whom he lived and worked, sharing their unending labours, their sorrows and their occasional joys. And, when in his latter years he sang of the first nightingale in April, his cracked and wavering old voice evoked that ache of mixed joy and sadness that the song of the nightingale itself brings on, particularly in the troubling beauty of an Anatolian spring. Aşık Veysel died in Şarkışla in the spring of 1971, and he was buried in the same field where his mother had given birth to him seventy-seven years earlier. His most famous song is 'Kara Toprak' 'Black Earth', in which he sings of the Anatolian soil that nourished him through all his days, and the refrain is his epitaph: 'My faithful sweetheart is the black earth; for though I wounded her with my hoe and shovel, she smiled and gave me red roses; my only true love is the black earth.'

At Şarkışla we turn left to head back to the south-west on the highway to Kayseri. After passing the town of Gemerek we go over the Beştepeler Pass at 1,359 metres, at the boundary between the provinces of Sivas and Kayseri.

About 28 kilometres farther along we come to the village of Sultanhanı. The village is named for the Seljuk caravanserai we see by the side of the road. An inscription says that the *han* was built by Alaeddin Keykubad I during the years 1232–36. The caravanserai repeats on a somewhat smaller scale the same plan that was used in the Sultan Hanı that Alaeddin Keykubad built on the Konya–Aksaray road, which we saw on an earlier itinerary. A short way farther along we make a diversion to the right to Bünyan. The only notable monument in Bünyan is Seljuk Ulu Camii. According to its dedicatory inscription, the mosque was built in 1256 for the emir al-Umara by the architect Kaluyan bin Karabuda. Oktay Aslanapa remarks on 'the heads of animals such as lions and gryphons set amongst scrolls in the decoration of the porch'. The mosque is almost square in plan, with the minaret rising from the north-east corner of the building. The prayer hall is divided into three equal north–south aisles by four pillars on the corners of a square, with the *mihrap* in a niche in the centre of the south wall.

Some 19 kilometres south of Bünyan we turn off to the right on a secondary road signposted for Elbaşı, four kilometres beyond which we come to the Seljuk caravanserai known as Karatay Hanı.

The caravanserai was completed in 1241 by the famous Seljuk vizier Celaleddin Karatay; after being in ruins for many years it was restored in 1964. Like most of the Seljuk caravanserais, it seems a miniature fortress, with its walls and corners studded with tower-like buttresses. The high porch, which projects outward 2.5 metres from the façade, framed by fluted and knotted pilasters at the corners, is said by Aslanapa to be 'the most monumental of all Seljuk architectural creations'. He also remarks that it 'has a wealth of figural decoration and might well be described as an epitome of Seljuk architecture'.

Returning to the main highway, we now continue towards Kayseri, passing a ruined Seljuk caravanserai known as Han Cami.

Four kilometres east of Kayseri we come to a partially ruined Seljuk *türbe* known as Çifte Kümbeti. This is an octagonal structure on a rectangular plinth, its conical outer roof of brick having collapsed to reveal its inner stone dome. The dedicatory inscription records that the *türbe* was built in 1247 by the princess Melike Adilye as the last resting-place of her mother, Melik al-Adil Abu Bakr ibn Eyub, wife of Sultan Alaeddin Keykubad I. There was a second *türbe* close by that has now disappeared, but the single surviving tomb is still called 'Çifte', or 'Double'.

During the last part of our journey we have been within sight of the lordly peak of Mount Erciyes, which since time immemorial has been a landmark for weary travellers approaching Kayseri, where we complete the last of our itineraries through the former lands of the Seljuk Sultanate of Rum.

APPENDIX 1: THE SELJUK SULTANS OF ROME

1077–86: Süleyman ibn Kutalmış

Interregnum

1093–1107: Kılıç Arslan I

1107–16: Melikşah

1116–56: Ruknuddin Mesut I

1156–88: Kılıç Arslan II

Division of the sultanate between the sons of Kılıç Arslan II
Küthuddin Melik Şah II
Ruknuddin Süleyman Şah II
Muhuddin Mesut Şah
Nüreddin Mahmud Sultan Şah
Müizeddin Tüğrül Şah
Müizeddin Kayser Şah
Nasreddin Bargıyaruk Şah
Nizamuddin Argun Şah
Arslan Şah
Sencer Şah
Giyaseddin Keyhüsrev I

1192–96: Giyaseddin Keyhüsrev I

1196–1203/4: Ruknuddin Süleyman Şah II

1204– ?: Izzeddin Kılıç Arslan III

1204–10: Giyaseddin Keyhüsrev I resumes reign

1210–20: Izzeddin Keykavus I

1220–37: Alaeddin Keykubad I

1237–46: Giyaseddin Keyhüsrev II

1246–61: Izzeddin Keykavus II

1246–65: Ruknuddin Kılıç Arslan IV

1246–57: Alaeddin Keykubad II

1265–83: Giyaseddin Keyhüsrev III

1283–98: Giyaseddin Mesut II

1298–1302: Alaeddin Keykubad III

1303–08: Giyaseddin Mesut II resumes reign

1308–24: Gazi Çelebi (?)

APPENDIX 2: GLOSSARY

acropolis: upper city, usually fortified
ahi: member of an Islamic fraternal organisation of guild members
bedesten: Turkish market building used for the sale of the most precious goods
beylerbey: governor general
beylik: Anatolian principality
capital: the uppermost element of a column
caravanserai: inn for travellers
citadel: inner fortress, usually on an acropolis
Corinthian: order of ancient Greek architecture
cornice: the projecting top course of a wall
çeşme: fountain
darülhadis: school for the study of the religious tradition of the Prophet
darülkura: school for the study of the Kuran
darüşşafaka: orphanage
darüşşifa: hospital
dershane: lecture hall of a *medrese*
drum: cylindrical or polygonal structure supporting a dome
eyvan: vaulted space recessed from a central hall or court
frieze: any horizontal zone covered with reliefs
gazi: warrior for the Islamic faith
griffin (gryphon): mythological beast, part eagle and part lion
hanikah: dervish oratory
Ionic: an order of ancient Greek architecture
kıble: direction of Mecca, towards which mosques are oriented
kümbet: Seljuk mausoleum
Kuran *kursu*: school for learning the Kuran
külliye: Islamic building complex
medrese: Islamic school of higher studies
mescit: small mosque
mihrap: niche in a mosque indicating the direction of Mecca
mimber: pulpit in a mosque
oculus: opening at the top of a dome
pendentive: spherical triangle that makes the transition from the circular cornice
    of a dome to its supporting arches

pilaster: an engaged or semi-detached pier

plinth: base of a statue or structure

portico: a colonnaded space, with a roof supported on at least one side by columns

şadırvan: ablution fountain

şerefe: balcony of a minaret

spandrel: the space between the exterior curve of an arch and the enclosing right angle

squinch: a surface making the transition between two adjacent and perpendicular arches and the cornice of the dome

tershane: naval shipyard and arsenal

tophane: armoury and ammunition storehouse

timarhane: insane asylum

tekke: dervish lodge

Turkish triangles: a polygonal structural belt composed of broken triangular surfaces

türbe: Turkish mausoleum

zaviye: Islamic shrine

APPENDIX 3: BIBLIOGRAPHY

Akdağ, Mustafa, *Türkiye'nin Iktisadi ve Ictimai Tarihi*, c. I, 1243–1453, Ankara, 1959

Angold, Michael, *The Byzantine Empire, 1025–1204, A Political History*, London, 1984

_____, *A Byzantine Government in Exile; Government and Society Under the Laskarids of Nicaea (1204–61)*, Oxford, 1984

Aslanapa, Oktay, *Turkish Art and Architecture*, London, 1971

_____, *Anadolu Selçuklarında Beylikler Devrinin Sonuna Kadar, Türk Sanatı*, Istanbul, 1973

Babinger, F., 'Ramadan Oghullari', in *The Encyclopedia of Islam*, new ed., vol. VIII, pp. 418–19 (eds C. E. Bosworth et al.), Leiden, 1978

Bates, Ülkü Ulusal, *The Anatolian Mausoleum of the Twelfth, Thirteenth and Fourteenth Centuries*, PhD thesis, University of Michigan, Ann Arbor, 1970

Barthold, W., *Turkestan down to the Mongol Invasion*, London, 1966

Bausani, A. 'Religion in the Saljuq Period', in *The Cambridge History of Iran*, vol. V (ed. J. A. Boyle), Cambridge, 1968, pp. 283–302

Boase, T. S. R. (ed.), *The Cilician Kingdom of Armenia*, Edinburgh and London, 1978

Bosworth, C. E., 'The Political and Dynastic History of the Iranian World (AD 1000–1217)', in *The Cambridge History of Iran*, vol. V, pp. 1–202 (ed. J. A. Boyle), Cambridge, 1968

_____, *The Islamic Dynasties: A Chronological and Genealogical Handbook*, Edinburgh, 1996

Bosworth, C. E., et al. 'Saldjukids', in *The Encyclopedia of Islam*, new ed., vol. VIII, pp. 936–78 (eds C. E. Bosworth et al.), Leiden, 1978

Boyle, J. A., 'Dynastic and Political History of the Il-Khans', in *The Cambridge History of Iran*, vol. V, pp. 303–421 (ed. J. A. Boyle), Cambridge, 1968

Bryce, W. C., 'The Turkish Colonization of Anatolia', *Bulletin of the John Rylands Library*, 38 (1955), pp. 18–44

Bryer, Anthony, and David Winfield, *The Byzantine Monuments and Topography of the Pontos*, 2 vols, Washington, DC, 1985

Cahen, Claude, *Pre-Ottoman Turkey*, New York, 1968

_____, *The Formation of Turkey: The Seljukid Sultanate of Rum, Eleventh to Fourteenth Centuries*, trans. and ed. E. M. Holt, London, 2001

_____, 'The Turkish Invasion: The Selchükids', in *A History of the Crusades*, vol. I, (ed. Kenneth M. Setton), pp. 135–76

_____, 'Karası', in *The Encyclopedia of Islam*, new ed., vol. IV, pp. 627–29 (eds C. E. Bosworth et al.), Leiden, 1978

_____, 'Kaykhusraw', in *The Encyclopedia of Islam*, new ed., vol. IV, pp. 816–17 (ed. C. E. Bosworth et al.), Leiden, 1978

_____, 'Kaykubad', in *The Encyclopedia of Islam*, new ed., vol. IV, pp. 817–18 (eds C. E. Bosworth et al.), Leiden, 1978

_____, 'Kayka'us', in *The Encyclopedia of Islam*, new ed., vol. IV, pp. 813–16 (eds C. E. Bosworth et al.), Leiden, 1978

Cary, M., *The Geographical Background to Greek and Roman History*, Oxford, 1949

Comnena, Anna, *The Alexiad*, English trans. E. R. A. Sewter, London, 1969

Czaplicha, M. A., *The Turks of Central Asia*, Oxford, 1918

De Plankol, X., 'Hamid', in *The Encyclopedia of Islam*, new ed., vol. III, pp. 132–33, (eds C. E. Bosworth et al.), Leiden, 1978

Erdmann, Kurt, *Das anatolische Kervansaray des 13. Jahrhunderts*, Berlin, 1961

Ertuğ, Ahmet (ed.), *The Seljuks; A Journey through Anatolian Architecture*, Istanbul, 1991

Ettinghausen, Richard, 'The Flowering of Seljuq Art', *Metropolitan Museum Journal*, 3 (1970), pp. 313–25

Fadıl, S. M., *The Decline of the Saljuquid Empire*, Calcutta, 1938

Foss, Clive, *Ephesus after Antiquity: A Late Antique, Byzantine and Turkish City*, Cambridge, MA, 1979

Friendly, Alfred, *The Dreadful Day: The Battle of Mantzikert*, 1071, London, 1981

Gabriel, Albert, *Monuments Turcs d'Anatolie*, 2 vols, Paris, 1931–34

Gardner, Alice, *The Lascarids of Nicaea: The Story of an Empire in Exile*, London, 1912

Gibbons, Henry Adams, *The Foundation of the Ottoman Empire*, London, 1968

Grousset, R., *The Empire of the Steppes*, New York, 1970

Hillenbrand, R., *Islamic Architecture*, New York, 1994

Hopwood, Keith R., 'The Byzantine–Turkish Frontier ca.1250–1300', in *Acta Viennensia Ottomanica*, (eds M. Kohbach, G. Prochaska-Eisl and C. Römer), Vienna, 1999, pp 153–61

Howorth, H. H., *History of the Mongols*, 3 vols., London, 1876–80

Işın, Ekrem (ed.), *Alaeddin'in Lambası, Anadolu'da Selçuklu Çağı Sanağı ve Alaeddin Keykubad, Istanbul*, 2001

Ibn Battutah, *The Travels of Ibn Battuta, A. D. 1325–1354*, 4 vols., trans. with revisions and notes H. A. R. Gibb, London, 1995

Ibn Bibi, *Anadolu Selçukı Devleti Tarihi*, trans. M. N. Gençosman, Ankara, 1941

Kafesoğlu, L., *Selçuklu Tarihi*, Ankara, 1992

Kafadar, Cemal, *Between Two Worlds: The Construction of the Ottoman State*, Berkeley, CA and Los Angeles, 1995

Kinnamos, John, *Epitome Historiarum*, English trans. C. M. Brand, *Deeds of John and Manuel Comnenus*, New York, 1976

Klausner, Carla L., *The Seljuk Vezirate: A Study of Civil Administration*, 1055–1194, Cambridge, MA, 1973

Konyalı, I. H., *Alanya (Alaiyye)*, Istanbul, 1946

Köprülü, Mehmet Fuat, *Osmanlı Devleti'nin Kuruluğu*, Ankara, 1959

_____, *Islam in Anatolia after the Turkish Invasion* (prologomena), trans. and ed. G. Leiser, Salt Lake City, 1993

_____, *The Seljuks of Asia Minor; Their History and Culture According to Local Muslim Sources*, tran. and ed. Gary Leiser, Salt Lake City, Utah, 1995

Köymen, Mehmet Altay, *Selçuklu Devri Türk Tarihi*, Ankara, 1963

_____, *Büyük Selçuklu İmparatorluğu Tarihi: Ikinci İmparatorluk Devri*, vol. V, Ankara, 1991

_____, *Büyük Selçuklu İmparatorluğu Tarihi: Alp Arslan ve Zamanı*, vol. III, Ankara, 1992

_____, *Büyük Selçuklu İmparatorluğu Tarihi: Kurtuluş Devri*, vol. I, Ankara, 1993

_____, *Selçuklu Devri Türk Tarihi*, Ankara, 1993

Kuban, Doğan, *Selçuklu Çağında Anadolu Sanatı*, Istanbul, 2001

_____, *The Miracle of Divriği*, Istanbul, 2001

Kuran, Abdullah, *Anadolu Medreseler*, vol. I, Ankara, 1969

Laiou, Angeliki, *Constantinople and the Latins: The Foreign Policy of Andronicus II, 1282–1328*, Cambridge, MA, 1972

Lambton, A. K. S., 'The Internal Structure of the Saljuq Empire', in *The Cambridge History of Iran*, vol. V, pp. 203–82 (ed. J. A. Boyle), Cambridge, 1968

Lang, David Marshall, *The Georgians*, New York, 1966

Langdon, John S, *Byzantium's Last Imperial Offensive in Asia Minor: The Documentary Evidence for and Hagiographical Lore about John III Ducas Vatatzes' Crusade against the Turks, 1222 or 1225 to 1231*, New Rochelle, NY, 1992

Leiser, Gary (ed.), *A History of the Seljuks: Ibrahim Kafesoğlu's Interpretation and the Resulting Controversy*, Carbondale and Edwardsville, IL, 1988

Le Strange, Guy, *Lands of the Eastern Caliphate*, Cambridge, 1930

Lloyd, Seton, and D. S. Rice, *Alanya (Alaiyye)*, London, 1958

Magdalino, Paul, *The Empire of Manuel I Komnenos, 1143–1180*, Cambridge, 1993

Marco Polo, *The Description of the World*, ed. A. C. Moule and P. Pelliot, London, 1938

Melikoff, I., 'Aydın-oghlu', in *The Encyclopedia of Islam*, new ed., vol. I, p. 783 (eds C. E. Bosworth et al.), Leiden, 1978

Melikoff, I., 'Danıshmendids', in *The Encyclopedia of Islam*, new ed., vol. II, pp. 110–11, (ed. C. E. Bosworth et al), Leiden, 1978

_____, 'Germiyan-oghullari', in *The Encyclopedia of Islam*, New Edition, Vol. II, pp. 989–96 (eds C. E. Bosworth et al.), Leiden, 1978

Merçil, E., 'Menteshe-oghullari' in *The Encyclopedia of Islam*, new ed., vol. VI, pp 1018–19 (eds C. E. Bosworth et al.), Leiden, 1978

Miller, William, *Trebizond: The Last Greek Empire*, New York, 1926

Mordtmann, J. H., 'Isfendiyar-oghlu', in *The Encyclopedia of Islam*, new ed., vol. IV, pp 108–9 (eds C. E. Bosworth et al.), Leiden, 1978

Mordtmann, J. H., and V. Menage, 'Dhu'l-Kadr', in *The Encyclopedia of Islam*, new ed., vol. II, pp. 238–40, (eds C. E. Bosworth et al.), Leiden, 1978

Muir, W., *The Mameluke or Slave Dynasty of Egypt, 1260–1517*, London, 1896

Nersessian, Serapie der, *The Armenians*, Westport, CT, 1959

Nicetas Choniates, English trans. H. Magoulias, *O City of Byzantium: Annals of Nicetas Choniates*, Detroit, 1984

Nicholson, Reynold A., *A Rumi Anthology*, Oxford, 2001

Norwich, John Julius, *Byzantium: The Apogee*, London, 1991

_____, *Byzantium: The Decline and Fall*, London, 1995

Ostrogorsky, George, *History of the Byzantine State*, trans. J. Hussey, Oxford, 1968

Öney, Gönül, *Beylikler Devri Sanatı XIV–XV Yüzyil (1300–1453)*, Ankara, 1989

Pitcher, Donald Edgar, *An Historical Geography of the Ottoman Empire*, Leiden, 1976

Prowdin, Michael, *The Mongol Empire: Its Rise and Legacy*, New York, 1961

Psellus, Michael, *Chronographia*, English trans. E. R. A. Sewter, London, 1953

Ramsay, William M., *The Historical Geography of Asia Minor*, London, 1890; reprinted New York, 1972

Redgate, A. E., *The Armenians*, Oxford, 2000

Riefstahl, R. M., *Turkish Architecture in South-western Anatolia*, Cambridge, MA, 1931

Rice, Tamara Talbot, *The Seljuks in Asia Minor*, London, 1961

Runciman, Steven, *History of the Crusades*, 3 vols, Cambridge, 1951–54

Sanaullah, F., *The Decline of the Saljuquid Empire*, London, 1938

Saunders, J. J., *The History of the Mongol Conquests*, London, 1971

Savvides, Alexis G. C., *Byzantium in the Near East: Its Relation with the Seljuk Sultanate of Rum in Asia Minor, the Armenians of Cilicia, and the Mongols, AD c. 1192–1237*, Thessaloniki, 1981

Sharp, John M. (ed.), *The Catalan Chronicle of Francisco de Moncada*, trans. by Frances Hernandez, El Paso, TX, 1975

Shaw, Sanford J., *History of the Ottoman Empire and Modern Turkey*, Vol. I, *Empire of the Gazis*, Cambridge, 1976

Sinclair, T. A., *Eastern Turkey: An Architectural and Archaeological Survey*, 4 vols., London, 1987–90

Sümer, Faruk, *Oğuzler Türkmenler*, Ankara, 1967

_____, 'Karaman-oghulları', in *The Encyclopedia of Islam*, new ed., vol. IV, pp. 618–25 (eds C. E. Bosworth et al.), Leiden, 1978

_____, *Selçuk Devrinde Doğu Anadolu'da Türk Beylikleri*, Ankara, 1990

Treadgold, Warren, *A History of the Byzantine State and Society*, Stanford, CA, 1997

Turan, Osman, *Selçuklar Tarihi ve Türk Islam Mediniyeti*, Ankara, 1965

_____, 'Anatolia in the Period of the Seljuks and the Beyliks,' in *The Cambridge History of Islam*, (eds P. M. Holt, A. K. S. Lambton and B. Lewis), Cambridge, 1970, vol.I, pp. 231–62

_____, *Selçuklar Zamanında Türkiye*, Istanbul, 1971

Unsal, Behçet, *Turkish Islamic Architecture*, London, 1959

Unver, S. A., *The Science of Medicine in the Seljuk Period*, Ankara, 1940

Uzunçarşılı, Ismail Hakkı, *Anadolu Beylikleri ve Akkoyunlu, Karakoyunlu Devirleri*, Ankara, 1988

Vryonis, Speros, Jr., *The Decline of Medieval Hellenism in Asia Minor and the Process of Islamization from the Eleventh through the Fifteenth Century*, Berkeley, CA, 1971

Wiet, G., 'Baybars I', *The Encyclopedia of Islam*, new ed., vol I, pp. 1124–76 (eds C. E. Bosworth et al.), Leiden, 1978

Wittek, Paul, *The Rise of the Ottoman Empire*, London, 1938

Woods, John E., *The Aqquyunlu: Clan, Confederation, Empire. A Study in 15th/9th Century Turko-Iranian Politics*, Minneapolis and Chicago, 1976

Yinanç, Mukrimin Halil, *Türkiye Tarihi Selçuklar Devri*, Istanbul, 1944

Zacharidou, E. A., *Trade and Crusade, Venetian Crete and the Emirates of Menteshe and Aydın (1300–1450)*, Venice, 1983

APPENDIX 4:
TURKISH SPELLING
AND PRONUNCIATION

Throughout this book, except in quotes from early sources, modern Turkish spelling has been used for Turkish proper names and for things that are specifically Turkish. Modern Turkish is rigorously logical and phonetic, and the few letters that are pronounced differently from how they are in English are indicated below.

Vowels are pronounced as in French and German – i.e. **a** as in father, **e** as in met, **i** as in machine, **o** as in oh, **u** as in mute. In addition, there are three other vowels that do not occur in English: these are ı (undotted), pronounced as the **u** in but; **ö**, as in German or as the **oy** in annoy; and **ü**, as in German or as **ui** in suit.

Consonants are pronounced as in English except for the following:

c as **j** in jam; e. g. **cami** (mosque) = jahmy
ç as **ch** in chat; e. g. **çorba** (soup) = chorba
g as in get, never as in gem
ş as in sugar; e. g. **çeşme** (fountain) = cheshme

Turkish words change form when modified by a preceding noun – e.g. Yeni Cami, the New Mosque, but Sultan Ahmet Camii, the Mosque of Sultan Ahmet.

INDEX